CW00920117

One of the most popular and extensive forms of eighteenth-century literature, the voyage-narrative, receives in this new study its first full treatment. It illustrates the very wide variety of published and unpublished material in this field, from self-satisfied official accounts to the little-known narratives of victims of the press-gang. There are names to conjure with: it includes a survey of writings about the Pacific – including Cook's voyages and Bligh and the Bounty; there is a major new study of William Dampier, studies of writings about the slave-trade, accounts of passengers – including Fielding and Mary Wollstonecraft, and autobiographies of seamen. This is a book about writing, rather than exploration and adventure, dealing with the devious routes from the actuality of experience to the production of self-serving narratives. While there are no new literary masterpieces to uncover, there are many new writers revealed, re-creating their adventures in narratives of great energy, vitality and interest, within the context of a century of British competitive sea-going imperialism.

CAMBRIDGE STUDIES IN EIGHTEENTH-CENTURY ENGLISH LITERATURE AND THOUGHT



*Some recent titles*

15 *Family and the Law in Eighteenth-Century Fiction: The Public Conscience in the Private Sphere*
by John P. Zomchick

16 *Crime and Defoe: A New Kind of Writing*
by Lincoln B. Faller

17 *Literary Transmission and Authority: Dryden and other Writers*
edited by Earl Miner and Jennifer Brady

18 *Plots and Counterplots: Sexual Politics and the Body Politic in English Literature 1660–1730*
by Richard Braverman

19 *The Eighteenth-Century Hymn in England*
by Donald Davie

20 *Swift's Politics: A Study in Disaffection*
by Ian Higgins

21 *Writing and the Rise of Finance: Capital Satires of the Early Eighteenth Century*
by Colin Nicholson

22 *Locke, Literary Criticism, and Philosophy*
by William Walker

23 *Poetry and Jacobite Politics in Eighteenth-Century Britain and Ireland*
by Murray G. H. Pittock

*A complete list of books in this series is given at the end of the volume.*

CAMBRIDGE STUDIES IN EIGHTEENTH-CENTURY
ENGLISH LITERATURE AND THOUGHT 24

# The story of the voyage

A

# VOYAGE

TO THE

# *SOUTH-SEAS*,

## In the YEARS 1740-1.

CONTAINING,

A faithful NARRATIVE of the Loss of his Majesty's Ship the *WAGER* on a desolate Island in the Latitude 47 South, Longitude 81:40 West: With the Proceedings and Conduct of the Officers and Crew, and the Hardships they endured in the said Island for the Space of five Months; their bold Attempt for Liberty, in Coasting the Southern Part of the vast Region of *Patagonia*; setting out with upwards of Eighty Souls in their Boats; the Loss of the Cutter; their Passage through the Streights of *Magellan*; an Account of their Manner of living in the Voyage on Seals, Wild Horses, Dogs, &c. and the incredible Hardships they frequently underwent for Want of Food of any Kind; a Description of the several Places where they touch'd in the Streights of *Magellan*, with an Account of the Inhabitants, &c. and their safe Arrival to the *Brazil*, after sailing one thousand Leagues in a Long-Boat; their Reception from the *Portuguese*; an Account of the Disturbances at *Rio Grand*; their Arrival at *Rio Janeiro*; their Passage and Usage on Board a *Portuguese* Ship to *Lisbon*; and their Return to *England*.

Interspersed with many entertaining and curious Observations, not taken Notice of by Sir *John Narborough*, or any other Journalist.

---

The Whole compiled by Persons concerned in the Facts related,

*VIZ.*

*John Bulkeley* and *John Cummins*,

Late Gunner and Carpenter of the WAGER.

---

*Bold were the Men who on the Ocean first*
*Spread the new Sails, when Ship-wreck was the worst:*
*More Dangers* Now *from* MAN *alone we find,*
*Than from the Rocks, the Billows, and the Wind.* WALLER.

---

*LONDON:*

Printed for JACOB ROBINSON, Publisher, at the *Golden-Lion* in *Ludgate-Street*. M.DCC.XLIII.

[Price Bound Three Shillings and Six-pence.]

*A Voyage to the South-Seas.* Title-page of the account by Bulkeley and Cummins of the wreck of the Wager, 1743.

# The story of the voyage

*Sea-narratives in eighteenth-century England*

PHILIP EDWARDS

CAMBRIDGE
UNIVERSITY PRESS

Published by the Press Syndicate of the University of Cambridge
The Pitt Building, Trumpington Street, Cambridge CB2 1RP
40 West 20th Street, New York, NY 10011–4211, USA
10 Stamford Road, Oakleigh, Melbourne 3166, Australia



First published 1994

Printed in Great Britain at the University Press, Cambridge

*A catalogue record for this book is available from the British Library*

*Library of Congress cataloguing in publication data*

Edwards, Philip.
The story of the voyage: Sea-narratives in eighteenth-century England / Philip Edwards.
p. cm. – (Cambridge studies in eighteenth-century English literature and thought)
Includes bibliographical references and index.
ISBN 0 521 41301 X (hardback)
1. English prose literature – 18th century – History and criticism.
2. Voyages and travels – History – 18th century – Historiography.
3. British – Travel – History – 18th century – Historiography.
4. Travelers' writings, English – History and criticism.
5. Ocean travel – History – 18th century – Historiography.
6. Sea stories, English – History and criticism.
I. Title. II. Series.
PR769.E38 1995
820.9′491′09033 – dc20 93–48138 CIP

ISBN 0 521 41301 X hardback

CE

# Contents

# Illustrations

# Preface

This book owes much to the Hakluyt Society, whose publications have been indispensable. I am grateful to the editors past and present whose work I have used, and to the Society for permission to use copyright material. I also have to thank Mr T. Beaglehole for permission to quote from J. C. Beaglehole's edition of Cook's journals, published by the Hakluyt Society.

For permission to make quotations from other works, I am grateful to Dr John C. Dann of the Clements Library, University of Michigan (Jacob Nagle's diary); Mr Graham Slater of the Epworth Press (John Newton's journal); the Colonial Williamsburg Foundation (John Harrower's journal); Messrs Routledge (Nicholas Owen's journal); the Banner of Truth Trust (George Whitefield's journal); Oxford University Press (Elizabeth Wynne's diary). Quotations from Joseph Banks's journals are from the edition by J.C. Beaglehole published in 1962 by the State Library of New South Wales.

In quoting from books published in the eighteenth century I have with very few exceptions used the original editions (sometimes the second if the first was not available). Sources of quotations are listed in the footnotes under short-titles which are given in full in the Bibliography.

There are a great many names of ships in *The Story of the Voyage*, and I have followed the precedent of my earlier book, *Last Voyages*, in not using italics for them. The convention of printing ships' names in italics seems to me a curious hangover from the eighteenth century, when commonly all proper names were put in italics. We rightly put the names of books in italics, because book-titles can get confused with the surrounding text ('She was fond of the wind in the willows'). But we do not put the names of places or people in italics. Is the name of a ship like the name of a place or person, or like a book-title? Decidedly the former, in my opinion.

Most of the work for this book has been done in the British Library, the London Library, and the University of Liverpool Library. I am grateful to the staff of these institutions for their help, particularly to Katy Hooper, the Special Collections Librarian at Liverpool. My thanks go also to John Smith, Cumbria County Librarian, and Harry Fancy, Whitehaven

Museum Curator, for aiding my work on John Roach. I am grateful to my colleague Paul Hair, and to Margaret Wilkes of the National Library of Scotland, for helpful replies to queries. The British Academy helped my work by a grant to assist working in London libraries.

I should also like to thank the University of Otago in New Zealand, for it was during a visiting professorship there in 1980 that, in the intervals of lecturing on Shakespeare, I began to explore eighteenth-century voyage-narratives. Finally, my warmest thanks to Howard Erskine-Hill for encouraging me to write this book, and for his support on a number of occasions when I needed it.

*Kendal*
*August 1993*

# 1

# Introduction

Relations of voyages and travels have at all times, and in all ages, since the invention of letters, been favourably received by the public: but, perhaps, in no age so well as in the present; writings of this kind being bought up with avidity and read with eagerness, more especially in this island, not only by the learned and polite, but also by the rude and illiterate.

This is the opening sentence of the preface to the English edition of *A Voyage to the Cape of Good Hope* (1785) by the Swedish naturalist Anders Sparrman, who had taken part in Cook's second voyage. Sparrman (or rather his translator) does well to point out that narratives of voyages in the eighteenth century were immensely popular across a very wide social range. King George III was frequently presented with handsome copies of such works, now in the British Library,[1] and the great library at Chatsworth contains a magnificent international voyage-collection made by Henry Cavendish, the eccentric millionaire-scientist (1731–1810). At the other end of the scale the public libraries of seaports such as Portsmouth, Whitehaven and Newcastle possess tattered copies of badly printed narratives on poor quality paper, with subscription lists of tradesmen of the area, containing the life and adventures of some local seaman, which were sold from door to door by their author. Lists of subscribers regularly confirm the wide social spread of readers (see p. 56).

'The peculiar Pleasure and Improvement that Books of Voyages and Travels afford, are sufficient Reasons why they are as much, if not more read, than any one Branch of polite Literature.' So wrote John Campbell in 1744.[2] Voyage-literature was not a new genre in the eighteenth century. Richard Hakluyt's great collection, *The Principal Navigations, Voyages, and Discoveries of the English Nation*, was published in 1589, with a much larger edition at the turn of the century. This record of English maritime endeavour, with its formidable share of stories of failure and disaster, was

[1] For example, C. J. Phipps, *A Voyage Towards the North Pole* (1774), dedicated to the king and beautifully illustrated. See Plate 1.

[2] John Harris, *Navigantium atque Itinerantium Bibliotheca*, Preface.

intended less as a celebration of the past than as a prelude to and herald of England's future imperial greatness overseas. Samuel Purchas's vast compilation, *Purchas His Pilgrims* (1625), though a continuation of Hakluyt, had less political edge and consciously addressed itself to the pleasure of the stay-at-home reader. There was no shortage in the literature of travel, by land as well as by sea, in the earlier seventeenth century, as the work of Thomas Coryate, Fynes Moryson, George Sandys testifies. There was a lull, for good reason, in the middle of the century. Towards the end of the century there is a strong sense of a new beginning, of something special happening, and what is really a new era of voyage-literature commences. It is perhaps the publication in 1694 of *An Account of Several Late Voyages and Discoveries to the South and North*, by Sir John Narborough and others, with its enthusiastic preface by Tancred Robinson, which properly marks the start of the new era, but so far as the general reader was concerned, there is no doubt that Dampier began it all with the extraordinary success of his *New Voyage Round the World* in 1697. In Chapter 2 I give a full account of the strange gestation period during which an adventurer without much education and with no experience of publishing gradually shaped the voluminous notes of his sea travels into the book which the age required and which everyone read. Throughout the succeeding century scientists, explorers and poets, as well as more ordinary readers, knew their Dampier.

On being asked how many books had the word 'voyage' in their title, the British Library's electronic *Eighteenth-Century Short-Title Catalogue* came up with 1,314 entries. Some of these were reprints and further editions of the same work, but against that we have to set all those voyage-publications without the operative word – all the journals, narratives, vindications, observations and histories. Perhaps two thousand works would be a reasonable estimate of published voyage-narratives in the eighteenth century. What has happened is that Hakluyt's hopes and Purchas's instincts have been justified. During the entire century British ships were all over the globe, creating, developing and maintaining an overseas empire; gaining and losing territory, exploring and fighting, carrying goods and people – soldiers, officials, brides, travellers, indentured servants and convicts. This empire-building was fiercely competitive; Britain was at war for about half the century. They were different wars, but though Spain was a consistent enemy it was France who was the real rival in a duel for world-domination.

At home the reading public could not get enough in the way of accounts of all the maritime activity involved in extending Britain's knowledge of the globe and her control of territories old and new. (They literally could not get enough, so fiction writers supplied them with more.) It was the same in other countries. English voyage-narratives were quickly translated into French, German or Dutch, and English readers could quickly read translations of major voyages undertaken by other European powers. When J. R. Forster translated the account of Bougainville's world-voyage, a German was giving a French narrative to English readers. The translation business was not just for the convenience of readers in Shropshire; it was also a weapon in the imperial war. Forster, who in 1772 was wholly committed to the cause of English supremacy in the fight, larded his translation with scornful comments about the French and plaudits for the English. In an audacious steal, the Scottish freelance John Callander simply appropriated the work of Charles de Brosses, *Histoire des navigations aux terres australes* (1756), and under the title of *Terra Australis Cognita* (1766–8) turned propaganda for French exploration in the southern ocean into propaganda for British exploration 'to promote the Commercial Interests of *Great Britain*, and extend her Naval Power'.

Besides the publication of accounts of individual voyages, there grew up a whole publishing industry of collections of voyages, multi-volume editions to go on the library shelves of Georgian houses. Some of these collections showed considerable care in collecting, translating and editing material, and with their introductory essays were serious contributions to geography and history. Others were parasitical, reprinting in abridged form what was easily available elsewhere. (There was a fine study of these collections in 1946 by G. R. Crone and R. A. Skelton.[3]) Among the more notable collections are A. J. Churchill's *Collection of Voyages and Travels*, 1704; John Harris's *Navigantium atque Itinerantium Bibliotheca*, 1705 (later revised by John Campbell); Thomas Astley's *New General Collection of Voyages and Travels*, 1745–7; Tobias Smollett's *Compendium of Authentic and Entertaining Voyages*, 1756; Alexander Dalrymple's *Historical Collection of the Several Voyages and Discoveries in the South Pacific Ocean*, 1770–1; James Burney's *Chronological History of the Discoveries in the South Sea or Pacific Ocean*, 1803–17; and John Pinkerton's *General Collection of the Best and Most Interesting Voyages and Travels*, 1808–14.

As early as 1710 the Earl of Shaftesbury drily noted that voyage-narratives 'are the chief materials to furnish out a library. . . . These are in our present days what books of chivalry were in those of our forefathers.'[4] True enough, voyage-narratives did have an impact on the imaginative life of the eighteenth century comparable to the impact of the world of chivalry on the imaginative life of the sixteenth century. And just as the force of that earlier impact can be judged by the epics of Ariosto and Spenser, so the force of the later can be found in the fiction of Defoe and Swift, and the poetry of Cowper and Coleridge. Even if writers show no

[3] 'English collections of voyages and travels'.

[4] *Advice to an Author*. Quoted by Frantz, *The English Traveller*, 8, see also 139–40.

direct influence in their work, many of them acknowledge in one way or another the grip of voyages on their imagination. Shelvocke's remarkable account of the shooting of an albatross (see Chapter 3) stuck in Wordsworth's mind and he suggested it to Coleridge when the latter was looking for a deed to be the cause of the Ancient Mariner's sufferings.[5] Cowper's 'The Castaway' is surely the most impressive tribute to the hold of voyage-narratives on the minds of eighteenth-century writers, but there is also his explicit note in *The Task* about the voyager, who 'spreads the honey of his deep research / At his return':

> He travels, and I too. I tread his deck,
> Ascend his topmast, through his peering eyes
> Discover countries, with a kindred heart
> Suffer his woes, and share in his escapes;
> While fancy, like the finger of a clock,
> Runs the great circuit, and is still at home.
>
> *The Task* IV.112–19

The voyage-narratives I am going to survey vary greatly in every respect. In length, in style, in format; in credibility; in motivation and intention; in tone of voice and cast of mind. Their authors vary from admirals and earls to the meanest victims of the press-gang. There are too few women, although three of the most spirited of the writings I shall discuss are by women: Anna Maria Falconbridge, Janet Schaw and Mary Wollstonecraft. (In spite of the 'wooden world' being largely a man's world, there were in fact a great many women at sea, but though they often kept journals they were less likely to write for publication.) With all their diversity, these narratives have one thing in common, and that is the ship. It is voyage in the narrower but for centuries accepted meaning of the sea-voyage that concerns me: the experience of being in the ship, as captain or seaman or passenger or prisoner. The land is always there of course, as harbour or hazard, land as described by the shipwrecked, or by the explorer-by-sea (the navigator as he was called), the trader or the slaver; but land-travel in itself has been excluded.

Even with this limitation, my subject is very extensive as well as very varied, and I offer only a highly selective view of it. Omissions will be very obvious; there is, for example, little on Cook's third voyage, or on the search for the north-west passage, or on the Darien colony, and there is much more about the Pacific than about the East Indies. Each of my chapters examines a group of related writings; I cannot try to do more than illustrate different aspects of a very large body of writings, some of which (for example, those relating to Cook or Bligh) are very well known,

[5] Lowes, *The Road to Xanadu*, 206. And see R. Holmes, *Coleridge: Early Visions* (London, 1989), 171–2.

some of which are perhaps known about, but rarely read, and some of which are almost entirely unknown. The availability of texts is a serious problem. Even with the better-known material, it is surprising how few of the original texts are accessible. There are hundreds of books *about* Cook and Bligh and Botany Bay, but the original writings themselves are not easily found, and the standard of documentation in even the best 'book about' can be scandalously offhand. One of the most interesting and important of all the writings I discuss, George Forster's *Voyage Round the World* of 1777, has never been reprinted, except in an admirable East German edition of Forster's works which is not on the shelves of the local bookshop or public library.

So this is a descriptive book; it seeks to make known, by examples, a voluminous and once very popular literature which has fallen out of sight, and which to my mind is of absorbing interest and vitality. My intention is pragmatic, empirical, exploratory; to collect, sort, compare, illustrate; Baconian not Cartesian, heeding above all Bacon's warning against the beckonings of the Idols to impose symmetry and pattern where none exists.[6] Within the various groups of writings, there are many features in common, but it is not unity in discourse that I present; rather individuality, variety, difference. Time enough to theorize when we know the material.

I have divided the book into three parts. The first is devoted to the writings of the 'founder', William Dampier, and includes the narratives of those associated with him: Lionel Wafer and Woodes Rogers. The second and largest part deals with writings about Pacific voyages between 1726 and 1798, beginning with Shelvocke and ending with Vancouver; it includes three of the century's best-known voyages: Anson, Cook and Bligh. The Anson chapter, however, is chiefly about the narratives emerging from the wreck of the Wager, Anson's store-ship. This chapter may seem disproportionately long and detailed; the wreck generated a whole series of conflicting accounts, and this body of writing, never fully examined, is of great interest in itself, and is an exemplary show-case of voyage-literature. In what I have to say about Cook and Bligh it will be quite clear that my purpose is not to retell the story of their voyages, but to examine the writings about the voyages.

The third part moves away from major voyages and reviews narratives under four headings. The first of these is the slave-trade, and this chapter is centred on the career of John Newton from slaver to hymn-writer. Next, I look at narratives written from the point of view of the passenger, and here the centre is Henry Fielding, who made his voyage to Lisbon a journey across the Styx. The third grouping is seamen's autobiographies,

6 Francis Bacon, *Novum Organum*, I, xxxviii–lxviii, in *Philosophical Works*, ed. J.M. Robertson (London, 1905), 263–74.

and the final (rather gloomy) chapter deals with the stories of transported convicts, indentured servants and shipwrecked sailors. Unavoidably, this third part has a piecemeal progression as I move from one writer to the next.

In my Conclusion I try to explain why I think this large and diversified branch of literature which I have been describing is important – more important than the travel fiction of the century, about which I have very little to say, although resemblances and links between the real and the imagined come to the surface on a number of occasions (see, for example, Wafer, Uring, Walker). The story of Robert Drury is indeed discussed, but I accept him as real and not, as sometimes has been supposed, a fiction.

My focus throughout the book is on the movement from experience into the written word, and on the mutations of the written word as it moves into print. The experience is inferred, not known; and the ideal paradigm of journal, manuscript draft and printed version, available from more than one individual engaged in the same venture, is seldom if ever found. Nevertheless, it is the indissoluble and unstable link between the writer, the world and the work (more fully argued about in my Conclusion) which has governed the writing of this book.

The prime question in exploring the nature of these writings is that of the motive for writing and the target aimed at. Obviously, for a great many of these writers, the main and sometimes the only motive for writing was money, but there are great differences in the scale of financial need. Quite a number of my writers were simply destitute, and they hoped that what they could make from selling their story would keep them alive (for example, Roach, Barker, Wills, Justice, Parker). For many others, less desperate, the rewards of publishing were an attractive means of adding to income, particularly after Hawkesworth had so immensely increased the going-rate for a major voyage-account to £6,000.

The next main motive was vindication or justification, rehabilitation or redress. Here we have, for example, William Bligh burnishing his image of righteousness, Alexander Campbell appealing against dismissal from the Navy, John Dean refuting charges of cannibalism, and George Shelvocke protesting about everything. Then, publication of a narrative could be a bid for promotion or employment (Colnett), or an attempt to get public and private support for a trading scheme (Meares).

As a motive for writing, the cause of science may be entangled with more self-serving ends, as was certainly the case with Johann Reinhold Forster, the much-maligned scientist of Cook's second voyage. In his *Observations* of 1778 (dedicated to the President and Fellows of the Royal Society – of which he was himself a Fellow), he described his aims in these ringing terms:

> My object was nature in its greatest extent; the Earth, the Sea, the Air, the Organic and Animated Creation, and more particularly that class of Beings to which we ourselves belong.

It will be seen that publication was for him of the first importance both for the money and for the advancement of his career.

The whole sad story (Chapter 5) of Forster's bitter dispute with Cook over the right to provide the official authoritative account of the second voyage is immensely revealing both of the outstanding importance of obtaining such rights, and of the great confusion that surrounded the publication of reports of expeditions.

The leaders of all expeditions sponsored by the Admiralty were of course bound to submit their full account to the Admiralty with their logs and journals. They were also instructed to collect at the end of a voyage all journals and records kept by their officers and other members of the ship's company. This precaution was a reasonable if ineffective measure to prevent the publication of unauthorized accounts of voyages which usually had (to say the least) politically sensitive objectives. There was no bar, however, against the eventual publication of an authorized account. But what was the nature and purpose of such an authorized publication?

It almost beggars belief that Lord Sandwich, First Lord of the Admiralty, should have chatted with a fellow-guest at Lord Orford's about Cook's first expedition, and have told him casually that he was looking for someone to 'write the voyage' – and then have accepted his fellow-guest's recommendation of Dr Hawkesworth – and then have given Hawkesworth not only Cook's papers but those of Byron, Wallis and Carteret – and then for us to find that Hawkesworth received so little in the way of direction that he felt himself free to organize and rewrite his material in any way he wanted, and resented being told very late in the day that he had to include all the navigational information which he had discarded as unimportant (pp. 83–4, 87).

This vagueness about the aims and purposes of an official publication, and in particular about the balance between the entertainment and edification of the general reader on the one hand, and the provision of scientific and technical information on the other, was part of an extraordinary lack of clarity in all major voyage-accounts. Schizophrenic dithering between the demands of science and the claims of the general reader was never resolved; it was there with Dampier at the beginning of the century and is still to be found in Meares at the end of the century.

On the one hand, there was the ideal, so frequently and eloquently expressed, of contributing to an international scientific archive: of serving the advancement of knowledge about unknown or little-known countries and oceans – about the people, the flora, the fauna, the terrain, the climate – and providing information about harbours, tides, winds, landfalls, for those who would follow and enlarge the bounds of human knowledge still further. Altruistic although all this was, it served patriotic ends; for all discoveries ministered to national pride. (Notice Banks's anxiety to get in with publication before the French; p. 83). And of course all officially sponsored voyages had opportunities for trade and settlement as primary objectives.

There is no dispute about the importance of the voyager's findings and observations to the Royal Society and to wealthy scientists such as Joseph Banks and Henry Cavendish, both of whom, it would seem, bought every travel publication of any importance. Nor is there any doubt that publications relating to earlier voyages were an essential item of equipment on every new voyage. We have the spectacle of Captain Cheap, Midshipman Byron and Gunner Bulkeley all examining (one by one) the same copy of Narborough's voyages on their bleak shipwreck island off the Patagonian coast. James Colnett, placed in charge of the Rattler for a south-sea exploration, went to the London booksellers to buy 'the various voyages of former navigators' (p. 126).

But there were not enough scientists, navigators, entrepreneurs and politicians to buy books in the quantities that would keep publishers in funds. It was the general public who made voyage-narratives so profitable to publish, and what the general public was assumed to need was a prime consideration with pretty well every writer discussed in this book, except perhaps the Forsters in their purely scientific publications, and George Vancouver, whose narrative could not have been intended to entertain anyone. No writer was really able to solve the problem of serving the two masters and achieve a satisfactory balance between scientific and technical information, and entertainment for the general reader. I describe Dampier's quite patent anguish and indecision in Chapter 2. At the end of the century, Arthur Young was still complaining of the way travel writers combined the telling of their story and making general observations.[7]

The uncertainty of the voyagers about their aim and their public made the gap which Defoe could enter. The preface to his *New Voyage Round the World* (1725) coolly raked the sea-going writers fore and aft for the 'tedious Accounts of their Log-work, how many Leagues they sail'd every Day; where they had the Winds . . .'. Sailors did not know how to make the most of their own stories – when, for example, 'they have had any Scuffle either with Native or *European* Enemies'. Their narratives 'have little or nothing of Story in them for the use of such Readers who never intend to go to Sea'.[8] Demonstrating to his readers how the task should be done, Defoe did not enlighten them with the information that *his* voyage round the world was wholly imaginary.

[7] Batten, *Pleasurable Instruction*, 32–3. [8] Defoe, *A New Voyage Round the World*, 2–3.

Smollett, more fairly, cut out the technical details from real voyage-accounts and improved the remainder. In the preface to his 1756 collection of voyages, he wrote that preceding collections were

> so stuffed with dry descriptions of bearings and distances, tides and current, variations of the compass, leeway, wind and weather, sounding, anchoring, and other terms of navigation, that none but mere pilots or seafaring people can read them without disgust. Our aim has been to clear away this kind of rubbish. . . . We have not only retrenched the superfluities, but endeavoured to polish the stile, strengthen the connexion of incidents, and animate the narration, wherever it seemed to languish.[9]

Smollett had the excuse that unlike Defoe he had actually been to sea, and had included a grisly account of his adventures as a naval surgeon's mate in *Roderick Random* (1748).

In any analysis of voyage-narratives of our period, authenticity is a major problem. I have challenged the authenticity of one of the accepted Wager narratives (pp. 75–6) and suggested that the 'inauthenticity' of one of the Cook narratives (second voyage) needs re-examining (p. 105). Robert Drury, recently rescued from his hijack by Defoe scholars, I accept as a real person (p. 166). It is quite possible that I have been taken in by a hoaxer somewhere in this book, and all credit to him if I have.

But authenticity is on the whole a less vexing problem than the continuing uncertainty about actual authorship. There are narrators who are mere inventions: in my judgement George Walker's life-story is an autobiography, written up by a Grub-Street hack as if it were the work of one of Walker's officers (pp. 189–91). Very occasionally, the working-up of a narrative by a literary person is acknowledged; see, for example, John Howell telling John Nicol's story – though the admission is in an afternote and only goes so far as initials. Where ghostings are not concealed they are usually anonymous (for example, Roach, p. 199, and Marra, p. 103). James Dalton's hair-raising and sometimes improbable adventures (pp. 210–11) were 'taken from his own Mouth in his Cell in Newgate'. Most often ghostings were unadmitted and can only be inferred.

A great many of the writers discussed in this book must have sought help. Dampier did not deny it, but fiercely rejected the accusation that therefore he was not the true author of his publications (p. 21). Cook had no confidence in himself as author, but after seeing what Hawkesworth had done with his journals for the first voyage, he determined to come into the arena himself. It was first necessary to by-pass J. R. Forster, and then *A Voyage Towards the South Pole and Round the World* appeared, 'written by James Cook'. In the preface he asked readers to excuse the lack of polish in an account 'given in my own words'; 'candour and fidelity', he thought,

9 Quoted by Crone and Skelton, 'English collections of voyages and travels', 110–11.

would 'balance the want of ornament'. As he was just about to set out on his third expedition, he was leaving his book 'in the hands of some friends' who have 'accepted the office of correcting the press for me'.[10] He did not say that the whole work had been written up for him by Canon John Douglas (pp. 122–3). Bligh's *Voyage to the South Seas* was written up for him by Joseph Banks and James Burney while he was away on his second breadfruit expedition. The disentanglement of the work of J. R. Forster from that of his son George in their major work, *A Voyage Round the World*, which purports to be by George alone, is a perplexing and complicated task (pp. 115–16).

The question of truthfulness in these narratives is a subject for my Conclusion. It will, however, very soon become clear that all voyage-narratives are self-serving, and that to watch (as we so often can) the development of a narrative is to see the record being adjusted, massaged and manipulated. There are one or two desperately honest and artless narrators – Elizabeth Justice, for example, and Roger Poole. The spectrum is very wide, between Cook's venial alterations and improvements in his journals and Shelvocke's breathtaking misrepresentations, but in general voyagers will not appear as a group of manly tars gripping their pens in fists more accustomed to handling ropes, setting down their recollections in simple and conscientious honesty. Voyage-literature is much more interesting than that. The writing, in all its deviousness, is a continuing involvement with and a continuing attempt to dominate the reality it is claiming to record.

The voyage-accounts which I discuss are almost wholly in prose. Both James Revel and (apparently) Robert Barker tried telling their stories in verse, and John Harrower, in his lonely diary, often moved into rhyme. The collection, *Naval Songs and Ballads*, made for the Navy Record Society by C. H. Firth in 1908, includes one or two rather painful attempts at verse story-telling; for example 'The Lighterman's Prentice Prest and Sent to Sea', and 'The Greenland Men'.[11] One R. Richardson, a seaman, wrote up Wallis's voyage as *The Dolphin's Journal Epitomized in a Poetical Essay* (see p. 95). But the only poetry of any moment in the following pages is J. F. Stanfield's worthy if embarrassing attempt to convert his unpleasant experiences aboard a slave-ship into an epic poem. However, it is essential to find room to salute William Falconer for his attempt to bring not only the events but the vocabulary of the sea within the compass of verse in his poem *The Shipwreck*, first published in 1762, and many times reprinted, with revisions.

Falconer was born in 1732, the son of an Edinburgh barber. He went to sea as a boy, and served in both merchant and naval ships. He was

[10] Cook, *A Voyage Towards the South Pole*, I, xxxvi.

[11] Firth, *Naval Songs and Ballads*, 201–2 and 249–52.

shipwrecked in the Mediterranean in 1750. He became a midshipman and later purser, and he married well. He compiled *An Universal Dictionary of the Marine* (1769). He was lost at sea in the Aurora, off the Cape of Good Hope, in 1769.

Falconer describes his intention:

> A scene from dumb oblivion to restore;
> To fame unknown, and new to epic lore.

The story is about the Britannia, on its way back to England from Venice via Crete. The disappointing first canto describes the captain, Albert ('a captive fettered to the oar of gain'), and among the others Palemon, hopelessly in love with the captain's daughter, who is forbidden him. Canto Two is in extraordinary contrast, as Falconer describes manoeuvring the ship in a violent storm.

> So Albert spoke; to windward, at his call,
> Some seamen the clue-garnet stand to haul –
> The tack's eased off; while the involving clue
> Between the pendent blocks ascending flew;
> The sheet and weather-brace they now stand by,
> The lee clue-garnet, and the bunt-lines ply:
> Then, all prepared, 'Let go the sheet!' he cries –
> Loud rattling, jarring, through the blocks it flies!
> Shivering at first, till by the blast impell'd
> High o'er the lee yard-arm the canvass swell'd;
> By spilling-lines embraced, with brails confined,
> It lies at length unshaken by the wind.
>
> To windward, foremost, young Arion strides,
> The lee yard-arm the gallant boatswain rides:
> Each earing to its cringle first they bend,
> The reef-band then along the yard extend;
> The circling earing round the extremes entwined,
> By outer and by inner turns they bind;
> The reef-lines next from hand to hand received,
> Through eyelet-holes and roban-legs were reeved;
> The folding reefs in plaits inroll'd they lay,
> Extend the worming lines, and ends belay.

Even with Falconer's explanatory notes these lines are hardly comprehensible. But it was a courageous initiative, and such passages as these stand up well against the sentimental conventional tone of the rest. Falconer may well say that he was 'perplexed in labyrinths of art'. But he produced something unique.

*The Story of the Voyage* is itself a coasting voyage; it puts in briefly at a number of selected ports and harbours. I am deeply conscious that if most of the writings I discuss are not well known to the general reader, they touch upon subjects on which scholars may have spent their entire working lives. I do not try to defend my ignorance, but I have to point out that this book is not in any way offering to contribute to the history of exploration, of naval campaigns, of the Pacific islanders, of sailing ships, of impressment, of the slave-trade, of New Zealand, of imperialism. It is concerned with all these subjects, and many more. But it is concerned with them as they appear through the lens of the writings under discussion. The object of study is the writings themselves: what the writers made of the events they were involved in, rather than, immediately and directly, the events themselves. That is to say, this book is not a study of eighteenth-century voyages and the profound effect those voyages had on human history; it is a study of the way those voyages were reported. Of course the book is immersed in what the writers were immersed in, and, in considering contexts, as I must, I can only hope that I have properly acknowledged all the help I have found in specialist works and that my blunders are small enough to be forgiven.

Though this book does not set out to add to or correct the history of imperialism, I do not pretend that I remain in some frozen state of indifference about the remorseless, unstoppable tide of invasion, dispossession, despoliation and cruelty which makes up so much of the story of the eighteenth century. The life of every single one of my writers was to some extent shaped by this huge movement of history, and what I have particularly wished to do is to discriminate between them as regards their own attitude to the global reshaping they were involved in. I wished above all to avoid the contemporary habit of collective punishment, which might lump them together as conscious or unconscious agents in an imperialist hegemonic conspiracy disseminating the values of the British power-structure.

As the last of the ages, the Age of Iron, took control of the world, it met on its way its earliest predecessor, the Age of Gold, and transformed it into its own grim semblance. I describe the uncanny percipience of Ovid in discussing Cook's explorations in Chapter 6. There were few if any of the people in Cook's ship who were not aware, as they made their stumbling contacts with the inhabitants of New Zealand or Tahiti, that this collision of cultures was a major moment in the historical process. No one who wrote about it, even if he was cheerfully confident about its outcome, was not thinking about the implications. And many deplored what was happening. It deeply undervalues the human spirit to be cynical about those who protested against, even about those who felt uncomfortable with, the arrogance of imperial domination. I refuse to regard them as collaborators, and hope I have given them their proper due. It was so *natural* for an English man or woman of the eighteenth century to think and speak contemptuously of the Irish, or the Catholics, or the Spaniards, or African slaves, or the South-Sea islanders, or the 'criminal class', that we should register *our* respect for those who showed *their* respect for the human dignity of peoples not of their own kin and colour or social class. The testing ground, the shibboleth, is the West African slave-trade. In the chapter on the slave-trade, I record many voices totally impervious to any consideration of humanity or decency in the treatment of Africans, but also many voices raised in protest well before abolitionism became fashionable.

It will be seen that I have given much less space in this book to the official accounts of figures of authority, the Ansons or Byrons or Vancouvers, who were consciously and willingly playing a leading part in the imperial endeavour, than to more ordinary people, petty officers and seamen, naturalists and surgeons, passengers and servants, and their unofficial accounts. And everywhere I have given special attention to words of fellow-feeling and indignation where the ill-treatment of others was concerned. I am particularly concerned to draw attention to those narratives in which the sea-journey was for the observer a quite painful moral journey of readjustment and revision of prejudgements (Janet Schaw's story, for example).

Within the wider world of international competitive imperialism, the wooden world which is my subject was itself an arena of much hardship, much cruelty, and much suffering. In Dr Johnson's tour of the Hebrides in 1773, the conversation turned to one of the guides who had been pressed into the Navy and had managed to get his release after nine months. Johnson said, 'Why, sir, no man will be a sailor, who has contrivance enough to get himself into a jail; for, being in a ship is being in a jail, with the chance of being drowned'.[12] It was this extraordinary jail, cramped and crowded, with livestock on deck and sick men below, pitching and rolling, with poor food, harsh discipline and constant danger, which was the instrument for enlarging the European world, for increasing the power and the territory of the European nations – and we are speaking of ships used for exploration and discovery, ships used to make war, ships used to convey slave-labour to West-Indian colonies or indentured labour to American colonies, ships used to carry cargoes to and from India and the East.

Of course, smooth agreeable voyages were not worth writing about. Stories from the sea will tend to concentrate on crisis and catastrophe. But quite apart from the many tales of shipwreck and disaster and captivity which are told, there are many accounts of the normal conditions of shipboard life which are pretty horrifying. The Navy of that time has much to answer for. In the chapter on autobiographies (Chapter 8) I

[12] Boswell, *Journal of a Tour to the Hebrides*, 247.

record some first-hand detail of the ferocity of flogging and 'starting', and of lives lived in the shadow of fear of the press-gang. It is worth noting here the writing of a singularly well-educated and literary naval officer, Edward Thompson, who moved from the merchant service to the Navy, and published his *Sailors Letters* in 1766. He was especially concerned with the difficult life of the midshipman, but he made the general comment, that 'the sea life is so opposite to human nature, that I am astonished so many engage in the pursuit, when so few approve it'.[13] He wrote of the life of junior officers as 'a state of vassalage', and spoke of 'the dirty road to preferment'. He was deeply concerned to bring more dignity, humanity and civility into the naval service, and was particularly indignant about the abuse of the 'despotick' authority of many captains who were 'not gentlemen nor men of education'. Thompson wrote with interest, intelligence and sensitivity about all that he saw, and it is notable that in the West Indies he deplored 'the cruel tyranny exercised over the slaves' as 'shocking to humanity'.[14]

Cruelty and tyranny were not confined to naval ships. Things were particularly bad in slaving ships, as will be seen, and it is evident from their treatment of the white crew that many captains of slavers were brutalized by their horrible trade. Even allowing for exaggeration by disgruntled subordinates there does seem to have been a large number of psychopathic sadists in command of ships of all kinds. There are some lurid details in the following chapters.[15] But 'despotick' captains were only a part of the harshness of sea-life. The depredations of scurvy, which took so long for its cause to be discovered and even longer for proper prophylactic measures to be taken, must come a high second in the list of adverse conditions. The extraordinary toll taken on Anson's expedition was before Dr James Lind published his treatise on scurvy in 1753, but the scourge continued in reduced form for many years. There were also the fatal fevers so hard to avoid in places like Batavia, where many of the crew on Cook's first expedition died.

One is obviously struck by the unnaturalness of life on these long voyages, with the harshness of the conditions, and the danger, and the severe discipline, and the cooping-up of men without women for long periods. But the paradox of the harshness and unnaturalness of life aboard ship, with the absence of so much that would belong to normal life, is that deprivation was also revelation. The starkness of the stripped-down existence, coupled with frequent contact with wholly different societies, made philosophers of a number of the writers in this book – though it has to be said that sometimes the illumination was slight, and did not last long.

[13] Thompson, *Sailors Letters*, I, 139. [14] *Ibid.*, II, 29.

[15] See also the horrifying allegations collected from the proceedings of the High Court of Admiralty by Rediker, *Between the Devil and the Deep Blue Sea*, 215–21.

# Part I

# 2

# William Dampier

## I

The flood-tide of eighteenth-century voyage-literature began, as we noted, with William Dampier's *New Voyage Round the World*, published by James Knapton in 1697. It was Knapton's first venture in travel writings, and he never looked back.[1] The book came out in February, and two further editions were called for before the year was out.[2] There were five editions all told by 1705; the work was many times reprinted in the collected editions of Dampier's writings, and (often abbreviated) in collections of travels. Everyone was familiar with it. It had a strong influence on writers such as Defoe, Swift and Coleridge. And, along with Dampier's later writings, it was constantly used by succeeding voyagers – Carteret, Cook and Banks, for example, and even Darwin.

Dampier was born in 1652 at East Coker in Somerset.[3] In a brief autobiographical sketch in his second publication[4] he wrote that it was not intended that he should become a sailor, but, when both his parents died, his guardians, 'having removed me from the *Latin School*, to learn *Writing* and *Arithmetick*, they soon after placed me with a Master of a Ship at *Weymouth*, complying with the Inclinations I had very early of seeing the World'. A very cold voyage to Newfoundland turned him against sea-going for a time, but the temptation of 'a *warm Voyage* and a *long one*' took him to Java, returning in 1672. He saw action in the second Dutch War in 1673, but fell ill and returned to his brother in Somerset.

In 1674, aged twenty-two, Dampier went to Jamaica to manage the estate of a neighbour, Colonel Hillier of East Coker. He left that employment after less than six months, took service in another plantation, but 'was clearly out of my Element', and went to sea again in a sloop trading round the Jamaican coast. Then this restless man took what turned out to

1 See P. G. Morrison, *Index of Printers, Publishers and Booksellers . . . 1641–1700* (Charlottesville, Va., 1955), for Knapton's earlier publications.

2 E. Arber, *Term Catalogues*, III (London 1906), 5, 17, 45, 113 and 469.

3 Wilkinson, *William Dampier*, 11–13, argues for 1651.

4 Dampier, *Voyages and Descriptions*, pt. II, chap. 1 (hereafter *VD*).

be a decisive step. 'I left that Employ also, and shipt myself aboard one Captain *Hudsel*, who was bound to the Bay of *Campeachy* to load *Logwood*.' In the thirteen weeks of 'this troublesome Voyage' he came into close contact with the 'privateers' (his euphemism for the buccaneers) who, for want of easier pickings, were cutting logwood.[5] The English had been exploiting the trade since the conquest of Jamaica in 1655.[6] Dampier decided to risk it. This was 'a Place where a Man might have gotten an Estate'. So in February 1676 he shipped himself to Campeachy Bay with the equipment he needed, 'Hatchets, Axes, Macheats (*i.e.* Long Knives), Saws, Wedges, &c. a Pavillion to sleep in, a Gun with Powder and shot, &c'. He joined a group of six logwood-cutters. 'It is not my Business to determine', he wrote, 'how far we might have a right of cutting Wood there', but in any case the trade was not sufficiently lucrative in itself, and he joined in marauding parties against Spanish settlements along the coast.

Dampier went back to England in 1678. He married, but left his wife to return to the West Indies in 1679 intending to resume the logwood trade. In Jamaica he changed his mind, acquired from its owner the title to an estate in Dorset, and was preparing to return to England when the offer came to join a trading voyage to the Honduras area. He thought this would be a way 'to get up some Money before my return'.[7] In fact it was over ten years, 1691, before he returned to England, and his adventures and observations over this long period form the subject of *A New Voyage Round the World*.

What happened was that when his ship got to Negril Bay in western Jamaica the crew decided to join the buccaneers, whose ships, under Captains Coxon, Sawkins, Sharp and others, they found lying there. After a little hesitation, Dampier also decided to join them. These buccaneers were an international collection (for example, French, English, Dutch) of professional sea-marauders preying on Spanish possessions by sea and land. (Henry Morgan had been the leading Englishman until in 1674 he gained the extraordinary respectability of being appointed lieutenant-governor of Jamaica and knighted.) Dampier's odyssey in this company is summed up as follows by W. H. Bonner.

> Thus from Christmas 1679 to September 1691 Dampier was one of a large number of West Indian buccaneers, under first one captain then another, attacking Porto Bello, crossing and recrossing the Isthmus of America on foot, living in Virginia for thirteen months, rounding the Horn and cruising in the South Sea along the coast of Peru and Chile and Mexico, sailing away to the Philippines, Formosa,

[5] Logwood (so called from the blocks or billets in which it was marketed) was the tree *Haematoxylon campechianum*, extensively used to give a reddish-brown dye.

[6] Floyd, *Anglo-Spanish Struggle*, 55–8.

[7] Dampier, *A New Voyage Round the World*, Introduction, p. iii (hereafter *NV*).

and Celebes, Australia, and the Nicobar Islands (northwest of Sumatra). Here, properly speaking, Dampier's career as a buccaneer ended; for, tired of buccaneers and their ways, he left them, after piratical escapades of eight and a half years.[8]

From the Nicobars, Dampier went in an open boat to Sumatra; he travelled to Tonquin and Malacca, and then spent several months as the gunner of the English fort at Bencouli (Bengkulu) in Sumatra. He arrived back in England in September 1691 with Prince Jeoly, 'the Painted Prince', whom he had lately acquired. Jeoly was a tattooed south-sea islander taken prisoner and put on sale in Mindanao. A friend of Dampier's had bought him and committed him to his charge. Dampier sold him for ready money. The Painted Prince 'was carried about to be shown as a Sight'; but the poor man soon died of small-pox at Oxford.[9]

For six years, until the publication of *A New Voyage Round the World*, there is almost no information about Dampier. That he was at Corunna in 1694 indicates he was getting employment of some kind to keep his wife and himself alive.[10] But it is clear that the preparation of *A New Voyage* was a time-consuming, laborious process, and it is legitimate to assume that Dampier was banking on his book to secure his future. He must have amassed a huge quantity of notes during his travels. He explains that when he took part in the march across the Panamanian isthmus, 'I took care before I left the Ship to provide myself a large Joint of Bambo, which I stopt at both ends, closing it with Wax, so as to keep out any Water. In this I preserved my Journal and other Writings from being wet, tho I was often forc'd to swim.'[11] When Dampier broke with the buccaneers, he and his companions tried out the 'canoa' in which they hoped to get to Sumatra, and it capsized.

When our things were stowed away, we with the *Achinese* entered with joy into our new Frigot, and launched off from the shore. We were no sooner off, but our Canoa overset, bottom upwards. We preserved our lives well enough by swimming, and dragg'd also our Chests and our Cloaths ashore; but all our things were wet. I had nothing of value but my Journal and some Drafts of Land, of my own taking, which I much prized, and which I had hitherto carefully preserved. Mr. *Hall* had also such another cargo of Books and Drafts, which were now like to perish. But we presently opened our Chests and took out our Books, which, with much ado, we did afterwards dry; but some of our Drafts that lay loose in our Chests were spoiled.

We lay here afterwards 3 Days, making great fires to dry our Books. The *Achinese* in the mean time fixt our Canoa, with Outlagers on each side; and they also cut a good Mast for her, and made a substantial sail with Mats.

8 Bonner, *Captain William Dampier*, 11.

9 Dampier *NV*, chap. 20 (end).

10 Masefield, *Dampier's Voyages*, I, 3.

11 Dampier *NV*, 16.

The Canoa being now very well fixt, and our Books and Cloaths dry, we launched out the second time, and rowed towards the East side of the Island, leaving many Islands to the North of us.

Dampier *NV*, 487.

What these 'Books' contained was both a narrative of happenings and an extremely detailed account of weather, scenery, the people of different countries, buildings, trees, vegetation, crops, birds, beasts and fish. Wholly untrained, Dampier was a natural Baconian scientist, fascinated by everything he saw, amassing information and recording phenomena, and doing his unassisted best to classify and explain what he observed. Having brought all this material home, he now had to decide how to convert it into a book.

The clearest evidence of his indecision and his toil is in the manuscript version of *A New Voyage*, which is in the British Library (Sloane 3236), and which, though often mentioned, has never been properly discussed. Evidently Dampier had written a first draft of his book and was not satisfied with it. He had then marked all the places where he wished to alter or amplify what he had written, and had gone to the expense of having this draft copied out (471 pages) leaving a wide margin on the left-hand side of the page to accommodate his new material. The places where revision was needed were marked by the scribe '(A)', '(B)', '(C)', etc. And then Dampier has filled the left-hand margin with his corrections and additions. (See Plates 2 and 3).

However, the version of the book which was eventually published bears little resemblance to this amplified manuscript version. The printed book is very much longer. Almost every incident has been reworked and enlarged, and a huge amount of new material on natural history and geography, and on the appearance and customs of the inhabitants of different countries, has been added. Bits of the amplified manuscript version turn up in all sorts of different places in the printed version. Sometimes the weaving-in of new material is quite crude: a 1,200-word account of the Moskito Indians is simply inserted in the middle of one of the original sentences.[12]

Was Dampier advised to make these far-reaching changes which quite transform the nature and scope of his work? There has been a lot of speculation on whether Dampier got others to help him to write his book. The suspicion that a rough seaman could not unaided have produced a work which was read throughout the world was perhaps inevitable. Charles Hatton, who met Dampier, provides the characteristic note of condescension. Dampier was 'a blunt fellow, but of better understanding than wou'd be exspected from one of his education. ... He is a very good navigator, kept his journal exactly, ... but, you must imagine, had

[12] *Ibid.*, 7–11.

assistance in dressing up his history.'[13] Lemuel Gulliver's statement, that he had advised 'my cousin Dampier' 'to hire some young gentleman of either university' to put his notes in order, is not evidence.[14] It would be quite remarkable if Dampier had never sought assistance; the question is about its extent. Dampier himself, in a fighting preface to his third publication, *A Voyage to New Holland* (1703), protested against being charged 'with Insufficiency, as if I was not my self the Author of what I write', although he considered it 'far from being a Diminution to one of my Education and Employment, to have what I write, Revised and Corrected by Friends'. This insistence on being 'the Author of what I write' while conceding revision by others (a distinction which may well have been contributed by one of the 'Friends') is worth attention. It is no good starting from a characterization of Dampier as a plain and simple fellow. His was an enigmatic and complex personality, and his talents were very unusual. The changes made between the Sloane manuscript and the published text are often sophisticated improvements which suggest an experienced literary editor. On the other hand, almost every retelling of an incident includes additional eye-witness material which could not have been provided by an editor. Revision seems to have been a collaboration to which Dampier contributed by far the most. Above all, the hesitation and tentativeness and sheer *naïveté* with which the final work is fashioned, and is offered to the reader as it proceeds, are the mark of one conceivable person only, Dampier the traveller and observer on his way to becoming Dampier the writer.

Here is an example of the reworking of an incident which may well be the responsibility of a more expert literary hand. Dampier is with Captain Swan, who had been willing to take his ship on the westward venture across the Pacific. They had had difficulty in persuading the crew to accept that, and the privations of their passage before they made a landfall at Guam were such that 'the Men began to murmur against Captain *Swan*, for persuading them to come this Voyage'. Dampier had been suffering for a long time from 'a Dropsy'. Here, first, is the manuscript account, one of Dampier's marginal additions to his original narrative.

While wee stayed here I was one day washing myself with some others a litle way from the town & Captain Swan coming that way came pretty neer where I was & said smiling ah Dampier you would haue poysoned them you are too Lean but I belieue sd he they would haue saued you aliue for you haue soe litle flesh that it will not giue them a meale – ffor if we had misd the Island Capt Swan had certainly ben kild & Eaten & all of us that promoted coming this way

(f. 185v).

[13] *Hatton Correspondence* (Camden Society, 1878), II, 224; quoted by Bonner, *Captain William Dampier*, 33.

[14] 'Letter from Capt. Gulliver to Cousin Sympson', prefacing the 1735 edition of *Gulliver's Travels*.

And here is the printed version

> It was well for Captain *Swan* that we got sight of it before our Provision was spent, of which we had but enough for 3 days more; for as I was afterwards informed, the men had contrived first to kill Captain *Swan* and eat him when the victuals was gone, and after him all of us who were accessary in promoting the undertaking this Voyage. This made Captain *Swan* say to me after our arrival at *Guam, Ah!* Dampier, *you would have made them but a poor Meal*; for I was as lean as the Captain was lusty and fleshy.
>
> Dampier *NV*, 283–4.

There are a number of cosmetic changes which may have come from an adviser but which may just as well be the sign of an increasingly diplomatic Dampier. Some of the more abusive references to his colleagues are toned down. For example, on the march back across the isthmus, 'all the persuasions I could use were not of force sufficient to worke on their stubborne natures', becomes 'But all the Arguments I could use were not for force sufficient to convince them'.[15] It has clearly been thought wiser to gloss over instances of incompetence, cowardice and failure in the face of Spanish arms. This is particularly the case with the long-planned and totally unsuccessful engagement in May 1685 with the Spanish treasure fleet *en route* from the Philippines. Concerning the massacre of fifty men, including Basil Ringrose, during a raid on the Mexican coast in February 1686, it is not easy to perceive in the printed text that the slaughter was the result of not obeying orders to stay together. The manuscript reads, 'They lay all along in the path as they were killed one and one and not two a brest any where by which it was easy to guess that their own folly ruined them . . .' (f. 173).

Basil Ringrose was another writer among the buccaneers. He wrote an excellent account of the early stages of the very adventures in which Dampier was involved, and had sent the manuscript back to London where it was published the year before his death. Now, a major motive in Dampier's revisions, countering as it were the tactful suppression of English incompetence, is to distance himself from the buccaneers. In the printed version he enlists Basil Ringrose as an ally in his moral separation from his shipmates. 'He had no mind to this Voyage; but was necessitated to engage in it or starve.' Ringrose is 'my ingenious Friend'. In the manuscript he is only 'the Ingenious M. Ringrose', and there is no mention of his distaste for what he was doing. Dampier's presentation of himself (and it is certainly not an editor's presentation of him) is a continuing anxiety in the printed text. This is not the case in the manuscript, though it does contain some interesting evidence of his sensitiveness about his occupation and his concern for the good will of his future

[15] f. 4v, and *NV*, 15.

readers. For example, there is a comically pretentious 'Preamble' to the main voyage into the South Seas, which finds no place in the printed text. It justifies his right to spend his life as he thinks fit, but – were the adventures he was engaged in legal?

> If it is objected that the point of right was not so well studyed in these aduentures as it ought to haue been I can only say that the Pollitical rights, Alliances and Engagements betweene Empires and states are too high for me to discuss.
>
> (f. 30).

His only desire, he says, is to serve his country. Concerning his decision to join Captain Swan in order to go to the East Indies, he writes as follows.

> I came into these seas this second time more to Endulge my cureosity then to gett wealth though I must confess at that time I did think the trade Lawfull yet had never followed it but in hopes to mak such descoveryes as might in time conduce to the benifit of my nation.
>
> (f. 128).

This is one of the marginal additions in the manuscript and it marks Dampier's increasing stress on the purity of his motives, and on the argument that he was using the buccaneers as a form of transport. That he once thought the trade lawful, or that its lawfulness was not a matter for him, is not brought up in the printed version.

The concluding page and a half of the manuscript, in Dampier's own handwriting, is an angry, paranoid, sometimes incoherent apologia which throws much light on Dampier and on the personality which he afterwards shaped as he revised his work. The challenge (imaginary or real?) that he was answering was: How can a person who is not in charge of a ship or conducting an expedition claim to be making discoveries of his own? His defence is (a) that he could have been master of a ship if he had so chosen; (b) that his journal was known to be full and accurate, and it had no rival; and (c) that being a master was no guarantee of the ability to provide the record of events and places which a 'discovery' demands. Here is the text.

> It may be demanded by som why I took these voyages & Descoverys of mine seing I was neither master nor mate of any of the ships; to such demands I answer that I might haue ben master of the first I went out in if I would haue accepted it for it was known to most men that were in the seas that I kept a Journall & all that knew me well did ever judg my accounts were kept as exact as any mans besides most if not all that kept Journalls either lodged them [when they] gott to Europe or ellse are not yet returned nor euer likely to come home[;] therefore I think I may most justly challenge as a right to those dyscoverys then any other man yet I can plainly see that some men are not soe well pleasd as if it came from any of the commanders that were in the south seas though most off them I think all besides Captain Swan were wholy incapable of keeping a sea journall & took noe account of any actions

> neither did they make any obseruations in those partes yet such is the opinion of most men that nothing pleaseth them but what comes from the highest hand though from men of the meanest capacitys. But I feare I am to prolex in this Discurse I am only to answer for myself & if I haue not giuen a Dyscription of those places to the satisfaction of my frinds I must beg pardon & desire them to [blame?] the defects they finde in these my writings on the meaness of my information and not in me whoe haue ben faithfull as to what is written of my own knowledg or in getteing the best information I could.
>
> (f. 233r and v).

From protesting too much that his subordinate position was of no consequence, Dampier moved, as we shall see shortly, to a position of deliberate vagueness about his status.

Comparison of Dampier's manuscript draft with his final printed text makes nonsense of what we often read about him and his personality. 'There was no honester mind than his', wrote W. H. Bonner in 1934, calling his writings 'a modest mariner's simple journals'. His manipulation of the record is well shown in his attempts to explain to his reader why, at Mindanao in the Philippines in January 1687, when the crew seized the ship and sailed leaving Captain Swan ashore, he found himself on board with the mutineers.

In the original version, as copied out by the scribe, Mr Harthop comes aboard. The crew proposes him as captain, but he refuses to accept, urging them to do nothing hasty, and goes ashore to fetch Captain Swan. The ship weighs anchor and sails without him. This version continues like this:

> Severall of us were hartily sorry for Captain Swan and those that tarried behind for 36 men stayed with him and I wish more would have stayed with him but had not money to maintaine our selves and we were loath to lay ourselves vnder the yoake of a Mahometan . . .
>
> . . . Of two Evills I thought to chuse the least and therefore came away with the ship with a resolution to leave her the first place wee came to neare an English ffactory.
>
> (f. 199).

So the first explanation is that Dampier was very uneasy about abandoning the captain, but had not the money to live ashore, and did not like being subject to Muslim rule; but he intended to leave the ship at the first opportunity. In the margin of the manuscript Dampier has inserted in his own handwriting all sorts of additions. (See Plate 3.) These develop the idea that he was coerced and did not voluntarily stay aboard the ship: they would not let him go. After the words, 'loath to lay ourselves vnder the yoake of a Mahometan', he has added 'yet would haue put these things to a venture but could not haue the liberty to leaue the ship'. This lack of liberty is enlarged on in a further additional note:

When mr harthop went ashore 2 of the men one wm williams and another whose name I haue forgot were by much Intreaty permitted to goe ashore but I could not haue that Liberty nor D[r] Coppenger though we endeavourd to perswade them to it for Coppenger they could not spare they haueing noe other Chyrorgeon abord & from me they would not parte for feare they should want a man to nauegate the ship.

(f. 199).

Herman Coppinger was the surgeon's mate, and Dampier's story is now that the two of them were forcibly kept aboard because they were needed for their different skills.

Following his original words 'neare an English ffactory', Dampier first inserted a concluding phrase suggesting a curious half-way house between reluctance and conscription; '& at present made of nesesity a vertue'. And in the margin there is yet another thought (a time-honoured excuse!):

I could not refuse it though I endeauourd it; but in goeing with them I thought I should in time perswade them to return & fetch Capt Swan & the rest of them away but I mist of my aim ...

In the end it looks as though Dampier decided, or was advised, to drop all this defensive protestation. In *A New Voyage* the fact that Mr Harthop was allowed to go ashore and that the ship sailed without him is suppressed. 'He perswaded them to be reconciled again, ... But they were deaf to it, and weighed again while he was aboard. ... They suffered no man to go ashore, except one *William Williams* that had a Wooden Leg, and another that was a Sawyer.'[16] It is an inference that Dampier, along with Harthop and Coppinger, was not allowed to leave the ship, but this is never stated. Rather meanly, Dampier puts the final blame on the captain. 'A Captain of any Prudence or Courage' would have come to see for himself what was happening and would have put a stop to the mutiny.

Dampier's fundamental reason for reorganizing and enlarging the narrative of his odyssey was a radical change of purpose. At some point he formed a wholly new conception of what his work should strive to be. It must always have been his intention to publish at some time and in some form his voluminous notes on turtles and monkeys and manatees, on plantains and avogato pears and coconuts, on harpooning and dug-out canoes and methods of dyeing. But the manuscript version is solely a narrative of events and a description of places (mountains, harbours, settlements, etc.). Even so, Dampier was already having problems in combining actions and topography, as his characteristic candour in sharing his perplexities with his readers makes evident. He abruptly breaks off his account of the ignominious defeat of the buccaneers by the

[16] Dampier *NV*, 374.

Spanish treasure convoy and says he will now describe the western coast of South America (which takes him twenty-three pages (ff. 95v–118v). What he has already written, he says,

is only matter of fact being the severall passages and transactions of many men drawn together by divers wayes into these remote places of the world which I am now goeing to describe.

... I had once thought of writeing this parte first but to rush on to the description of a Country before it is manifest that a man hath been there and knows it seems very odd in my opinion.

But every man may doe what he pleaseth as to the reading of it for his own satisfaction – he may enter on this part first or the other.

It may well be that Dampier's model in this first version of his travels was Basil Ringrose's narrative, which was published in 1685 the 'The Second Volume' of the English translation from the Dutch of John Esquemeling's *Bucaniers of America* (first edition 1684).[17] Ringrose superimposed a story of events on a kind of log which pays special attention to navigational information, including many sketch-maps of coasts and harbours. (Dampier's manuscript had such sketch-maps, but they did not survive into the printed version.)

In 1694, three years after Dampier got back to England, and three years before the publication of *A New Voyage*, there appeared a book which may have triggered Dampier's change of direction.

*An Account of Several Late Voyages & Discoveries to the South and North. By Sir John Narborough* [and others]. *To which are Annexed a Large Introduction and Supplement Giving an Account of other Navigations to those Regions of the Globe.*

*London: Printed for Sam. Smith and Benj. Walford, Printers to the Royal Society.*

The matter-of-fact journals of Narborough and other recent travellers provided no kind of model for Dampier. But the anonymous 'Introduction and Supplement', which were in fact by Tancred Robinson, Fellow of the Royal Society, may have seemed to Dampier an invitation to bring forward that mass of material which he was keeping in reserve.

The Advantages of taking judicious and accurate Journals in Voyages and Itineraries, are so great and many, as the Improvement of *Geography*, *Hydrography*, *Astronomy*, *Natural* and *Moral History*, *Antiquity*, *Merchandise*, *Trade*, *Empire*, &c., that few Books compare with them either for Profit or Pleasure.[18]

Robinson demonstrates the intense enthusiasm of the early years of the Royal Society for amassing information. His introduction is a hymn of what voyagers can do to improve the stock of knowledge in the world and

17 The author's name is sometimes given as Exquemelin or Oexmelin.

18 Narborough, *An Account of Several Late Voyages and Discoveries*, v (italic/roman reversed).

hence improve the condition of mankind. He recounts the knowledge already passed on by earlier travellers to the southern ocean and the northern ice as though it were the foundations of the tower of truth. Of Barents's voyages in the 1590s he writes: 'These *Dutch* Navigations were written by *Gerart de Veer*, and contain great Variety of curious Observations, to which Mr. *Boyle* owns himself much beholden in the composing his History of Cold.'[19]

Robinson was particularly concerned about the great southern continent – on which Dampier had his own precious notes. The crime was not to publish. Recently, he wrote, several ships had passed into the South Sea, but he was unable to record what they had to offer to the sum of knowledge, 'not having seen any Journals or Voyages'.[20]

> 'Tis to be lamented, that the *English Nation* have not sent along with their *Navigators* some skilful *Painters*, *Naturalists*, and *Mechanists*, under publick *Stipends* and *Encouragements*, as the *Dutch* and *French* have done, and still practise daily, much to their Honour as well as Advantage.

The keenness of the Royal Society to use seamen as the agents of science went back to its early days. The *Philosophical Transactions* for 1666 contained 'Directions for Seamen, bound for far Voyages', designed to increase the Society's '*Philosophical* stock by the advantage, which *England* injoyes of making Voyages into all parts of the World'. Seamen were encouraged 'to keep an exact *Diary*'. What they wanted them to look out for fitted very well with Dampier's own interests, for example, 'To keep a register of all changes of Wind and Weather at all houres, by night and by day, shewing the point the Wind blows from, Whether strong or weak: The Rains, Hail, Snow and the like, the precise times of their beginnings and continuance, especially *Hurricans* and *Spouts*'.[21]

Dampier would not have read the *Philosophical Transactions*, nor would the Royal Society have intended to recruit buccaneers to the cause of science, but it is not in the least unlikely that he read Robinson and identified himself with the skilful naturalist whose observations Robinson craved. It is a possibility that the Secretary of the Royal Society himself, Sir Hans Sloane, encouraged Dampier towards the more scientific content of *A New Voyage*. Sloane, an avid collector of everything, had gone to Jamaica in 1687 as physician to the Duke of Albemarle and spent fifteen months gathering plants.[22] He had a passion for the narratives and maps of the buccaneers, and presumably gave good money for the manuscripts of Ringrose, Coxon, Sharp and others, which are now in the British

[19] *Ibid.*, xviii. [20] *Ibid.*, xiii. [21] Frantz, *The English Traveller*, 15–16 and 22–3.

[22] His two magnificent volumes on the natural history of Jamaica, *A Voyage to the Islands*, with 'large Copper-Plates as big as the Life', were not published until 1707 and 1725.

Library.[23] Sloane later acquired the early draft of Dampier's narrative which we have been examining, and when Dampier became a celebrity he arranged for the painting of his portrait by Thomas Murray (see Plate 4). It is only surmise that he advised and encouraged Dampier *before* the publication of *A New Voyage*, but there must have been someone to give Dampier the confidence to dedicate his work to Charles Montague (later Earl of Halifax), the President of the Royal Society. And perhaps to help him with the phrasing.

Yet dare I avow, according to my narrow sphere and poor abilities, a hearty Zeal for the promoting of useful knowledge, and of anything that may never so remotely tend to my Countries advantage: And I must own an Ambition of transmitting to the Publick through your hands, these Essays I have made toward those great ends, of which you are so deservedly esteemed the Patron. This hath been my design in this Publication, being desirous to bring in my Gleanings here and there in Remote Regions, to that general Magazine, of the knowledge of Foreign Parts, which the *Royal Society* thought you most worthy the Custody of, when they chose you for their *President*.

Dampier *NV*, sigs. A2 and A2v.

It is a measure of Dampier's change of direction that in the preface to *A New Voyage* he actually apologizes for including 'a Thread' of the 'Actions of the Company among whom I made the greatest part of this Voyage'. These actions were not included 'to divert the Reader with them' but to provide a scaffolding for his observations. It is his refrain that he is writing not to entertain or divert but to edify. The plainness of his style is offered as a guarantee of the seriousness of his purpose. 'As to my Stile, it cannot be expected, that a Seaman should affect Politeness; for were I able to do it, yet I think I should be little sollicitous about it, in a work of this Nature.'[24]

Dampier's frequent and disarming confessions show that his 'Method' of combining static descriptions of peoples, places and natural history with a narrative of events was never finally and satisfactorily settled. He states in the preface, for example, that 'the Reader will find as he goes along, some References to an Appendix, which I once designed to this Book', which would include 'a Chapter about the Winds in different parts of the World'. 'But such an Appendix would have swelled it too unreasonably; and therefore I chose rather to publish it hereafter by its self, as opportunity shall serve.' The fine 'Discourse of Winds' was published in 1699 in the rather strange collection of pieces that would not fit, entitled *Voyages and Descriptions*.

It was, of course, disingenuous of Dampier to disclaim any interest in the excitement of adventure in his new text. Action is certainly subordinated to observation. But one reason for soft-pedalling the adventures was

[23] See Elliott Joyce, in Wafer, *A New Voyage*, xxvi–xxviii.

[24] Dampier *NV*, sig. A3v.

to keep a misty veil over the crudities of buccaneering life, and the nature and extent of his own participation. And there is no doubt at all that some of the incidents in the manuscript version have been enlivened for the printed text in a spirit that no one could call scientific. Here is, as an example, one of the most famous passages in the book, the perilous journey in an open boat from Nicobar to Sumatra, after breaking with the buccaneers.

The evening of this 18th Day was very dismal. The Sky looked very black, being covered with dark Clouds, the Wind blew hard, and the Seas ran high. The Sea was already roaring in a white fome about us; a dark night coming on, and no Land in sight to shelter us, and our little Ark in danger to be swallowed by every Wave; and what was worst of all, none of us thought our selves prepared for another World. The Reader may better guess, than I can express, the confusion that we were all in. I had been in many eminent dangers before now, some of which I have already related, but the worst of them all was but a play-game in comparison with this. I must confess that I was in great conflicts of Mind at this time. Other dangers came not upon me with such a leisurely and dreadful solemnity: A sudden Skirmish or Engagement, or so, was nothing when ones blood was up, and pusht forward with eager expectations. But here I had a lingring view of approaching death, and little or no hopes of escaping it; and I must confess that my Courage, which I had hitherto kept up, failed me here; and I made very sad reflections on my former Life, and lookt back with horrour and detestation, on actions which before I disliked, but now I trembled at the remembrance of. I had long before this repented me of that roving course of life, but never with such concern as now. I did also call to mind the many miraculous Acts of Gods Providence towards me, in the whole course of my Life, of which kind, I believe few Men have met with the like. For all these I returned thanks in a peculiar manner, and this once more desired Gods Assistance, and composed my mind, as well as I could, in the hopes of it, and as the event shew'd, I was not disappointed of my Hopes.

Submitting our selves therefore to Gods good providence, and taking all the care we could to preserve our lives, Mr. *Hall* and I took turns to steer, and the rest took turns to heave out the Water, and thus we provided to spend the most doleful night I ever was in. About 10 a clock it began to Thunder, Lighten and Rain; but the Rain was very welcom to us, having drunk up all the Water we brought from the Island.

Dampier *NV*, 496–7.

The earlier version is much more cheerful, and there is no hint of this spiritual stock-taking.[25] The printed version is patched up out of several separate passages in the manuscript. There, the night of the eighteenth day passes quite peacefully: 'Wee lay down and sett the Malayas to steer haveing a small gale at N.E.' It was on the nineteenth day that 'in the night Mr Hall and I tooke turnes to the Helme and had a fresh gale all

[25] ff. 228v–30v.

night'. And it was on the twenty-first day (which has disappeared in the final account) that they had to bale out but at least had the comfort of fresh water.

> every sea would flape in over our Gunnalls but that wee soone hove out againe[;] in the night we had much thunder and raine which refreshed vs for all our water was spent.

The final dramatized emotional set-piece cannot be attributed simply to the hand of an editor, because the printed version contains new circumstantial technical details about the sail and the 'outlagers' which could only have come from Dampier's own notes or recollections.[26]

In the final printed version, Dampier manages to keep his own status and position extremely vague. That he was the commander of a ship would seem to be the intended inference of such a statement as 'I had a good observation of the Sun, and found myself in lat. 54 deg. 52 min. South',[27] or 'Some of our men were a little disheartned; but it was no more than I ever expected'.[28] On the other hand, there is simultaneously the continuous dissociation of himself from the buccaneers' activities. He makes a clear division between the select gentlemanly few who need the money or want to travel, and the rest – a surly, unreasonable, avaricious, violent, insubordinate lot. To some extent this separation may have been valid. The presence among the buccaneers of such educated and literate men as Basil Ringrose and the surgeon Lionel Wafer (see below, p. 32) suggests that plundering was not the sole objective of them all. Dampier includes among the reluctant buccaneers Captain Swan, who on Mindanao told him 'that what he had already done of that kind he was forc'd to; but now being at liberty, he would never engage in any such design: For, said he, there is no Prince on Earth is able to wipe off the Stain of such actions'.[29]

'Our business was to pillage', Dampier wrote. He clearly played his part in the incessant shore-raids and the harrying of Spanish shipping. But there is no reason to doubt that he was voyaging more for 'Knowledge and Experience' than for the uncertain delights of marauding.[30] His self-righteousness, however, and stern disapprobation of the buccaneering trade look like a late development. J. C. Beaglehole was right to say that the buccaneers provided Dampier with 'a convenient way of seeing the world'[31] and it is clear enough from the early draft of his work that he was often enough disgusted by the attitudes and activities of his companions.

[26] A notorious suppression that has nothing to do with maintaining the seriousness of the discourse is the omission of the seizure of a Danish vessel off the African Coast in 1683. Dampier was with Captain Cook in the Revenge. They boarded a thirty-six-gun Danish ship and took it by force. They renamed it the Batchelor's Delight and continued their cruise in it.

[27] Dampier *NV*, 82. [28] *Ibid.*, 5. [29] *Ibid.*, 364 (see also 278). [30] *Ibid.*, 440.

[31] Beaglehole, *The Exploration of the Pacific*, 166.

But it is also clear that as he revised his work he thought it prudential to establish a moral chasm between himself and buccaneering.

Dampier revolutionized his book by expanding it to include all his 'observations'; but his perplexities about managing his discourse remain and are without doubt the source of a great deal of the pleasure that the book gave. *A New Voyage* earned great respect for the abundance of its information, but its literary success was in part a matter of the reader being able to patronize the author for his *naïveté* in blending actions and descriptions, anecdotes and phenomena. When he was sick of the dropsy, Dampier wrote, he heard that 'the Natives say, that the best remedy they can find for it is the Stone or Cod of an Allegator (of which they have 4, one near each Leg, within the Flesh) pulverized and drunk in Water. ... I would have tried it, but we found no Allegators here ...'.[32]

Dampier consistently expresses his admiration for the skills and his respect for the customs of what he calls 'the Natural Inhabitants' of the countries he visited, always excepting the Australian aborigines. African slaves, however, who seem to have been present in small or very small numbers in the ships he was in, are scarcely within his vision as he writes. They are mentioned on the crossing of the isthmus, with fear that they will abscond with equipment (which they do) or might knock them on the head while they slept (which they do not). About the inhabitants of New Holland, or Australia, Dampier had nothing good to say. He found their appearance and manners repulsive, and considered them strangely uncooperative in not being willing to carry barrels of water in exchange for clothes.[33] These are the exceptions. At the other extreme are the Moskito Indians from Honduras.[34] It was customary to have several of them on board; they were chiefly useful for their skill in 'striking' fish, turtles and manatees with 'Harpoons and Turtle-irons'. They lived very independent lives. It was of course the adaptability and amenability of these cooperative Indians that commended them to the buccaneers.

Dampier's admiration for the dexterity and ability of 'primitive' peoples rests on an implicit conviction of general European superiority. 'They have no names among themselves; and they take it as a great favour to be named of any of us; and will complain for want of it.' 'They learn our Language, and they take the Governor of *Jamaica* to be one of the greatest Princes in the World.'[35] At the same time, Dampier is too much interested

32 Dampier *NV*, 255–6.

33 For the far-reaching effect of Dampier's renowned expression of dislike for the aborigines, see Bernard Smith, *European Vision and the South Pacific*, 125–6.

34 The Moskito Indians of the Atlantic coast were in fact a mixed race from interbreeding with African slaves. Their cooperation with the English, and their slaving raids on tribes in the interior, are described by Floyd, *Anglo-Spanish Struggle* (e.g. 22–3 and 64–7). The notorious raids reappear in the narratives of Uring (see p. 147) and Roach (p. 201).

35 Dampier *NV*, 86–7 and 10–11.

in the appearance, clothing, buildings, customs, family relationships and so on of the many different peoples he describes to spend time asserting superiority. The quality of his attitude and his interest is well shown in a notable passage expressing his scepticism about cannibalism.

As for the common opinion of *Anthropophagi*,[36] or Man-eaters, I did never meet with any such people: All Nations or Families in the World, that I have seen or heard of, having some sort of food to live on, either Fruit, Grain, Pulse, or Roots, which grow naturally, or else planted by them: if not Fish and Land-Animals besides; (yea, even the People of *New-Holland*, had Fish amidst all their penury) would scarce kill a man purposely to eat him. I know not what barbarous Customs may formerly have been in the World; and to sacrifice their Enemeies to their Gods is a thing that hath been much talkt of with relation to the Savages of *America*. I am a stranger to that also, if it be, or have been customary in any Nation there; and yet, if they sacrifice their Enemies it is not necessary that they should eat them too. After all, I will not be peremptory in the Negative, but I speak as to the compass of my own knowledge, and know some of these Cannibal stories to be false, and many of them have been disproved since I first went to the *West Indies*. At that time how barbarous were the poor *Florida Indians* accounted, which now we find to be civil enough? What strange stories have we heard of the *Indians*, whose Islands were called the Isles of *Cannibals*? Yet we find that they do Trade very civilly with the *French* and the *Spaniards*; and have done so with us. I do own that they have formerly endeavoured to destroy our Plantations at *Barbadoes*, and have since hindred us from settling the Island *Santa Lucia* by destroying 2 or 3 Colonies successively of those that were settled there; and even the Island *Tobago* has been often annoyed and ravaged by them, when settled by the *Dutch*, and still lies waste (though a delicate fruitful Island) as being too near the *Caribbees* on the Continent, who visit it every Year. But this was to preserve their own right, by endeavouring to keep out any that would settle themselves on those Islands, where they had planted themselves; yet, even these People would not hurt a single person, as I have been told by some that have been Prisoners among them.

Dampier *NV*, 485–6.

## II

Of the several accounts of the doings of the buccaneers which overlap with Dampier's, the most interesting is that of Lionel Wafer, ship's surgeon, whose book *A New Voyage and Description of the Isthmus of America* was published in 1699, two years after Dampier's book, by the same publisher, James Knapton. Unlike Dampier, Wafer decided (as did so many of his predecessors in Hakluyt and Purchas) to make the story of his adventures a prelude to the quite separate, and very extensive, commentary on the territory and its inhabitants. Wafer had the great advantage over

[36] The text reads '*Authropophagi*'.

Dampier of having lived among the Indians and his well-written description of them is a more serious contribution to ethnography than Dampier's more tangential experience could possibly provide.

Wafer was several times in Dampier's company, including the first stages of the main south-sea voyage under Captain Cook, 'tho' he forgot to mention me in that part of his Voyages'.[37] The focus of comparison is on the march back across the isthmus in 1681. Wafer's leg was hurt in a gunpowder accident. Unable to keep up with the main party, he went ahead at his own speed with a small group of others similarly outpaced, including Richard Gopson, 'an ingenious Man, and a good Scholar; and had with him a *Greek* Testament which he frequently read, and would translate *extempore* into English to such of the Company as were dispos'd to hear him'.[38] Gopson reached the safety of the ships in the Caribbean, but was so exhausted that he very soon died. Another member of the group was William Bowman, who slipped off a branch into a flooded river and was carried downstream; miraculously he survived, in spite of the weight of '400 pieces of Eight' on his back. 'He was a weakly Man, a Taylor by Trade.'[39]

Unlike Dampier, Wafer did not keep a journal. 'Yet I have not trusted altogether to my own Memory; but some Things I committed to Writing, long before I return'd to England; and have since been frequently comparing and rectifying my Notices, by Discoursing such of my Fellow-Travellers as I have met with in London.'[40] Dampier incorporated an early draft of Wafer's narrative in his own first version (the Sloane manuscript). Presumably it was a joint decision that each should publish separately a much expanded redaction of his own work.

It is not to disparage Wafer's trustworthiness to say that the absorbing narrative of his adventures often reads like fiction. Here is a representative passage. It is the conclusion of an account of a deluge that caused a great flood and separated Wafer from his companions. He found a precarious safety overnight by climbing into a hollow tree.

> While I was Praying and Meditating thus on my sad Condition, I saw the Morning Star appear, by which I knew that Day was at hand. This cheared my drooping Spirits, and in less than half an hour the Day began to dawn, the Rain and Lightning ceas'd, and the Waters abated, insomuch that by the time the Sun was up, the Water has gone off from my Tree.
>
> Then I ventured out of my cold Lodging; but being stiff and the Ground slippery, I could scarce stand. Yet I made a shift to ramble to the Place where we had made our Fire, but found no Body there. Then I call'd out aloud, but was answer'd only with my own Eccho; which struck such Terror into me, that I fell down as dead, being oppress'd both with Grief and Hunger; this being the 7th Day of our Fast, save only the *Maccaw*-berries before related.

[37] Wafer, *A New Voyage*, 29. [38] *Ibid.*, 5. [39] *Ibid.*, 10. [40] *Ibid.*, lxviii.

Being in this Condition, despairing of Comfort for want of my Consorts, I lay some time on the wet Ground, till at last I heard a Voice hard by me, which in some sort revived me; but especially when I saw it was Mr. *Hingson*, one of my Companions, and the rest found us presently after, having all sav'd themselves by climbing small Trees. We greeted each other with Tears in our Eyes, and returned Thanks to God for our Deliverance.

Wafer, *A New Voyage*, 13.

As we know, such stories as this were written up by Wafer some time after the event. Then (as we can see by comparison with the version in Dampier's manuscript) they were revised. In his Hakluyt Society edition Elliott Joyce usefully gives examples of the changes. He thinks that 'a competent sub-editor' was responsible for the greater sophistication of the printed version.[41] But it is striking that the changes in Wafer's stories are trifling compared with the wholesale reorganization and rearrangement which we found in the stories of Captain Swan's conversation with Dampier on Guam and of the boat journey to Sumatra. The narrative order, the language, and the tone of comment remain unaffected.

If we get the sense of *déjà vu* in reading Wafer it is not Wafer's fault. What seems to us the conventional stuff of travel fiction is in fact the source of the conventions of eighteenth-century travel fiction, as Percy Adams's book, *Travel Literature and the Evolution of the Novel*, shows.[42] Wafer's printed accounts may have journeyed some distance from 'what actually happened' but their story-book air seems to derive from Wafer's own presentational style, wherever that was formed, rather than from imitation of accepted patterns by him or an editor. He helped later fiction to masquerade as fact.[43]

In the real world too, Wafer's account of the isthmus had a very great influence and here it is necessary to return to Dampier. In *A New Voyage* Dampier relates with his usual dispassionate detachment the mistakes, misjudgements, misunderstandings, cowardice, deceit and treachery which led to the total failure of the buccaneers' attempt to plunder Guayaquil on the west coast (modern Ecuador) in 1684.[44] He pays particular attention to what became of 'three Barks coming from *Guiaquil*, laden with Negroes' – a thousand of them, 'all lusty young Men and Women'. They intercepted these slave-ships, but after the failure of the raid contented themselves with carrying off 'about forty of the stoutest Negro-Men'. Then follows a remarkable passage, of which there is no trace in the earlier manuscript version, in which Dampier relates, though

41 *Ibid.*, lxii. 42 See index to Adams, *Travel Literature*, under 'Wafer'.

43 An excellent example of fact looking like fiction is Wafer's account of the bleeding and curing of a chieftain's wife (Wafer, *A New Voyage*, 18–19). The only alteration here was to delete a sentence which implied the equality of Indians and Europeans.

44 Dampier *NV*, 153–8.

it 'may seem to the Reader but Golden Dreams', what might have happened if they had carried off the slave-ships.

> There never was a greater opportunity put into the hands of men to enrich themselves than we had; to have gone with these *Negroes*, and settled our selves at *Santa Maria*, on the *Isthmus* of *Darien*, and employed them in getting Gold out of the Mines there.
>
> Dampier *NV*, 158.

For not only had the buccaneers driven the Spaniards from this area, but the Indians, 'who were mortal Enemies to the *Spaniards*, . . . were our fast friends, and ready to receive and assist us'. Access to the northern coast of the isthmus made the position ideal for trade.

> In a short time we should have had assistance from all parts of the *West Indies*; many thousands of Privateers from *Jamaica* and the *French* Islands especially would have flockt over to us; and long before this time we might have been masters not only of those Mines, (the richest Gold-Mines ever yet found in *America*) but of all the coast as high as *Quito*: And much more than I say might then probably have been done.
>
> Dampier *NV*, 159.

These golden dreams of Dampier's were closely related to those of William Paterson for establishing a Scottish presence in the West Indies, which realized themselves in the terrible disaster of the Darien colony, the first contingent of which sailed to its painful fate in July 1698, a year after the publication of *A New Voyage*. Paterson had obtained from Dampier a copy of Wafer's journal, and this was read by the directors of the company formed to promote the Scottish colony. Wafer himself was spirited up to Edinburgh, and, under the promise of a commission to lead an expedition, was milked of his knowledge about Golden Island, off the Panama coast.[45] Both Dampier and Wafer were summoned for questioning in London by the Lords of Trade and Plantations, who were deeply hostile to Scottish colonial initiatives. Neither man was closely involved with planning the Scottish venture, but their optimistic tone about the potentialities of Darien had a great, and tragic, effect.[46]

## III

Dampier's dream of enriching himself by organizing slave labour to work Panamanian gold mines remained a dream on paper; and what brought him fame and prosperity was the book in which he wrote down that dream. Charles Hatton wrote to his brother, Viscount Hatton, in May

45 Elliott Joyce, in Wafer, *A New Voyage*, li–liv; and Prebble, *Darien Disaster*, 106–8.

46 For a full account of Wafer's report on conditions on the isthmus and its effect on the Darien enterprise, see Prebble, *Darien Disaster*, 66–7.

1697, 'Dampier's Voyage takes so wonderfully, 2 editions are already sold of, and he tells me he is fitting y^e^ second part for y^e^ press'.[47] The Royal Society praised him in the *Philosophical Transactions* for 1697 for the diligence of his observations in parts of the world 'for the most part unknown to English Navigators'.[48] He was granted a sinecure in the Customs, and Sir Hans Sloane arranged for his portrait to be painted. He dined with Pepys, the Secretary of the Navy, in August 1698, and there met John Evelyn, who recorded his meeting with the 'famous buccaneer', and found him 'a more modest man than one would imagine' (modest in the sense of well behaved).[49] The 'good Reception and universal Approbation' of *A New Voyage*[50] made him an authority to be consulted on all sides.

Dampier's main reward was, however, something of a poisoned chalice. Charles Montague, President of the Royal Society, brought him to the attention of the Earl of Orford, First Lord of the Admiralty, and he was asked to submit proposals for a major voyage of exploration. These proposals (which Masefield printed in his second volume, pp. 325–7) were for a voyage with two ships lasting three years to explore 'Terra Australis' ('that vast space surrounding ye South Pole') and 'ye remoter part of the *East India Islands*'. He was offered one ship, the Jolly Prize, which in June 1698 he turned down as unfit. He accepted in its stead the Roebuck, although at the conclusion of the voyage this ship, in Dampier's words, 'founder'd thro' perfect Age near the Island of *Ascension*'.[51]

He was now genuinely a captain, and immune from any accusation of not directing his own discoveries. He took the ship over in August 1698 and eventually sailed from the Downs in January 1699. Before leaving England, he deposited the manuscript of his second volume with James Knapton. It was published in February as *Voyages and Descriptions, Vol. II*.[52] It is an odd compilation of what had been left over from the previous volume. The first section described what had happened to Dampier in 1688–9 after reaching Sumatra (chiefly his journey to Tonquin). The second section goes right back to Dampier's first years in the Caribbean, 1674–6. The third section is his most scientific work, his Discourse on Winds. The first two sections, though enlivened by well-told anecdotes, tend to ramble and straggle (to use two of his favourite words). The Tonquin journey, in Conradian waters, offers many glimpses of Conradian wanderers and exiles, even in those early years. Perhaps the

47 *Hatton Correspondence*, II, 225; quoted by Bonner, *Captain William Dampier*, 33.
48 Frantz, *The English Traveller*, 18.
49 Evelyn, *Diary*, ed. Dobson (London 1908), 445.
50 Funnell, *A Voyage Round the World*, Preface.
51 Dampier, *A Voyage to New Holland*, Dedication, sig. A3 (hereafter *VNH*).
52 The handsome Argonaut edition of 1931, by C. Wilkinson, based on the edition of 1729, inexplicably used the title *Voyages and Discoveries*.

best story in the second section is the tragedy of the mysterious and romantic figure of 'Indian Warner'.

> I have been informed that this Captain *Warner*, whom they mentioned, was born at *Antego*, one of our *English* Islands, and the Son of Governour *Warner*, by an *Indian Woman*, and bred up by his Father after the English manner; he learned the *Indian* Language also of his Mother; but being grown up, and finding himself despised by his *English* Kindred, he forsook his Father's House, got away to St *Lucia*, and there lived among the *Caribbe Indians*, his Relations by the Mother side. Where conforming himself to their Customs he became one of their Captains, and roved from one Island to another, as they did. About this Time the *Caribbees* had done some spoil on our *English* Plantations at *Antego*: and therefore Governour *Warner*'s Son by his Wife, took a Party of Men and went to suppress those *Indians*; and came to the place where his Brother the *Indian Warner* lived. Great seeming Joy there was at their Meeting; but how far it was real the Event shewed; for the *English Warner* providing plenty of Liquor, and inviting his half Brother to be merry with him, in the midst of his Entertainment ordered his Men upon a signal given to murder him and all his *Indians*; which was accordingly performed. The Reason of this inhumane Action is diversly reported; some say that this *Indian-Warner* committed all the spoil that was done to the *English*; and therefore for that Reason his Brother kill'd him and his Men. Others that he was a great Friend to the *English*, and would not suffer his Men to hurt them, but did all in his power to draw them to an amicable Commerce; and that his Brother kill'd him, for that he was ashamed to be related to an *Indian*. But be it how it will, he was call'd in question for the Murder, and forced to come Home to take his Tryal in *England*. Such perfidious Doings as these, beside the baseness of them, are great hindrances of our gaining an Interest among the *Indians*.
>
> Dampier *VD*, pt. II, 5–6.

(Needless to say, Colonel Philip Warner, Deputy-Governor of Antigua, was acquitted of the charge of murder. He claimed that the Indian was not his half-brother, and had been killed in fair fight. His accuser was convicted of perjury.[53])

It can be argued that the third section of the book, the Discourse on Winds, is Dampier's most notable achievement. It is a very serious disquisition, and argues an extraordinary attentiveness and intelligence in marshalling and analysing his observations. J. C. Shipman's book, *William Dampier: Seaman-Scientist* (1962), records the respect given to Dampier's work over the centuries by seamen and meteorologists alike: Sir William Shaw's four-volume *Manual of Meteorology* of 1942 'quotes in full detail Dampier's now classic description of a typhoon'.[54] The literary register of these scientific observations is very interesting indeed.

53 See Masefield, *Dampier's Voyages*, II, 111; and the documentation in Hulme and Whitehead, *Wild Majesty*, 89–106.

54 Shipman, *William Dampier*, 14.

The Clouds that precede a Hurricane are different from the North Banks, in this, that whereas the Clouds preceding Norths are uniform and regular; of an exact blackness even from the Horizon to the upper edg of it, and that as streight and even as a Line stretched out. On the contrary, the Hurricane-Clouds tower up their Heads, pressing forwards as if they all strove for precedency; yet so linked one within another, that all move alike. Besides, the edges of these Clouds are guilded with various and affrighting Colours, the very edg of all seems to be of a pale fire colour, next that of a dull yallow, and nearer the Body of the Cloud of a Copper Colour, and the Body of the Cloud which is very thick appears extraordinary Black: and altogether it looks very terrible and amazing even beyond expression.

Dampier *VD*, pt. III, 71.

The elements are humanized and provided with emotions as though the reality of the phenomena depended upon a response both aesthetic and sympathetic in the reader-observer. This animistic view of nature is strikingly original. Dampier was writing in total ignorance of the 'hylozoistic' debate about nature recounted in Barbara Stafford's *Voyage into Substance.* Stafford's time-bracket of 1760–1840 precludes discussion of Dampier's important work, which was of course read by all the later voyagers whom she *does* discuss (for example, Banks) and which presumably influenced them in their 'vitalizing' of natural objects.

These sea-breezes do commonly rise in the Morning about Nine a Clock, sometimes sooner, sometimes later: they first approach the shore so gently, as if they were afraid to come near it, and oft-times they make some faint breathings, and as if not willing to offend, they make a halt and seem ready to retire. I have waited many a time both ashore to receive the pleasure, and at Sea to take the Benefit of it.

It comes in a fine, small, black Curle upon the Water, whenas all the Sea between it, and the shore not yet reach'd by it, is as smooth and even as Glass in Comparison; in half an Hour's time after it has reached the shore it fans pretty briskly, and so increaseth gradually till 12 a Clock, then it is commonly strongest, and lasts so till 2 or 3 a very brisk gale; about 12 at Noon it also veres off the Sea 2 or 3 Points, or more in very fair Weather. After 3 a Clock it begins to dye away again, and gradually withdraws its force till all is spent, and about 5 a Clock, sooner or later, according as the Weather is, it is lull'd asleep, and comes no more till the next Morning.

Dampier *VD*, pt. III, chap. 4.

Interspersed among such remarkable endeavours to create a scientifically accurate description by way of anthropomorphism are frequent homely examples of personal experience. In Chapter 6, 'Of Storms', Dampier describes 'a very violent Storm, sailing from Virginia'. By an error of the master and 'him that con'd', the ship broached to. The master 'raved like a mad Man' and no expedient would 'bring her . . . to her Course'.

I was at this time on the Deck with some others of our Men: and among the rest one Mr. *John Smallbone*, who was the main Instrument at that time of saving us all. Come! said he to me, let us go a little way up the Foreshrouds, it may be that will make the Ship wear; for I have been doing it before now. He never tarried for an Answer, but run forward presently [meaning immediately], and I followed him. We went up the Shrouds Half-mast up, and there we spread abroad the Flaps of our Coats, and presently the Ship wore.

Dampier *VD*, pt. III, 64.

Dampier was away in the Roebuck for a little more than two years, returning to England in the early summer of 1701. The first part of his narrative of the expedition, *A Voyage to New Holland* was published in 1703, the complete version not appearing until 1709. His difficulties with this narrative were increased by losing 'many of my Books and Papers' in the sinking of the Roebuck. The querulous and defensive preface to what he calls 'this *Third Volume*' of his '*Voyages and Descriptions*' strongly asserts its dedication 'to such Readers at home as are more desirous of a Plain and Just Account of the true Nature and State of the Things described, than of a Polite and Rhetorical Narrative'. This aspiration does not extend to details about the almost continuous quarrels with his subordinates. Indeed, he never mentions any of his officers by name, but speaks in general of 'this Vexatious Voyage; wherein the Ignorance and Obstinacy withal, of some under me, occasion'd me a great deal of Trouble' and of 'many Difficulties, the Particulars of which I shall not trouble the Reader with'.[55] As J. A. Williamson put it, 'Dampier's qualifications to lead a difficult expedition lay solely in his literary talent'.[56] When it came to it, he lacked the personal qualities for successful command, however good a seaman and navigator he may have been.

The main source of friction was Lieut. George Fisher, R.N., his first lieutenant. Feuding began when the ship was still in the Downs and grew steadily worse until Dampier physically assaulted Fisher, put him in irons and set him ashore in a Portuguese goal in Bahia. For this treatment Dampier was court-martialled on his return from the voyage. The bitter testimonies to the court on both sides of this lacerating relationship are printed in the second volume of Masefield's *Dampier's Voyages*. Dampier was found guilty of 'very hard and cruel usage' of Fisher and was fined the whole of his pay for the voyage. It was the opinion of the court that Dampier was not a fit person to be employed as a commander of any of Her Majesty's ships.

Because the Roebuck's departure was so much delayed, Dampier approached Australia from the west via the Cape of Good Hope rather than from the east via Cape Horn. His exploration was confined to the

[55] Dampier *VNH*, 44 and 45. [56] Dampier *VNH*, ed. Williamson (1939), xxx.

north-western and northern coasts. He was anxious to win the confidence of the aborigines and hoped they would prove amenable to commercial projects and developments.

> I intended especially to observe what Inhabitants I should meet with, and to try to win them over to somewhat of Traffick and useful Intercourse, as there might be Commodities among any of them that might be fit for Trade or Manufacture, or any found out in which they might be employed.
>
> Dampier, *VNH*, pt. II, 4.

Contact was very slight, however, and tended to be frustratingly confrontational. Dampier turned away from Australia to explore New Guinea, New Britain and New Ireland. Vegetation, the birds, beasts and fish, are described in his narrative in the usual minute detail (accompanied by drawings); some of the best pages are about the inhabitants, particularly the mixed people of Timor. This information was highly prized by succeeding travellers, but a modern reader may feel that a great deal of the life that sparkles no naively and refreshingly in *A New Voyage* has disappeared in this third and last of Dampier's narratives.

## IV

Dampier sailed on two further major expeditions. He obtained the command of a privateer, the St George, sponsored to take advantage of the War of the Spanish Succession by harrying French and Spanish shipping. He sailed from Ireland in 1703 in company with a second ship, the Cinque Ports, returning in 1707 with little achieved. He wrote nothing about this voyage, but in 1707 his publisher James Knapton brought out *A Voyage Round the World. Containing an Account of Captain Dampier's Expedition into the South-Seas in the Ship St. George.* This was by William Funnell, 'Mate to Captain *Dampier*', and it is consistently belittling in its presentation of Dampier, disagreeing with his judgements and painting him as faint-hearted and indecisive. ('Our men would have set the Village on fire but the Captain being ashore would not suffer them.'[57]) Funnell's attitudes both to animals and to people are repulsive. He describes baiting sea-lions and getting Indians hopelessly drunk with equal delight. Eventually he broke away from Dampier and went off to India in a prize ship.

In response, Dampier published a *Vindication of his Voyage*, with 'some small Observations' on 'Mr. Funnel's Chimerical Relation' (reprinted by Masefield), an angry, bitter, abusive document, disputing facts and attacking Funnell for his behaviour and moral standards. Whoever is in the right, it is clear that Dampier had been unable to exercise control and had reacted violently to all questioning of his authority.

[57] Funnell, *A Voyage Round the World*, 79.

Dampier's final employment at sea was not as captain but as pilot on another privateering expedition, financed by Bristol merchants who fitted out two ships, the Duke and the Dutchess, under the command of Woodes Rogers. This was another three-year voyage (1708–11), and unlike the cruise of the St George it was extremely lucrative for its backers. Once again, Dampier published no account of this voyage, and he plays a subdued and unflattering role in Woodes Rogers's famous narrative, *A Cruising Voyage Round the World* (1712). This buoyant and self-confident account, many times reprinted, is utterly different in tone from anything Dampier wrote. The fierce discipline that Rogers imposed on his ships is somehow intensified in the no-nonsense authority of his text. All his dealings, however stern, are supremely reasonable, no other policy decision would have been correct, no alternative version of events would have been true. He mentions 'several unhappy Differences arising at and before our Attempt on *Guiaquil*. This made me so particularly relate all that pass'd material in that Attempt, so that I doubt not any ones contradicting this Journal to my Disadvantage. ... Not being willing to make the Reader a Party-taker, or trouble his Patience to read over unreasonable Feuds, I have left 'em as much as possible out of my Journal.'[58] The constant use of ''em' for 'them' is all part of the plain-man good sense which Rogers cultivates. 'I rather chuse to keep to the Language of the Sea',[59] and indeed the colloquial directness of his style is quite an achievement.

It had been a requirement of 'the Employers' that all major decisions during the voyage should be confirmed in written agreements signed by the senior officers. The texts of these agreements are cleverly used by Rogers to confirm his own wisdom, or, when things go wrong (as with the failure to capture the Acapulco treasure-galleon), to demonstrate his reservations about these communal decisions and his certainty that if *his* advice had been taken all would have been well. At one point there was a dispute about whether Captain Dover should be put in command of a prize. The resolutions and counter-resolutions on this subject Rogers contemptuously called 'a Paper-War amongst our selves'. 'I am sorry to trouble the Reader with these Disputes.' Unfortunately, 'this Dispute is against my Desire already put in Print, from the publick Notes of the Voyage, otherwise I had left it wholly out of my Journal, as I had done several other of our Differences'.[60]

Among the signatories of some of these agreements is Alexander Selkirk. *A Cruising Voyage Round the World* contains the celebrated story of his rescue after four years on Juan Fernandez, where he had been left by the captain of the Cinque Ports, with whom he had quarrelled, on Dampier's previous

[58] Rogers, *A Cruising Voyage*, 237. [59] *Ibid.*, 1. [60] *Ibid.*, 309 and 311.

voyage. The familiar story of the 'Man cloth'd in Goat-Skins, who look'd wilder than the first Owners of them' is very well told, though it ends in an uncharacteristically pious tone.

> We may perceive by this Story the Truth of the Maxim, That Necessity is the Mother of Invention, since he found means to supply his Wants in a very natural manner, so as to maintain his Life, tho not so conveniently, yet as effectually as we are able to do with the help of all our Arts and Society. It may likewise instruct us, how much a plain and temperate way of living conduces to the Health of the Body and the Vigour of the Mind, both which we are apt to destroy by Excess and Plenty, especially of strong Liquor, and the Variety as well as the Nature of our Meat and Drink: for this Man, when he came to our ordinary Method of Diet and Life, tho he was sober enough, lost much of his Strength and Agility. But I must quit these Reflections, which are more proper for a Philosopher and Divine than a Mariner, and return to my own Subject.
>
> Rogers, *A Cruising Voyage*, 130–1.

Rogers also takes a high moral tone about gambling – surprising in a commission of banditry, piracy and pillage. There was another signed resolution on this score and there it appears that the evil of gambling was that 'some by chance might thus too slightly get Possession of what his Fellow-Adventurers have dangerously and painfully earn'd'.

Rogers claims to have treated the Spaniards whom he captured with civility and tolerance, in spite of his sly little jokes about their religion. He also expresses indignation at inhumanity towards Indians. But about the African slaves he occasionally had aboard his attitude is unequivocal. They were 'the most troublesome Goods we had'. They were 'punish'd severely' when they tried to run away.[61] They were carried about to be sold, not for service. There were also women, in a different category. At one point 'one of our Negro Women' gave birth on board to 'A Girl of a Tawny Colour'. The father could not have been one of Rogers's men.

> But to prevent the other she-Negro (call'd *Daphne*) from being debauch'd in our Ship, I gave her a strict Charge to be modest, with Threats of severe Punishment, if she was found otherwise. One of the *Dutchess*'s black Nymphs having transgressed this Way, was lately whip'd at the Capston. This I mention to satisfy the censorious, that we don't countenance Lewdness, and that we took these Women aboard, only because they spoke *English*, and begg'd to be admitted for Landresses, Cooks and Semstresses.
>
> Rogers, *A Cruising Voyage*, 279.

What Rogers calls 'our long and fatiguing Voyage' came to an end in October 1711. In March 1715, William Dampier died in London, aged sixty-two. His life had reached a peak with the publication of *A New Voyage Round the World*, when he was forty-four, and began to decline even as his

[61] *Ibid.*, 190 and 228.

career seemed to be reaching new heights. He was essentially an observer, and, in spite of his lack of sophistication, a writer. Though he did not lack initiative in making decisions about his life, he was happier when events were taking their course than when he was trying to shape them. He was a sad failure as a leader. The personality that emerges from the historical documents is of a moody, withdrawn and irascible man. The personality that emerges from the writings is altogether different. Partly it is his own self-creation, dictated by a shrinking from exposure and accusation, but it is not difficult to get behind image and self-presentation to find a diffident enthusiast, making notes even as he trailed his musket on a buccaneering raid. The town, he once remarked, 'has a good handsom Church. One thing I have observed in all the *Indian* Towns under the *Spanish* Government ... that the Images of the Virgin *Mary* and other Saints ... are still painted in an *Indian* Complexion, and partly in that dress; but in those Towns which are inhabited chiefly by *Spaniards*, the Saints also conform themselves to the *Spanish* Garb and complexion.'[62]

Dampier's originality lay in his absorption in everything that was around him and his zest for collecting the most detailed information in all sorts of areas which quickly became the provinces of specialists and professionals. J. C. Beaglehole wrote: 'Dampier was a natural genius: he had the scientific mind and observed with an intentness as painstaking as it was unusual, he recorded his observations with precision and vividness, not because of training or an interest in the academic'.[63] The hesitation and uneasiness in his writings as regards the proportions and balance of observation and actions are a clear indication that although travel-writing had had an immensely long history it was now entering a new phase, and Dampier had few models to follow. He was, indeed, engaged with a much bigger problem than he realized: the discomfort of the new travel-literature about its readership. Later in the century, as official scientific expeditions were organized and 'observation' was revolutionized in its classificatory procedures, the reviews which represented the all-important lay readership were still unhappy about the proper division between information and experience in travel accounts.[64]

[62] Dampier *NV*, 123. [63] Beaglehole, *The Exploration of the Pacific*, 166.
[64] See Pratt, *Imperial Eyes*, 87.

# Part II

# 3

# A disconsolate black albatross

The best-known example of the impact of eighteenth-century voyage-narratives on imaginative literature is the albatross in Coleridge's poem, 'The Ancient Mariner'. It was Wordsworth who (in 1797) thought of the shooting of an albatross, described in Shelvocke's *Voyage Round the World*, when Coleridge was in need of a crime which would bring 'the spectral persecution' on his hero.[1] In *The Road to Xanadu*, John Livingstone Lowes wrote at length about the fundamental importance that this borrowing came to have on the structure of the poem as a whole. Wordsworth said he had been reading Shelvocke a day or two before. The passage in Shelvocke's book, published in 1726, was concerned with his attempt to get through the Straits of Le Maire and round Cape Horn. The weather was dreadful, with continual squalls of sleet, snow and rain, 'and the heavens were perpetually hidden from us by gloomy, dismal clouds'. There was no sign of life; no fish to be seen –

> nor one sea-bird; except a disconsolate black *Albitross*, who accompanied us for several days, hovering about us as if he had lost himself, till *Hatley*, (my second Captain) observing, in one of his melancholy fits, that this bird was always hovering near us, imagin'd, from his colour, that it might be some ill omen. That which, I suppose, induced him the more to encourage his superstition, was the continued series of contrary tempestuous winds, which had oppress'd us ever since we had got into this sea. But be that as it would, he, after some fruitless attempts, at length, shot the *Albitross*, not doubting (perhaps) that we should have a fair wind after it. I must own, that this navigation is truly melancholy, and was the more so to us, who were by ourselves without a companion, which would have somewhat diverted our thoughts from the reflection of being in such a remote part of the world, and as it were, separated from the rest of mankind to struggle with the dangers of a stormy climate, far distant from any port to have recourse to, in case of the loss of masts, or any other accident; nor any chance of receiving assistance from any other ship.
>
> Shelvocke, *Voyage Round the World*, 73.

Shooting albatrosses later became a matter of course on southern voyages. Naturalists seemed to think it their duty to shoot as many as they

[1] Wordsworth to Isabella Fenwick, quoted by Lowes, *The Road to Xanadu*, 203.

could (see p. 100), and very frequently the birds were cooked and eaten. Often enough there was comment on their huge wing-spread. Shelvocke's passage is quite remarkable in investing the bird with an identity, and imagining it to have feelings, and in responding to its presence. Not that Shelvocke shared his second captain's illusions about the bird's sinister powers; he makes it clear that the contrary winds went on for weeks after the death of the bird. But his association of the solitary dark bird with their own despondency, danger and isolation, 'separated from the rest of mankind', is unusually sensitive and imaginative.

The passage impressed Wordsworth, but it did not impress William Betagh, the captain of the marines in the same ship. 'After all your whining', he wrote, "tis plain it better suted your scheme to be without captain *Clipperton*'.[2] Shelvocke had two particular purposes in composing this passage; one was to discredit Simon Hatley, who, with Betagh and others, deserted him later in the voyage; and the other was, by making much of the misery and danger of being alone, to conceal the fact that he had deliberately separated himself from his sister-ship.

George Shelvocke was an educated man of good family who had served as a naval officer, and in 1718, when he was about forty-three years old, he was chosen by a group of 'gentlemen adventurers' to command two privateers, the Success and the Speedwell, being sent to harry the Spaniards in the South Seas.[3] But the partners soon decided that they could not trust him and they put John Clipperton (who had been Dampier's mate in 1704) in overall command, leaving Shelvocke in command of the smaller ship, the Speedwell. The two ships soon lost contact, and it seems certain that Shelvocke, not brooking his deposition, gave Clipperton the slip, and decided to take the Speedwell on a privateering expedition on his own account. He claimed that off the Brazilian coast his crew mutinied and forced him to agree to turn buccaneer and share the booty with them, cutting out the sponsors. When he returned after a three-year voyage in 1722 he was arrested at the behest of the 'adventurers'. He seems to have escaped and avoided charges being laid against him, but clearly he needed to vindicate himself. He submitted an account of his voyage to the Admiralty, and then in 1726 published 'a more compleat and perfect account of my proceedings'. He hoped that his narrative would be helpful to future navigators, and would also be acceptable to his 'Land-reader', whom he had endeavoured to 'entertain with a true voyage, after he has been so long amused by the fictitious circumnavigations, and extra-

[2] Betagh, *A Voyage Round the World*, 58.

[3] Some of these biographical details are from W. G. Perrin's introduction to the reprint of Shelvocke in 'The Seafarer's Library' (1928). Unfortunately the reprint is inaccurate, and it does not give Shelvocke's important prefatory material.

ordinary adventures that have lately appeared in print'.[4] Shelvocke was a spirited writer, but his best passages by far are those like the albatross passage in which he was romancing or misrepresenting the facts.

His narrative is full of reckless and pugnacious abuse of his officers and crew, and of Clipperton. Clipperton was not a gentleman and did not like gentlemen – 'the very thoughts of having any thing like a Gentleman in his ship terrified him'. Moreover, not being a naval person, he was 'a stranger to regular discipline'. As for putting a drunkard like him in command of the expedition, 'no body that had a thorough knowledge of him wou'd have given him the charge of a Collier'.[5] Hatley (who had been Woodes Rogers's third mate) was no better. He could not accuse Betagh, a marine officer, of lack of seamanship, but he could despise his incompetence and cowardice. Contempt for everyone else and pity for himself he could turn on like a tap.

> It was a melancholy reflection to me, that after having been 30 years an Officer in the service, under the best regulated discipline in the world, I should now be harass'd with continual mutinies, and exposed to the unthinking malice, and unaccountable humours of my own ship's company. For I must ingenuously profess, I dar'd not punish them as they deserv'd; and was certain that some of my chief Officers privately approved of their actions, as I afterwards found by their conduct.
>
> Shelvocke, *Voyage Round the World*, 26.

Two years after the appearance of Shelvocke's narrative, William Betagh published his *Voyage Round the World*. Shelvocke's 'pretended narrative' was 'intirely a deception, and his whole conduct an indignity to his country'. He was publishing his own narrative 'to undeceive mankind' about an account which was a 'libel invented to give a gloss to all his evil actions' – 'the most absurd and false narrative that was ever deliver'd to the publick'.[6] Considering the offensiveness of Shelvocke's comments on him, the violence of Betagh's tone is understandable, but it does not improve what seems to be a very good case against Shelvocke. The two narratives are an angry dialogue, and we can neither wholly trust nor wholly discredit either of the disputants, though the balance of credibility is certainly on Betagh's side. (He had the additional advantage of using a journal kept in Clipperton's ship.)

The keystone of Shelvocke's narrative is the mutiny at St Catherine's Island, Brazil, and he gives a very lengthy account of it. The ringleader was 'one Matthew Stewart', who presented Shelvocke with a letter signed by all the petty officers and most of the crew, and a set of articles proposing the sharing out of all plunder equally among the ship's company with 5

[4] Shelvocke, *A Voyage Round the World*, xxxii. [5] *Ibid.*, xxii and xxv.

[6] Betagh, *A Voyage Round the World*, Dedication, 2, and 323.

per cent extra for Shelvocke. Shelvocke pooh-poohs 'the needless tautologies, insignificant expressions, incoherency and dull confusion with which the Articles, etc., were drawn up'. And he did all he could, he wrote, 'to destroy their project'. But the mutineers grew impatient with delay, and proposed to demote Shelvocke and put Stewart in command. Shelvocke says he swore that he 'never would submit to any alteration that might bear the least likelihood of being prejudicial to the Gentlemen adventurers'. And he went on protesting and pleading until in the end he decided the best thing to do was to win time by signing the articles. He apologizes to the reader for dwelling so minutely on the particulars of this affair, but it was necessary 'to vindicate myself from an aspersion that has been spread, which intimated as if myself had been the promoter of this change'.[7]

This aspersion is certainly repeated by Betagh, who calls the entire mutiny a put-up job, 'a masterpiece of machiavilian politicks'. Stewart was Shelvocke's creature. He was 'a young man of good sense and good education' who came from Glasgow. He was Shelvocke's steward, waiting on the officers in the cabin, until in the Canaries Shelvocke astonished them by making Stewart first mate, 'tho' not seaman enough to distinguish between a brace and a bowline'. He was instructed by Shelvocke in each step of the mutiny; if there had been a real mutiny they could easily have quelled it. Betagh considerably weakens, not his case against Shelvocke but his right to moral indignation, by not denying that he too, along with all the other officers, eventually agreed to sign the articles.[8] I think Betagh was right in claiming that the mutiny was Shelvocke's invention. In which case, Shelvocke's pain and distress at the crude English of the articles is a master-stroke.

Betagh's comments on life aboard the Speedwell are amusing enough. Shelvocke actively discouraged journal-keeping. Betagh's ensign, Hamilton, 'a gentleman of a good family in *Scotland*', started a mock journal. He made a solemn entry about the capture of a dung-barge. '"This geud day we a taen a sma vashel lodded wi turd."' There was great laughter at this, and Shelvocke sent his son (also called George) to enquire the reason. Shelvocke then came down himself in a fury and asked Hamilton 'what business he had to keep a journal? adding that he was a saucy fellow, and there should be no pen and ink work aboard his ship'.[9] Betagh disliked son George almost as much as he disliked the father. He 'contributed much to the company's uneasiness. ... He knew nothing of sea affairs. ... His imployment in London was to dangle after the women, and gossip at the tea-table; and aboard us, his whole business was to thrust himself into all

[7] Shelvocke, *A Voyage Round the World*, 36–44. [8] Betagh, *A Voyage Round the World*, 34–8.
[9] *Ibid.*, 103–4.

society, overhear every thing that was said, then go and tell his father: so that he was more fit for a boarding school than a ship of war.'[10] (He later became a Fellow of both the Royal Society and the Society of Antiquaries.)

It was a long voyage and Shelvocke's is a long book. But the whole activity of the voyage, cruising off the west coast of South America, seems petty and paltry. The men started muttering: 'if this was making their fortune, they had better have staid at home and begged in the streets'.[11] In fact, Shelvocke felt it expedient (as will be seen) to underplay his conquests; in the end the pickings were rich for him and for those few who stayed with him to the end. The stayers did not include Betagh and Hatley, who were detached to go off raiding in the Mercury, a small ship they had seized – Betagh says it was nothing more than a lighter. Shelvocke swore they had resolved to desert, and that their plans were foiled by the Spaniards, who captured them. He also claimed that the Spaniards treated Betagh very well and made him an officer in the Navy, because he was an Irish Catholic. Betagh denies all this: that there was any intention to desert, that he was a Catholic, even if as an Irishman he had been brought up in the faith, and that he had served with the Spaniards.

Shelvocke went on cruising until the Speedwell was wrecked on Juan Fernandez. He gives a vivid description of the wretchedness and peril of their situation, of their struggle to survive, and building a new boat to take them off. However, Betagh, writing now not with first-hand knowledge but with information from David Griffith, a midshipman, claims that Shelvocke deliberately wrecked his ship with the idea of ridding himself of all obligation to the sponsors. And looking more closely at Shelvocke's dramatic account with this in mind we may well think that the rhetoric is on a par with the simulated distress of the albatross passage; for example, 'the melancholy howlings of innumerable seals on the beach, ... rocky precipices, inhospitable woods, dropping with the rain'; 'with the first glimpse of daylight, we looked at each other like men awakened out of a dream'.[12]

They built their crazy ship and sailed away from this 'perfectly romantick' place, with its 'savage irregular beauty', leaving behind a dozen 'deserters'. They managed to take over a Spanish ship, the Jesus Maria, which they renamed The Happy Return, and in this they met up again with Clipperton and the Success. Shelvocke never has a good word for Clipperton, and claims that Clipperton (quite reasonably) wanted little to do with him. But Clipperton did suggest collaborating to intercept the Manila treasure ship. Shelvocke was all in favour but says that his men agreed only with 'the most resign'd willingness'. But treachery lay ahead.

[10] *Ibid.*, 20. [11] Shelvocke, *A Voyage Round the World*, 127. [12] *Ibid.*, 207–8.

William Morphew, another Irishman who had succeeded Betagh as the chief subject of abuse, transferred with two others to Clipperton's ship – which then gave him the slip. There are pages of indignation about this 'most cruel and perfidious piece of treachery'. At last Shelvocke had found the consort from which he had been so long and so sadly separated; they have before them a wonderful opportunity of fulfilling the object of their expedition, and 'through an excess of mean-spiritedness', he is tricked and abandoned – and 'plunged the deeper in the sea of despair'![13] Betagh's information was that as a condition of continuing in consort Clipperton had demanded the refunding of the prize-money that Shelvocke had already shared out.

Shelvocke's crew was getting very small, through desertion, death and capture, and he had to rely on 'our *Negro* prisoners' – about twenty of them – 'who proved to be very good sailors'. He was thinking of surrendering at Panama if the war with Spain were over, but eventually made it across the Pacific to China, in another captured ship, with rotten sails, and sickness and death aboard. In Canton he found his enemy Clipperton, whom he abuses for incompetence and drunkenness. He sold his ship, and found himself alone with his son – everyone else sneaked off. It is curious that in this epic of continuous self-justification Shelvocke never manages to convey the sense that anyone felt the least affection or loyalty towards him. He got a passage back to England where he arrived in August 1722, after an absence of three years and seven months. Betagh had written to the owners from Lima, and Shelvocke was arrested, though, as we noted, he got out (by bribery?) before charges were laid. Betagh claims that Shelvocke had made himself a rich man through cheating not only the owners but his own crew of their shares in the plunder. He also claims that Shelvocke's narrative deliberately conceals the extent of his loot. When Matthew Stewart reached England he too was arrested and an account book was found containing a note of the division of the spoils from the taking of the Concepción de Recova alone, amounting to £23,000. Stewart told Betagh that Shelvocke made £7,000 out of the voyage.

Shelvocke's 1928 editor, W. G. Perrin, could find nothing about Shelvocke's later life. 'He died in November, 1742, at the age of 66, apparently highly respected, at the official residence in Lombard Street of his son, who was then Secretary of the General Post Office.'[14] What one wrote about a voyage could be more important than the voyage itself. Betagh's challenge to Shelvocke's fashioning of events seems quite destructive, but apparently it had no long-term effect. Betagh dropped out of sight, but Shelvocke lived on, achieving a certain kind of immortality through an albatross that was really a red herring, carefully put in position.

[13] *Ibid.*, 327. [14] Shelvocke, *A Voyage Round the World*, ed. Perrin (1928), xix.

# 4

# The wreck of the Wager

## I

On Friday, 21 December 1764, the Honourable John Byron ('Foulweather Jack', grandfather of the poet) was writing up his log in H. M. S. Dolphin, anchored off Cape Virgin Mary, at the eastern entrance to the Magellan Straits. Byron was the commodore of a two-ship expedition under secret orders from the Admiralty to search the South Atlantic for land or islands which might be strategically important to Britain and then, moving into the Pacific, to go north in search of a passage into Hudson Bay. The Admiralty also gave him instructions on what to do if he touched upon the coast of Patagonia.

You are to make enquiry after the People who were Shipwrecked in His Majesty's Ship the Wager and left upon that Coast, and use your best endeavours to bring them home with you, taking all possible care to avoid giving any Kind of Umbrage of Offence to the Spaniards.

*Byron's Journal of his Circumnavigation*, 7.

That shipwreck had happened in 1741, twenty-three years earlier. As he wrote, Byron had open before him a copy of the account of the wreck and its aftermath by John Bulkeley and John Cummins, *A Voyage to the South-Seas*, first published in 1743, with a second edition in 1757.

This is the same place where the Wager's Crew mention there having seen a number of Horsemen waving to them with white Handkerchiefs to come on shore, & that tho' they were very desirous of knowing what these people were, it blew so hard that they could not come near the Shore & was obliged to stand off to Sea; Bulkeley, Gunner of the Wager says in his Book we could not by any means come to the knowledge of these People; whether they are unfortunate Creatures that have been cast away, or whether they are Inhabitants about the River Gallegoes we can't tell. Just as we came to an anchor I could see very plain with my Glass a number of Horsemen opposite to the Ship riding backwards & forwards & waving to us to come on shore exactly in the manner Bulkeley mentions to have seen them, as I was very anxious to know what these People were I immediately ordered my 12 Oar'd Boat out, & went toward the Shore in her very well armed. . . . When we came near the shore we saw I believe near 500 People some on foot but most on Horseback.

*Byron's Journal of his Circumnavigation*, 45.

The remainder of the sentence following 'says in his Book' is a direct quotation from Bulkeley. Byron does not quote Bulkeley's emphatic statement that 'the Indians we saw in the *Streights of Magellan*, are People of a middle Stature, and well-shaped'. Legend had had it since Magellan's day that the Patagonians were giants,[1] and the legend seems to have taken hold of Byron. The Indian chief 'was one of the most extraordinary Men for size I had ever seen till then. ... I never was more astonished than to see such a Set of People. The Stoutest of our Grenadiers would appear nothing to these.' These people 'in size come the nearest to Giants I believe of any People in the World'.[2] His second-in-command, a six-footer, appeared 'a mere shrimp to them'. Byron described these giants in a letter to Lord Egmont at the Admiralty, but it was not until his return home in 1766 that the news spread about these huge Patagonians. In the rest of the voyage Byron had only very partially carried out the Admiralty's instructions. He had landed on the western side of the Falkland Islands on 15 January 1765 and taken possession of them for His Majesty, but he left without being aware that there was a French settlement in the east, established in 1763 by Bougainville, who had formally taken possession of the islands for France. On reaching the Pacific, Byron made no attempt to look for the north-west passage, claiming his ships were not fit for it. Instead he went in search of the mythical riches of the Solomon Islands, which he failed to locate.

The story of the Patagonian giants became a sensation. (Helen Wallis suggests that the British government was content with the publicity as a screen for Byron's activities in the Falklands.[3]) Junior officers in the ship added to the inches. 'Their middle stature seemed to be about eight feet; their extreme nine and upwards', said the author of the first, unauthorized, printed account of the voyage in 1767.[4] Midshipman Charles Clerke told the Royal Society that 'there was hardly a man there less than eight feet, most of them considerably more'. However, it was the egregious John Hawkesworth, LL. D., commissioned by the Admiralty to write the official narrative of Byron's voyage (published in 1773 along with that of Wallis and Carteret, and that of Cook's first voyage) who 'gave final authority to Byron's giants'. Not only did he alter the words of Byron's journal to include phrases like 'gigantic stature', 'may indeed more properly be called giants than tall men', but, quite ignoring the evidence of actual measurement by Wallis and Carteret, wrote in his General Introduction,

[1] See the account in Adams, *Travelers and Travel Liars*, chap. 2.

[2] *Byron's Journal of his Circumnavigation*, 46. [3] *Ibid.*, 188. [4] *Ibid.*, 46 note.

concerning the giants, 'the concurrent testimony of late navigators ... will put an end to all the doubts that have been hitherto entertained of their existence'.[5]

The editor of Byron's journal for the Hakluyt Society, Robert E. Gallagher, makes it clear that even in this, his official account, Byron was given to extraordinary exaggeration and distortion. His pen seems to run away with him. In the Pacific in June 1765 he wrote, 'My people fall down daily in the Scurvy', and, on leaving the 'Isles of Disappointment', 'greatly grieved I could procure no Refreshment for our Sick here'. Captain Mouat, the commander in the same ship, wrote in *his* journal, 'found a great Quantity of Cocoa Nutts, and Pepper Grass, w$^{ch}$ were of infinite Service to our people a few of which were down with the Scurvy'.[6] Byron was never a stickler for the truth. Even so, though he may well have been awed by the menacing appearance of the painted Indians massed in front of him when his boat ran ashore, it is scarcely comprehensible that he should have reported on their appearance in the terms he used, and so become responsible for the recrudescence of the Patagonian myth.

For twenty-two years earlier, in 1741–2, Byron had actually lived among Patagonian Indians for several months. And in 1768, two years after he returned from his round-the-world voyage in the Dolphin, he published his story of those months. In this narrative he twice commented on the size of the Indians. 'These people were of a small stature, very swarthy, having long, black, coarse hair, hanging over their faces.' 'These Indians are of a middling stature, well set, and very active.'[7] Nowhere does he show any consciousness that some comment is needed on this marked difference from the size of the people he claims to have observed in his later visit. Although by 1768 he himself had published nothing regarding his round-the-world voyage, he must have been fully aware of the interest aroused by his reports on the abnormal size of the Patagonians. Percy G. Adams noted that the reviewer in *The Gentleman's Magazine* remarked that 'no mention is made of people on the coast of Patagonia of an uncommon height'.[8] It is a mystery how Byron could preserve the contradictory records of his two experiences entirely insulated from each other; I hazard a guess at the explanation at the end of this chapter.

Byron's earlier acquaintance with the Patagonian Indians was enforced, and forms part of the story of the wreck of the Wager. He was a seventeen-year-old midshipman in 1740, and he was serving in the Wager alongside Bulkeley and Cummins. The Wager was part of Captain George Anson's fleet, sent out to attack Spain's empire in the Pacific after Captain Jenkins's severed ear and popular feeling had pushed Walpole into a

[5] *Ibid.*, 188–91 and lxxvii–lxxix. [6] *Ibid.*, lxii.

[7] Byron, *A Narrative of the Honourable John Byron*, 33 and 144.

[8] Adams, *Travelers and Travel Liars*, 37.

Spanish war. There were four big fighting ships; Centurion, Gloucester, Severn and Pearl, with the Wager as store-ship, Tryal (an eight-gun sloop) and two 'pinks' as victuallers. The land-forces on the ships were provided from those pensioners of Chelsea Hospital who were not fit enough to desert on the way to Portsmouth docks. The wreck of the Wager on the west coast of Patagonia was only one of the misfortunes that dogged Anson. It is astonishing that this largely disastrous expedition should have been rated a triumph of British naval endeavour, and have made Anson's name a household word. It is only a little less astonishing that the tedious and bland official narrative of the voyage, published in 1748, should have become a best-seller, with over 1,800 subscribers and a string of fifteen editions by 1756.[9]

The Severn and the Pearl never reached the Pacific, the Wager was wrecked, the Tryal more or less came apart at Juan Fernandez, the disabled Gloucester had to be blown up in the Pacific. Only the Centurion survived to reach Macao. Anson's main enemy (apart from the weather) was not the Spanish squadron under Pizarro waiting to intercept him, but scurvy. Of approximately 2,000 men who manned the six fighting ships leaving England in 1740 only 145 came home in the Centurion in 1744. More than 1,300 perished from scurvy.[10]

Although Anson had failed to intercept the Manila galleon off the Mexican coast, he was given a second chance towards the end of his long voyage and in June 1743 he captured the Spanish galleon Nuestra Señora de Covadonga off the Philippines. Glyndwr Williams, editor of the narrative of the voyage, has described how in word and image the fight was transformed into the traditional triumph of a plucky little English ship against a much larger Spanish foe.

> In reality the odds were weighted heavily against the Spaniard. ... The *Centurion* was a specialist fighting ship mounting sixty guns, twenty-four of them heavy 24-pounders. ... The *Covadonga* was smaller than the *Centurion*, the heaviest of her cannon were only 12-pounders, and she was essentially a trading vessel.
>
> Anson, *Voyage Round the World* (1974), xiv.

Anson was thus able to return home with a mass of treasure, his share of which made him rich for life.

A very readable unofficial account of the Anson voyage was published in 1745, *A True and Impartial Journal of a Voyage to the South-Seas and Round the Globe in His Majesty's Ship the Centurion.* Its author was Pascoe Thomas, 'teacher of the Mathematicks on board the Centurion'.[11] Although he

9 Anson, *Voyage Round the World* (1974), ix, xvii and xix.

10 *Ibid.*, xv; and Pack, *The Wager Mutiny*, 13.

11 The list of subscribers provides an insight into the wide readership range of voyage-narratives. Many are described as mariners, some of them from the Centurion. There are clergymen (including the Dean of Carlisle and the Prebendary of Winchester), schoolmasters, surgeons, attorneys-at law, and many merchants – a brewer, a shipwright, a peruke-maker, an oculist, a linen-draper, for example. But there is not a woman among them.

writes that it is not his design 'to tell the World our Sufferings and Hardships on the Voyage', his book is of value for just that – its graphic, vivid accounts of what it felt like to live through violent storms and the scourge of scurvy. The South Atlantic storms took a heavy toll of the squadron; Thomas tells of one little-discussed problem. 'The heads' are the seamen's lavatories, set in the eyes of the ship, either side of the bow.

Her Decks were almost always full of Water, washing from Side to Side, the Gratings of the Heads were torn up, the necessary Houses there wash'd down, and the Seas continually breaking in at the Head Doors, no Person could attempt oftentimes, for many Days together, to go near them.

Thomas, *A True and Impartial Journal*, 21.

He was himself a victim of scurvy. Black spots spread on his body –

till almost my Legs and Thighs were as black as a Negro; and this accompanied with such excessive Pains in the Joints of the Knees, Ancles and Toes, as I thought, before I experienced them, that Human Nature could never have supported. It next advanced to the Mouth; all my Teeth were presently loose, and my Gums, over-charged with extravasated Blood, fell down almost quite over my Teeth; This occasioned my Breath to stink much.

Thomas, *A True and Impartial Journal*, 142.

Thomas was very indignant at the callousness of the officers towards scurvy-victims among the seamen, whom they abused as 'idle fellows'.

At an early point in his narrative, Pascoe Thomas becomes angry regarding the loss of some papers on which were written his calculations, by means of an eclipse of the moon, of the longitude of St Catherine's Island, Brazil, as 49° 53′ W (my atlas gives it as 48° 30′). He implies that the papers have been stolen.

I am sorry I should be obliged in this Place, in order to do Justice to myself, to take some notice of a certain Honourable Gentleman, who turn'd his Back on the Expedition, (for what Reason is best known to himself) and arrived in England long before us; and who, as I am credibly inform'd, is now, in conjunction with a Friend of his, and assisted by the Journals of some of our Officers, which they have lent them for that laudable Purpose, endeavouring to make a Monopoly of this Voyage, and to that end designs to publish *by Authority*; (an effectual Method to discourage others, and not unlike many arbitrary Proceedings on other Occasions.)

Thomas, *A True and Impartial Journal*, 10.

This 'Honourable Gentleman' was Richard Walter, the chaplain on board the Centurion. He had indeed left the ship at Canton, in December 1742, and returned home in an East Indiaman. He was not therefore a witness of the fight with the Covadonga, as Thomas was. The 'Friend of his' was Benjamin Robins, F. R. S., like Thomas a mathematician. Although he was deeply interested in naval matters he was not present on the Anson voyage. Robins's share in the writing of the official narrative has always been a matter of dispute.[12] The 1748 publication was described as 'Compiled from Papers and other Materials of the Right Honourable George Lord Anson and published under his Direction, By Richard Walter, M.A.' How much Robins had to do with shaping the narrative is immaterial. It is quite clear that Anson masterminded the entire work, and it is his viewpoint that is expressed, whether 'I' or 'we' or 'Mr. *Anson*' is credited with making the observation. Insecurity about tenses as well as haziness about the identity of the narrator constantly remind us that this very pedestrian account is a patchwork stitched together. But essentially it is the voyage as Anson chose it to be represented. At every point it confirms the wisdom of his judgement.

This official narrative contains some interesting pages about the loss of the Wager and the subsequent vicissitudes of the captain and the crew. None of this was known at first hand by Anson or Walter. The damaged Wager had fallen behind after rounding the Horn and was never seen again. The information in the narrative must have been garnered after the Centurion's return to England.

The basic story of the loss of the Wager is as follows. In the terrible storms experienced in trying to round Cape Horn, she had lost her mizen mast, and suffered considerable damage to the standing rigging. She lost contact with the other ships. Her captain, David Cheap, who had only just joined the ship following a reshuffle of command, was feeling his way up the western coast of Patagonia to the agreed rendezvous of Nuestra Señora di Socoro in latitude 45° (now Guamblin Island). On 13 May (1741), both the carpenter, John Cummins, and the gunner, John Bulkeley, saw land on the *port* beam, bearing NW by N. The second-in-command, Lieutenant Beans, said this was impossible. They had drifted into the Gulf of Peñas and what they could see to port was the Tres Montes peninsula. Cheap attempted to get out of the bay by turning south. He was unluckily disabled by a fall. At 4.30 a.m. the ship hit a rock and went aground wedged between two rocky islets off what is now Wager Island, 47° 50′ S, 75° 0′ W. The anarchy and confusion which marked the following weeks began at once, with some of the crew becoming hopelessly drunk on the vast quantities of liquor which the ship was carrying for the entire fleet. Most of the ship's company got safely ashore and split up into groups, making shelters and scavenging for food. There were some visits from Indians in canoes, but they stopped coming, seemingly because some of the crew tried to interfere with the women.

Order of a kind was established for bringing stores ashore from the ship,

[12] Anson, *Voyage Round the World* (1974), xxi and xxv.

protecting them, and distributing rations of flour and liquor. A ration of a pint of wine a day for each man, or half a pint of brandy, later increased, must have contributed to the constant quarrelling. Drink certainly played its part in a row with the midshipman Henry Cozens at the centre, which ended with Captain Cheap shooting him fatally at point-blank range.

Getting off the island depended entirely on the skill of the carpenter Cummins, who cut the long-boat in two, lengthened her by twelve feet and decked her. She was now fifty feet long with a nine-foot beam. They had three other boats: a yawl, a barge and a cutter. There were about a hundred men to be taken off; forty-five had died in or after the wreck, and seven had decamped. The great question was whether they were to head north or south. Captain Cheap wanted to go north in the hope of rejoining Anson. The great majority, led by Bulkeley, wanted to head south, through the Magellan Straits, to reach the haven of Portuguese Brazil.

The captain prevaricated and temporized until the others, convinced that he had no intention of accepting the southern course, decided to divest him of command and take him along by force. But they acceded to his request to be left on the island, and they allowed him the yawl. At the end of October, eighty-one men set sail in the long-boat, now named the Speedwell, together with the barge and the cutter, under the nominal command of Lieutenant Beans, though Bulkeley the gunner was in fact in charge. With Cheap there stayed behind the surgeon William Elliot and Lieutenant Hamilton of the Marines (whose commanding officer, Captain Pemberton, was in the Speedwell). Two midshipmen, Byron and Alexander Campbell, then changed their minds about the southern venture and, with seven others, took back the barge to rejoin the captain. Eventually the Speedwell was on her own, making painful progress through the Magellan Straits, with men and boys constantly dying of starvation. As they turned north again, a party of eight, including the midshipman Isaac Morris, was stranded ashore and left behind. At the end of January 1742, three months after leaving Wager Island, the Speedwell, with a mere thirty survivors, reached Rio Grande and later Rio de Janeiro. The survivors split into two groups. Robert Beans and his party got back to England ahead of Bulkeley, Cummins and the cooper John Young, who took nearly a year to reach home (1 January 1743).

Only four of Cheap's party survived a hazardous journey north, Cheap himself, Byron, Campbell and Hamilton, reaching Chiloe by travelling with Indians and surrendering to the Spaniards, who treated them reasonably. Cheap, Hamilton and Byron got back to England in April 1746, Campbell in May. Isaac Morris, with two others left behind by the Speedwell, returned in July – three and a half years after Bulkeley, Cummins and Young.

## II

The account of these events which is given in the authorized narrative of Anson's voyage is, as is to be expected, extremely favourable to Captain Cheap, stressing his care and concern for his ship and his men. Cozens was shot because the captain thought he was heading a mutiny, and 'this incident, however displeasing to the people, did yet, for a considerable time, awe them to their duty, and rendered them more submissive to the Captain's authority'.[13] (*Pour encourager les autres!*) Cheap is commended for his wish to go north, capture a Spanish vessel and make for Juan Fernandez. The southward route, 'infinitely more hazardous and tedious', 'had the air of returning home', and 'this circumstance alone rendered them inattentive to all its inconveniencies, and made them adhere to it with insurmountable obstinacy'. The long-boat party freed the captain at the last minute, 'as they well knew what they had to apprehend on their return to *England*, if their Commander should be present to confront them'.

This last is an outrageously disingenuous remark. Anson and Walter make no mention at all of the fact that by the time they wrote these words there had been a court martial to enquire into the loss of the Wager (1746). Cheap and his officers had been acquitted of responsibility for the loss of the ship, but Lieutenant Beans was reprimanded on several counts. No charges whatsoever were brought against those who had repudiated Cheap's authority on the island – and for a time actually made a prisoner of him. But Anson and Walter were content to leave in print the insinuation that the long-boat party was guilty of mutiny.

To make matters worse, all the information in this account, so heavily slanted against Bulkeley and Cummins (who are never named) is derived from the Bulkeley and Cummins narrative, *A Voyage to the South-Seas*, published on their return in 1743. Here is some of the evidence.

Anson/Walter:
She struck on a sunken rock, and soon after bilged, and grounded between two small Islands, at about a musquet shot from the shore.

*Voyage Round the World* (1748), 146.

Bulkeley/Cummins:
The Ship struck abaft on a sunken Rock ... she struck, bilged, and grounded between two small Islands ... not above a Musket-shot from the Shore.

*Voyage to the South-Seas* (1743), 18.

Anson/Walter:
they at last pointed a four pounder, which was on the quarter-deck, against the

[13] Anson, *Voyage Round the World* (1748), 144.

hut, where they knew the Captain resided on shore, and fired two shots which passed but just over it.

*Voyage Round the World* (1748), 147.

Bulkeley/Cummins:

... brought a Quarter-deck Gun, a four Pounder, to bear on the Captain's Hut, and fir'd two Shot, which went just over the Captain's Tent.

*Voyage to the South-Seas* (1743), 21.

The Anson narrative has no other source for the events on Wager Island than Bulkeley and Cummins. Differences and additions are entirely a matter of interpretation and comment. A good example of their use and abuse of the earlier narrative is the tendentious treatment of the crucial shooting of Cozens by Cheap.

It was not in the least doubted, but there were some violent measures in agitation, in which *Cozens* was engaged as ringleader.

The purser fires a pistol at Cozens – and here with rare imagination the Anson narrative makes him cry out '*that the dog had pistols*':

The Captain ... rushed out of his tent; and not doubting but it had been fired by *Cozens* as the commencement of a mutiny, he immediately shot him in the head without farther deliberation.

Anson, *Voyage Round the World* (1748), 149.

All this is built on some words of Bulkeley, who was trying to find some explanation for the Captain's impulsive and reckless act.

His preceding Behaviour ... might probably make the Captain suspect his Design was Mutiny; tho' this we must aver, that Mr. *Cozens* neither on this or any other Occasion, appeared in Arms since the Loss of the Ship.

Bulkeley, *Voyage to the South-Seas* (1743), 32.

As will be seen, it became something of a habit to rely on Bulkeley and Cummins for facts in a narrative aiming to discredit them. The wreck of the Wager, the events on the island, and the homeward struggle of the survivors, generated some powerful writing, but Bulkeley and Cummins is the platform where it all starts.

The title-page of the 1743 publication, *A Voyage to the South-Seas* (see the Frontispiece), reads 'The Whole compiled by Persons concerned in the Facts related, viz. *John Bulkeley* and *John Cummins*, Late Gunner and Carpenter of the Wager'. Presumably the publication was undertaken jointly and the profits were to be shared, but although the text is based on a jointly kept journal, the writing-up is clearly Bulkeley's responsibility; he writes of himself in the first person and generally refers to Cummins as 'the Carpenter'. Bulkeley was a married man with children, and he had previously been able seaman, master's mate and midshipman in various ships.[14] As

[14] Bulkeley, *Voyage to the South-Seas* (1927), 211.

gunner in the Wager he was a warrant-officer, and he took charge of one of the watches. The assured tone of the dedication and the preface may seem altogether too literary for a professional seaman. So may the clever (rather free) quotation from one of Waller's poems on the title-page.

> Bold were the Men who on the Ocean first
> Spread the new Sails, when Ship-wreck was the worst:
> More Dangers Now from MAN alone we find,
> Than from the Rocks, the Billows, and the Wind.

Possibly they had assistance with the dedication and the preface. But there is no evidence of ghosting in the consistent texture of the writing in the body of the book. Bulkeley's literacy is confirmed by the parting shot of the second edition (1757). Apropos the continuing injustice he was subject to, he takes the opportunity –

> to recommend to the candid reader, the perusal of that excellent Book, entitled, *The Christian Patern, or, The Imitation of Jesus Christ, by Thomas à Kempis*: which book I brought with me through the various Scenes, Changes, and Chances of the Voyage, and Providence made it the Means of comforting me.
>
> *Voyage to the South-Seas* (1757), 242.

At the end of their protracted voyage home, Bulkeley and Cummins, with John Young the cooper, travelled from Lisbon to Portsmouth in H. M. S. Stirling Castle. When they arrived at Spithead, the captain refused to allow them ashore until he had a reply from the Admiralty to a letter he had written. The letter presumably raised the question of their having been responsible for mutiny, an accusation which Bulkeley claimed Lieutenant Beans had spread abroad in Lisbon. After two weeks a letter came from the Admiralty instructing that they should have their liberty. 'After we had staid a few Days with our Families', writes Bulkeley, 'we came to *London* to pay our duties to the Lords of the Admiralty.[15] We sent in our Journal for their Lordships Inspection: They had before received a Narrative from the Lieutenant.' Bulkeley pauses to discredit Lieutenant Beans's narrative on the grounds that he had not kept a journal but had relied on his memory. He goes on that the Lords of the Admiralty kept their journal 'for some Time' and then ordered them 'to make an Abstract by way of Narrative, that it might not be too tedious for their Lordships Perusal'. A committee of enquiry was then set up, but it was considered improper to open the proceedings before 'the Arrival of the Commodore [Anson], or else Capt. *Cheap*'.

> And it was also resolved, that not a Person of us should receive any Wages, or be employ'd in his Majesty's Service, till every Thing relating to the *Wager* was more plain and conspicuous.
>
> Bulkeley, *Voyage to the South-Seas* (1743), 219.

[15] Here and elsewhere I have filled out dashes in the original; e.g., 'L---ds of the A-------y'.

At this point, as the second edition puts it, 'we were offer'd a considerable Sum by the Booksellers of *London*, to publish our Journal to the World'. They asked the Lords of the Admiralty for permission, and their Lordships said it was nothing to do with them: 'you may do as you will with it'. So they published, ending the preface thus:

Till the Commodore's Arrival we cannot know our Fate; at present we are out of all Employment, and have nothing to support ourselves and Families, but the Profits arising from the Sale of our Journal; which perhaps may be the Sum Total we shall ever receive for our *Voyage to the South-Seas*.

Bulkeley's journal of the voyage out was lost in the wreck, but 'from the time we were Ship-wreck'd, the Carpenter and myself were exceeding careful in writing each Day's Transactions'.[16] That their publication is to some extent a transcription of that journal is clear enough. Here are some entries for mid-July.

*Saturday* the 18th, launched the Boat, sent her to the Wreck, and brought ashore one Cask of Beef; it is believed some Guns were heard from the Sea: The Watch reported they have heard them two Nights past. Great Disturbances among the People. Wind at E.N.E. and Frosty weather.

*Sunday* the 19th, launch'd the Boat, sent her to the Wreck, hook'd a Cask supposed to be Beef; but when towed ashore, we found it contained nothing but Hatchets; we took up along Shore, Abundance of Checque Shirts in Dozens, also Caps, Bales of Cloth, and Pieces of Beef and Pork.

*Wednesday* the 22nd. This Day began to build a House to dwell in, finding our Stay here, will be much longer than we at first expected.

The 23rd, took up along Shore several Pieces of Beef and Pork, Shirts, Caps, Frocks, Trowsers, Pieces of Cloth, with other serviceable Things, and Wax Candles of all Sizes.

*Saturday* the 25th, hard Showers of Rain and Hail; the Wind at North. Shot several Sea-Gulls, Geese, Hawks, and other Birds: The Carpenter had this Day given him by one of the People, a fine large Rock Crab, it being the first of the Kind we ever saw here.

Although *Voyage to the South-Seas* is based upon the journal entries, it has to be recognized that its driving force is the need for justification and vindication, 'to clear our Characters' as the preface puts it, against the charges of inciting mutiny which it was believed Beans had laid in Lisbon and repeated in his testimony to the Admiralty. In the absence of a legal hearing suspicion hung about them. The penalty for mutiny was death. Bulkeley and Cummins were writing for their lives. There is understandably a partisan tone in their narrative, but the general veracity of what they relate is upheld by the fact that no charges were pressed against them.

They themselves believed they would be charged, and so did the public.

[16] Bulkeley, *Voyage to the South-Seas* (1743), 20–1.

In the revised 1757 edition Bulkeley was able to give details of Cheap's return and the summons to the court-martial. An officer of the court told Bulkeley (not knowing who he was) that 'I believe the Gunner and the Carpenter will be hang'd, if no Body else'. In Portsmouth, Cheap told some of Bulkeley's friends that he did not think it would be in his power to save them from hanging (as if he wanted to!). It was later argued (by Byron, for example, in his narrative) that Bulkeley and Cummins got off on a technicality; namely, that since naval service (i.e., entitlement to wages) ceased at the moment of wreck, so did naval discipline and its fearsome strictures. It is true that the law was clarified as a direct result of the Wager case, but it is impossible to believe that the logic of this argument would have held the court back if it had believed there was a strong case against Bulkeley and Cummins. The only person to suffer even reprimand was Beans, who was in the long-boat with them, and who laid the charges no doubt thinking thereby to save his own skin. Captain S. W. C. Pack, whose book is firmly entitled *The Wager Mutiny*, wrote that 'they owe their acquittal not only to the unpopularity of the Board, but to the strength of public opinion, and also to the fact that their miraculous escapes had caught the public fancy'.[17] This is a little unfair to the case that Bulkeley and Cummins made out. Would it not be truer to say that they won? In *Voyage to the South-Seas* they were writing for their lives and they won. They were not charged with mutiny.

In the preface, Bulkeley wrote that he was aware that it was considered wrong for 'Persons of our Stations' to take the initiative on the island. But, he goes on, 'There was a Necessity for Action, and a great deal of it too'. With Cheap sulking in his tent, asserting an authority he was unable to exercise, there was paralysis on the island. Bulkeley and Cummins were wholly responsible for organizing the escape. Cummins worked at reconstructing the long-boat until it became an obsession. A seaman was found 'cutting up an Anchor-Stock for Fire-Wood, which had been designed for a particular Use for the Boat; at Sight of the Fellow's Folly he could not contain himself: This Affair . . . for some time impaired his Understanding, and made him delirious . . .'.[18]

While Cummins was at work on 'the Means of our Deliverance', Bulkeley was planning the route. At the end of July he found Byron in his tent reading the captain's copy of Narborough's voyages 'to these Seas'. He borrowed it and was convinced that as the converted long-boat would be no kind of a fighting ship they had no alternative but to go through the Magellan Straits and make for Brazil. A paper was drawn up making out the case for this route and it was signed 'by all the Officers on the Spot, except the Captain, Lieutenant, Purser, and Surgeon, and by all the

[17] Pack, *The Wager Mutiny*, 246. [18] Bulkeley, *Voyage to the South-Seas* (1743), 67.

Seamen in general, except the Captain's Steward'. The midshipmen Byron and Campbell were among the signatories. The captain asked for time, and then produced his arguments for going north to seek Anson. There was a long debate, with Beans staying quiet, until finally Cheap submitted.

Gentlemen, I am agreeable to take any Chance with you, and go any Way: but would have you consider of it, and defer your Determination till all is ready to go off the Spot.

Bulkeley, *Voyage to the South-Seas* (1743), 57.

At this point, Bulkeley rather surprisingly makes it clear that he challenged Cheap's authority. If the captain went with them, he was told he would not be allowed 'to weigh, to come to an Anchor, to alter Course, without consulting your Officers'. Cheap replied, 'Gentlemen, I was your Commander till the Ship parted'. 'We answered, Sir, we will support you with our Lives, as long as you suffer Reason to rule.' Two days later Cheap, still emphasizing the danger of the southern course, said, 'I am determined to take my Fate with you, or where the Spirit of the People leads'.

However, as August went on, Bulkeley found that efforts were being made to win adherents for the northern course.

There is a Sort of a Party-rage among the People, fomented by a kind of Bribery that has more Influence on the Seamen than Money; there are some daily bought off by Rum, and other strong Liquors. Unless a Stop is put to these Proceedings, we shall never go off the Spot.

Bulkeley, *Voyage to the South-Seas* (1743), 69–70.

Beans now came out more openly on the side of Bulkeley, who drew up another paper reiterating the agreement to go south. 'We do, notwithstanding, find the People separating into Parties, which must consequently end in the Destruction of the whole Body.' A unanimous confirmation was sought. According to Bulkeley, Lieutenant Beans said that if the captain would not sign it 'he should be confin'd for shooting Mr *Cozens*, and he would take the Command on himself'. Cheap's response to the paper was, 'Have I not told you before, that I do not care which Way I go, Southward or Northward? I will take my Fate with you.' But he would not sign. To everyone's surprise, the Lieutenant said nothing.

Captain Pemberton, in charge of the marines, now came to the fore, agreeing to the transfer of command to Beans if the captain refused to sign. Bulkeley's account of the ensuing crisis needs extensive quotation.

At the same time Captain *Pemberton* told the People, he would stand by 'em with his Life, in going through the *Streights of Magellan*, the Way proposed in the Paper. The People gave three Cheers, crying aloud for *England*. The Captain hearing the

Noise, got out of Bed to his Tent-Door, and call'd the People, enquiring what they wanted; then sent for all the Officers: He was then told, since he refus'd signing the Paper, and had no Regard for the Safety of our Provisions, the People unanimously agreed to take the Command from him, and transfer it to the Lieutenant. Hearing this, with an exalted Voice, Captain *Cheap* says, Who is he that will take the Command from me? Addressing himself to the Lieutenant, Is it you, Sir? The Lieutenant reply'd, No, Sir. The Terror of the Captain's Aspect intimidated the Lieutenant to that Degree, that he look'd like a Ghost. We left him with the Captain, and returned to Captain *Pemberton*'s Tent, to acquaint him of the Lieutenant's refusing the Command.

We had not been long here before Captain *Cheap* sent for us. I was the first Person call'd for; at my entering his Tent, I saw him seated on a Chest, with a cock'd Pistol on his Right Thigh; observing this, I desir'd Mr. *Jones*, who was the Mate he always rely'd on for Navigation, to tell the Captain, I did not think proper to come before a cock'd Pistol: Notwithstanding I was arm'd, I drew back, altho' I had my Pistol cock'd, and there were several Men near me arm'd with Muskets. The Captain's personal Bravery no Man doubted of; his Courage was excessive, and made him rash and desperate; his shooting Mr. *Cozens* was a fatal Proof of it; he was grown more desperate by this unhappy Action, and was observ'd since seldom to behave himself with any Composure of Mind. . . . I had no Desire of falling by the Hand of Captain *Cheap*, and should be greatly disturb'd to be compell'd, for my own Preservation, to discharge a Pistol at a Gentleman against whom I never had any Spleen, and who was my Commander.

When Mr. *Jones* acquainted him with what I desired him, the Captain threw his Pistol aside, and came out of his Tent; he told the People, he would go with them to the Southward; he desired to know their Grievances, and he would redress them: They all call'd out for their Sea-Store of Provisions to be secur'd [these were the provisions set aside for the long-boat journey], and the rest equally divided. Here the Captain show'd all the Conduct and Courage imaginable; he was a single Man against a Multitude, all of 'em dissatisfy'd with him, and all of 'em in Arms: He told 'em the ill Consequence of sharing the Provisions, that it was living To-day and starving To-morrow; but the People were not to be satisfy'd, the Officers had now no Authority over 'em, and they were some Time deaf to their Persuasions; nay, it was with Difficulty that they could dissuade 'em from pulling down the Store-Tent, and taking away the Provisions by Force; they remov'd the Provisions out of the Store-tent, then fell to digging a Hole to bury the Brandy; the Sea-Store to be secur'd, the Remainder to be immediately shar'd. Had this been comply'd with, the Consequences might have been very terrible: However, to pacify 'em in some Shape, it was agreed, that every Man should have a Pint of Brandy *per* Day, which, by Calculation, would last 'em three Weeks. On this they seem'd very easy, and went to their respective Tents.

The Captain told his Officers, that he would act nothing contrary to what was agreed on for the Welfare and Safety of the Community. Finding the Captain in a Temper of Mind to hearken to Reason, I said to him, Sir, I think it my Duty to inform you, that I am not the Person whom you imagine to be the Principal in this Affair. The Captain answer'd, How can I think otherwise? I reply'd, Sir, the Paper I read to you was your Lieutenant's Projection: There sits the Gentleman, let him disown it, if he can. The Captain turning himself to the Lieutenant, says, Mr. *Bulkeley* has honestly clear'd himself. We then drank a Glass of Wine, and took our Leaves. At Night the Captain sent for Mr. *Cummins* and me to sup with him; we were the only Officers present with him: When I was seated, I said, Sir, I have my Character at Stake, for drawing back from your cock'd Pistol: Had I advanc'd, one of us must have dropt. The Captain answer'd, *Bulkeley*, I do assure you, the Pistol was not design'd for you, but for another; for I knew the Whole before. We then talk'd of indifferent Things, and spent the Evening in a very affable Manner.[19]

September came and went, with many disturbances among the seamen, visits from Indians, and, in the improving weather, reconnaissances of the coast in the barge. On 6 October, Beans brought word from the captain that his resolution 'was to be Captain as before, and to be governed by the Rules of the Navy'. This was not accepted. 'We think him a Gentleman worthy to have a limited Command, but too dangerous a Person to be trusted with an absolute one.' On 8 October, according to Bulkeley, Captain Pemberton was preparing to take Cheap prisoner – for having shot Cozens. 'We now are convinc'd the Captain hath no Intention of going to the Southward', so it was proposed to take him forcibly. Bulkeley now drops into the third person.

It was reckon'd dangerous to suffer the Captain any longer to enjoy Liberty; therefor the Lieutenant, Gunner, Carpenter, and Mr. *Jones* the Mate, resolv'd next Morning to surprize him in his Bed.

Bulkeley, *Voyage to the South-Seas* (1743), 90.

It was a party of seamen who were sent in to do this. Cheap was bound and moved from his tent.

All his Things were mov'd to the Purser's Tent; As he was coming along, he said, Gentlemen, you must excuse my not pulling my Hat off, my Hands are confin'd. Well, Captain *Beans*! you will be call'd to an Account for this hereafter. The Boatswain, after the Captain's Confinement, most barbarously insulted him, reproaching him with striking him, saying, Then it was your Time; but now, G--d d--n you, it is mine. The Captain made no Reply but this, You are a Scoundrel for using a Gentleman ill when he is a Prisoner. When the Captain was a Prisoner, he declared, he never intended to go to the Southward, having more Honour than to turn his Back on his Enemies; and farther, he said, Gentlemen, I do not want to go off in any of your Craft; for I never design'd to go for *England*, and would rather chuse to be shot by you; there is not a single Man on the Beach dare engage me; but this is what I fear'd.

Bulkeley, *Voyage to the South-Seas* (1743), 93.

19 *Ibid.*, 74–7 (paragraphing not original).

On Sunday, 11 October, Captain Cheap restated his position.

He had rather be shot than carried off a Prisoner, and that he would not go off with us; therefore desired me to ask the People to suffer him to remain on the Island: The People readily agreed to his Request; and also consented to leave him all Things needful for his Support, as much as could be spared. Lieutenant *Hamilton* and the Surgeon chose to stay with him. We offer'd him also the Barge and Yawl, if he could procure Men to go with him. The Question was propos'd before the whole Body; but they all cry'd aloud for *England*, and let him stay and be d---n'd; does he want to carry us to a Prison? There is not a Man will go.

Bulkeley, *Voyage to the South-Seas* (1743), 97.

Articles were prepared giving command to Lieutenant Beans. The signatories included the three remaining midshipmen, John Byron, Alexander Campbell and Isaac Morris. Bulkeley then said goodbye to Cheap.

As soon as the above Things were deliver'd, we got ready for sailing. I went and took my Leave of the Captain: He repeated his Injunction, That at my Return to *England*, I would impartially relate all Proceedings: He spoke to me in the most tender and affectionate Manner; and, as a Token of his Friendship and Regard for me, desir'd me to accept of a Suit of his best Wearing-Apparel: At parting, he gave me his Hand with a great deal of Chearfulness, wishing me well and safe to *England*. This was the last Time I ever saw the unfortunate Captain *Cheap*. However, we hope to see him again in *England*, that Mr. *Cummins* and myself may be freed from some heavy Imputations to our Prejudice laid on us by the Gentleman who succeeded him in Command, and who, having an Opportunity of arriving before us in *England*, not only in the Places he touch'd at Abroad, but at Home, has blacken'd us with the greatest Calumnies; and, by an imperfect Narrative, has not only traduc'd us, but made the whole Affair so dark and mystical, that till the Captain's Arrival the Lords of the Admiralty will not decide for or against us. But if that unfortunate Captain never returns to this Country, let us do so much Justice to his Character, to declare, that he was a Gentleman possess'd of many Virtues; he was an excellent Seaman himself, and lov'd a Seaman; as for personal Bravery, no Man had a larger Share of it; even when a Prisoner he preserv'd the Dignity of a Commander; no Misfortunes could dispirit or deject him, and Fear was a Weakness he was entirely a Stranger to; the Loss of the Ship was the loss of him; he knew how to govern while he was a Commander on Board; but when Things were brought to Confusion and Disorder, he thought to establish his Command ashore by his Courage, and to suppress the least Insult on his Authority on the first Occasion; an Instance of this was seen on the Boatswain's first appearing ashore; shooting Mr. *Cozens*, and treating him in the Manner he did after his Confinement, was highly resented by the People, who soon got the Power in their own Hands . . .

At Eleven in the Forenoon, the whole Body of People embark'd, to the Number of eighty-one Souls; fifty-nine on Board the Vessel, on Board the Cutter twelve, and in the Barge ten: At Noon got under Sail, the Wind at N.W. by W. The Captain, Surgeon, and Mr. *Hamilton*, being on the Shore-side, we gave them three Cheers; which they return'd.

Bulkeley, *Voyage to the South-Seas* (1743), 103–5.

The remarkably handsome tribute to Cheap may have been written as an obituary, but the passage would obviously stand to Bulkeley's advantage as a tribute to his own fair-mindedness and lack of malice, should Cheap ever turn up again.

The journey of the Speedwell through the Magellan Straits and up the South American coast to Rio Grande was appalling. The boat was difficult to handle, searching out the correct passage was a constant nightmare, the weather was dreadful, and the food available on the crowded vessel totally inadequate. In *Robinson Crusoe*, the hero laughs hollowly when, on visiting the wreck, he finds a lot of money. '"O drug!" said I aloud, "what art thou good for? ... I have no manner of use for thee ..." However, upon second thoughts, I took it away.' Wise man. In the Speedwell, the sailors, hungry, vermin-ridden and sick, had hung on to *their* money through thick and thin, and, incredibly, they now began to trade for the scanty daily allowance of flour.

*Sunday* the 15th [November] ... This Day several People drove a Trade with their Allowance, giving Silver Buckles for Flower, valued at twelve Shillings *per* Pound, and before Night it reach'd to a Guinea, the People crying aloud for Provisions, which are now so scarce, that several on Board are actually starving though Want.

*Thursday* the 19th, Fresh Gales at W. N.W.: with Hail and Snow. This Morning cast loose, and sail'd out, but could make no Hand of it; our Boat will not work to Windward; put back from whence we came, and sent the People ashore to get Muscles. This Night departed this Life Mr. *Thomas Caple*, Son of the late Lieutenant *Caple*, aged twelve Years, who perish'd for want of Food. There was a Person on Board who had some of the Youth's Money, upwards of Twenty Guineas, with a Watch and Silver Cup. Those last the Boy was willing to sell for Flower; but his Guardian told him, he would buy Cloaths for him in the *Brazil*. The miserable Youth cry'd, Sir, I shall never live to see the *Brazil*; I am starving now, almost starved to Death; therefore, for G-d's Sake, give me my Silver Cup to get me some Victuals, or buy some for me yourself. All his Prayers and Intreaties to him were vain; but Heaven sent Death to his Relief, and put a Period to his Miseries in an Instant. Persons who have not experienc'd the Hardships we have met with, will wonder how People can be so inhuman to see their Fellow-Creatures starving before their Faces, and afford 'em no Relief: But Hunger is void of all Compassion; every Person was so intent on the Preservation of his own Life, that he was regardless of another's, and the Bowels of Commiseration were shut up.

Bulkeley, *Voyage to the South-Seas* (1743), 132–3, 135–6.

There were deaths every day; some hours beforehand, the dying 'are taken light-headed and fall a joking and laughing; and in this Humour they expire'. The oldest man in the party, Thomas Maclean, the cook, aged eighty-two, survived until almost the end of the voyage.

## III

It was at 'Freshwater Bay', south of Buenos Aires (the latitude is given as 37° 25′ S), that the party of eight was stranded ashore. The reasons given by Bulkeley for sailing without them are not convincing. The weather was bad; 'we expected every Minute the Vessel would founder at her Anchor'; 'We saw no Probability of the People coming Aboard'; it was 'every Man's Opinion that we must put to Sea or perish'.[20] They floated a cask ashore with firearms and necessaries, and a letter. They could see the party ashore; they 'made Signals wishing us well; at which we got under Sail, and left our Brethren'.

Isaac Morris's account of the adventures of the stranded party, *A Narrative of the Dangers and Distresses* ... was published in London (probably in 1750) as 'a Supplement to Mr Bulkeley's Journal, Campbell's Narrative, and Ld. Anson's Voyage'. Morris testifies that Bulkeley had faithfully related the manner of leaving Wager Island and the dealings with Captain Cheap. But he does not accept Bulkeley's insistence that they had no choice in the Speedwell but to sail without them. They received the floated message that the Speedwell could not stand in to fetch them off, but the next day conditions were good.

> To our great Surprize, we saw the Schooner with her Ensign hoisted at the Topping-lift, and under Sail from us.... The most probable Reason we could give for such inhuman Treatment was, that, by lessening the Number of their Crew, they might be better accommodated with Room and Provisions.... We could not help looking on it as the greatest Act of Cruelty thus to maroon us under a false Pretence of an utter Impossibility of taking us on board with them.
>
> Morris, *A Narrative*, 14–15.

When Bulkeley came to prepare the second edition of *Voyage to the South-Seas*, 1757, he included much of Morris's narrative, but not this passage.

Morris's story is excellently told. As usual, there is a strong contrast between the vitality of recollected incident and the deadness of the literary fill-in, such as 'After deliberating upon our unhappy Circumstances, and comforting each other with imaginary Hopes ...', or 'the compassionate Reader will paint our Distress in his Imagination in stronger Colours than can be described by Words'.

They established a mode of living on the shore, living on seals, training the puppies of wild dogs and breeding pigs. Two attempts to make their way to Buenos Aires ended in failure. The harmony of the party began to break; they were very fearful of disintegration. They divided themselves into two watches, and took a solemn oath 'never to quit each other'. One day Morris's watch was returning from an expedition.

[20] *Ibid.*, 162.

When we were got within a Stone's Cast of our Hut, I perceiv'd our Dogs very busy at a small Distance wagging their Tails in a very fondling Manner. Being a-head of my Companions, I passed on without much regarding it, thinking they had lighted on a dead Colt. But when I came to the Hut I was quite confounded; the Hut was rifled, and all our Necessaries taken away. In the utmost Consternation I ran back to my Comrades, whom I saw standing where I had left the Dogs: Seeing me running eagerly towards them, they cry'd out, *What's the Matter,* Isaac? I told them our Hut was pull'd down, and every thing taken away. *Ay*, said they, *and something worse has happened; for yonder lie poor* Guy Broadwater *and* Ben. Smith *murder'd.*

Morris, *A Narrative*, 35–6.

They never found the other two men. Morris and his remaining three companions set out once again to trek north and were once again defeated. They now had no ammunition, and no fire, and it was winter. At one point Morris was foraging alone.

To my Astonishment, I discover'd about a Dozen of Horses galloping down the sandy Bay towards our Hut, and, as they came nearer, I plainly saw Men on their Backs, & that they were *Indians*, 'Twas in vain to fly; I imagined nothing but Death approaching, and prepared to meet it with all the Resolution I could muster up. I ran towards them, and fell on my Knees, begging my Life with all the Signs of Humility I could make; when I heard a Voice saying, *Don't be afraid,* Isaac! *we are all here.* This revived me. The *Indians* alighted, and whilst some were intent on examining the Hut, others stood with drawn Knives, ready to dispatch us in case we made any Resistance.

Morris, *A Narrative*, 45–6.

The Indians had captured his comrades, who had managed to insist that there was a fourth who must not be left behind. So, wrote Morris, 'I had the Happiness of being taken Prisoner with them'.

Although the Indians bartered their captives among themselves, the English sailors were treated with 'great Humanity'. After several months travelling they were brought before the king, who spoke some Spanish, and who declared his enmity to the Spaniards who had robbed his people of their territory and driven them into the mountains. They spent many months in the Indian town working as menials; but 'tho' we were their Slaves, we were treated very humanely, and they would suffer no one to use us ill'. There were four captured Spanish women in the town, 'and the King told us, with a smile, he would give us each a Wife'.[21] That is all Morris writes, but they evidently accepted the gift, for they were later reported as saying 'that they had each of them a *Spanish* Woman given him to Wife, and that some of them had left Children behind them'.[22]

Eventually they persuaded the king to take them to Buenos Aires, where

[21] Morris, *A Narrative*, 53. [22] Campbell, *The Sequel to Bulkeley and Cummins's Voyage*, 98.

they were ransomed by the 'President of the English Assiento House, Mr. Gray'. They refused to become Catholics, and were made prisoners-of-war on board Admiral Pizarro's ship, Asia – 'treated more like Slaves than Prisoners of War'.

## IV

It was now 1745, four years after the wreck of the Wager. Morris was astonished to find on board the Asia his fellow-midshipman Alexander Campbell, whom he had last seen defecting from the southward enterprise and turning back in the barge with Midshipman Byron to join Captain Cheap on the island. The story of Campbell, Byron and Cheap is told in the separate narratives of the two midshipmen; Campbell's in 1747, Byron's not until 1768. Cheap's own account, a bland and colourless affair, survives only (strangely enough) in Bulkeley's second edition.

Campbell's narrative was entitled simply *The Sequel to Bulkeley's and Cummins's Voyage to the South-Seas*. He published as did his precursors for the money he might make and to vindicate himself, having been denied further employment by the Navy because of allegations against him – in his case allegations by his captain, David Cheap.

> All I have to say in Behalf of the following Sheets, is, that they are void of Art, Malice, or Misrepresentation. The Facts related in them are undeniable, dress'd in the plain unsophisticated Language of an honest Tar, whose principal View in publishing them, is to clear his Character from a very gross Calumny. Most of the Hardships I suffered in following the Fortune of Captain *Cheap*, were the Consequence of my voluntary Attachment to that Gentleman, and the Distresses I underwent with him, and for him, are such as perhaps have never been equall'd. In Reward for this the Captain has approved himself the greatest Enemy I have in the World. . . . I now find myself destitute of Employment, and without the least Prospect of being provided for in the Service of my King and Country.
>
> Campbell, *The Sequel to Bulkeley and Cummins's Voyage*, ii.

Campbell had separated from Cheap, Byron and Hamilton in Santiago, and Cheap, arriving back in England first, had reported 'that I had enter'd into the *Spanish* Service'. Campbell learned this when *he* got back in May 1746 and unsuspectingly reported to the Admiralty. What Campbell does not say is that Cheap had also charged that Campbell had become a Catholic while he was in Spanish hands, and that this was the reason why he separated from the others and chose not to come home with them in a French ship. Campbell is silent about his conversion, but it seems to be a fact.

Campbell reckons there were twenty left behind on Wager Island. They had two boats, the barge and the yawl. When the Speedwell had left,

Cheap brightened up. 'He became very brisk, went about every where to get Wood and Water, made Fires, and proved an excellent Cook.'[23]

They set sail from the island, but the yawl was swamped and sank. As they could not all get into the barge, they left behind four marines.

> When we departed, the four poor Wretches stood on the Beach, gave us three Cheers, and cry'd, GOD *bless the* KING! Our Hearts melted with Compassion for them, but there was no helping their Misfortune. Their Names were *Smith*, *Hobbs*, *Hertford*, and Corporal *Croslet*.
>
> Campbell, *The Sequel to Bulkeley and Cummins's Voyage*, 46.

However, they were forced to go back, and they resolved to pick the marines up. But alas, they had disappeared. They found one musket, and their ammunition.

Campbell records violent quarrels, chiefly over food, and the death from starvation of John Bosman. Six men went off in the barge to get food, and neither they nor the barge were seen again. (The Spaniards later found it with two survivors.) Now without any boat, Cheap and his tiny party were taken over by Indians and carried north in their canoes. Elliott the surgeon died. The Indians 'were looking upon themselves as our Masters, and we finding ourselves obliged to submit to them in all Things'. Famished and lousy, they were forced to paddle and bail, and march without shoes over rough tracks. Campbell describes in detail Indian methods of fishing and so on, but he has nothing good to say about his hosts. After many months they arrived at Chiloe, where they were well treated by both Indians and Spaniards.

In spite of this story of continued misfortune and misery, Campbell contends that if only the main party had come north, they could have captured Chiloe and the Lima ship.[24]

Cheap, Campbell, Byron and Hamilton were two years in Santiago. They were able to get funds, but Campbell claims Cheap cheated him of his fair share. He broke with them, and travelled overland with Pizarro's officers to Buenos Aires, and there found the little band of his former shipmates. He writes that in the Azores he *was* asked to join the Spanish service, but he refused.

Campbell bitterly contrasts his utter rejection by the Navy with the immediate promotion given to the Honourable John Byron. The latter had been promoted to lieutenant during his absence, and on his return was given command of a twenty-gun sloop, to be followed in a few months by his appointment, as captain, to the frigate Syren.[25] Byron's own account of things was, as we have seen, not published until as late as 1768, two years after his round-the-world expedition, and twenty-seven years

[23] *Ibid.*, 29. [24] *Ibid.*, 77.

[25] Pack, *The Wager Mutiny*, 219; *Byron's Journal of his Circumnavigation*, xx.

after the wreck. What his motives were for not publishing earlier, or for publishing at that particular time, are not at all clear. It was hardly a question of waiting until his captain was no longer alive, for Cheap died in 1752. Whatever the reason, his publishers, S. Baker and G. Leigh, capitalized on the renown of the recent voyage. The title is *The Narrative of the Honourable John Byron (Commodore in a Late Expedition round the World)*. (See Plate 5.)

The narrative presents itself as an attack on Bulkeley and Cummins. Their reminiscences are so selective 'that they appear evidently to have been put together with the purpose of justifying those proceedings which could not be considered in any other light than that of direct mutiny'. 'It will be obvious to every reader, why a licentious crew should hearken to any factious leader rather than to the solidity of their captain's advice.'[26] But he grants that in the law which existed at that time, 'this ungovernable herd' may not strictly have been mutineers, since their employment in the Navy ceased at the time of the wreck.

Byron's style is very starchy, but it has its own humour.

> It would have redounded greatly to the tenderness and humanity of captain Cheap if at this time he had remitted somewhat of that attention he shewed to self-preservation.
>
> Byron, *The Narrative*, 110.

He makes no scruple of copying directly from the narrative he is abusing, especially the account of the wreck itself. But he has his own material, such as the story of the boy who had to be stopped from eating the liver of a drowned man, and of the dog which he befriended and later ate. He claims, surely falsely, that he joined the long-boat party only because he thought the captain was to be with them, and that he left when he found otherwise.

The best of the narrative is its record of the humiliations of travelling north with the Indians on whom they became totally dependent. Byron goes beyond Campbell in offering a classic rendering of the inversion nightmare, in which the relationship of superior to inferior, civilized to savage, master to slave, is turned upside-down. Indeed, he invokes one of the most potent (and common) versions, that of the Christian prisoner of the infidel Turk: he and Campbell were 'working like galley slaves all day'.[27] He claims he was kicked and beaten and kept away from the fire. Once he crawled into a wigwam and found himself with two women, one old and the other young and pretty, who took pity on him and allowed him to sleep by them.

His position (as he describes it) was complicated by the attitude of the Indians to Cheap. The Indians' contempt for the midshipmen was

[26] Byron, *The Narrative*, vi–vii. [27] *Ibid.*, 164.

increased by the recognition that they were Cheap's subordinates. And Cheap got off lightly because he was accepted as the chief. Byron's account of the enfeebled Cheap complacently accepting the Indians' acknowledgement of his superiority, allying himself with the new power-structure and assenting to the maltreatment of his own officers, is startling. Byron moves into the grotesque in his picture of degenerate authority. The torment of lice, he wrote, was intolerable.

> But we were clean in comparison to captain Cheap; for I could compare his body to nothing but an ant-hill, with thousands of those insects crawling over it; for he was now past attempting to rid himself in the least from this torment, as he had quite lost himself, not recollecting our names that were about him, or even his own. His beard was as long as a hermit's; that and his face being covered with train-oil and dirt, from having long accustomed himself to sleep upon a bag, by the way of pillow, in which he kept the pieces of stinking seal. . . . His legs were as big as mill-posts, though his body appeared to be nothing but skin and bone.
>
> Byron, *The Narrative*, 166.

It will be seen that the reverence for authority and discipline which inspires Byron's preface does not carry through into the body of his narrative. Nor does he follow up his initial onslaught on Bulkeley and Cummins. Probably different parts were written at different times; much is vague and general, but the incised particularity of a number of passages suggests notes written soon after the actual incidents.

There was one further narrative concerning the Wager disaster. This was published in 1751, as *An Affecting Narrative of the Unfortunate Voyage and Catastrophe of his Majesty's Ship Wager ... The Whole compiled from authentic Journals, and transmitted by Letter to a Merchant in London, from a Person who was an Eye Witness of all the Affair ...* In E. G. Cox's *Reference Guide to the Literature of Travel* (1935–49), vol. II, this is attributed to John Young (the cooper), and the attribution is accepted by G. B. Parks in *The New Cambridge Bibliography* (1971) and by Glyndwr Williams in his edition of Anson's *Voyage Round the World*. S. W. C. Pack, in his book on the Wager, calls the narrative 'the best written of the many stories', and quotes from it many times, finding the observations 'penetrating' (p. 82) and remarking on one occasion that 'we may be justified in relying more on the cooper's version' (p. 102).

It is surely the case, however, that the book is a fake. Its record of incidents is based entirely on Bulkeley and Cummins, and what Pack quotes are the endless moralizings which have been spliced into the borrowed framework. It is Grub-Street work, and it looks as though the hack was hired to do the job, because once again Bulkeley and Cummins are turned against themselves, and the narrative is made at every point to support the captain and established authority. It is easy to see why Young the cooper has been given the authorship. Young was the only other member of the crew to be with Bulkeley and Cummins to the end, and must therefore be responsible for any narrative that stays with those two. But it is only at the very end of the book that the hack implies this identification, which is of course essential for his credibility.

Mr. *Bulkeley*, the Carpenter, and your humble Servant, as soon as we came from off the Vessel, repaired to Change; where we made ourselves known to some Gentlemen of the *British* Factory whom we there met with.

*An Affecting Narrative*, 158.

At this point Bulkeley reads as follows:

We *Englishmen*, when we came ashore, went immediately on the *Change*. I was pretty well known to some Gentlemen of the *English* Factory.

Bulkeley, *Voyage to the South-Seas* (1743), 49.

It is hard to see how anyone could be impressed by the interminable moralizing of the sententious narrator, or his refined literary touches: 'Those who are deaf to the most sonorous Blasts of *Æolus*, or whom *Neptune*'s utmost Fury cannot terrify, are yet startled by these shocking Incidents'. Two examples of interpretative amplification are worth giving. In the first he has access to Cheap's thoughts on the proposal to go to the south.

In his Heart he absolutely disapproved their Scheme: but he saw, the Violence of their present Inclinations would push them on Extremities, if he testified his Dislike of it; he studied therefore prudently to temporise with them: hoping, either some Incident might occur, to alter their views, or that their Passions would by degrees subside, and they might become ... more conformable to Authority.

*An Affecting Narrative*, 49.

The second ornamentation provides dialogue for the rascally mutineers when Lieutenant Hamilton and the surgeon decline to join the main party.

On one of the Fellows crying out, very opportunely, 'Sink their Body's, my Boys, if the silly Sons of Bitches will run to the Devil, what's that to any one', and another answering, 'Aye, by G-d, *Jack*, you're in the Right', all acquiesced: and these two Gentlemen were allowed, without further Abuse, to stay with the Captain – to his great Consolation.

*An Affecting Narrative*, 71.

The most passionate part of the narrative is a refusal to accept Bulkeley's account of his farewell to Cheap (see above, p. 68).

Just as we were going off, Bulkeley would run to take a final Adieu of that Gentleman, and give him a friendly Embrace. He return'd seemingly much affected with the tender Reception he had found, and the melting Farewell at parting. Some of the Circumstances we fancied were of his own Invention, as they were quite unsuitable with the gallant Spirit of that haughty Officer, whose Genius and Disposition were formed to command, but never could descend to cringe and wheedle.

*An Affecting Narrative*, 81–2.

This is an interesting example of a reader's scepticism about a written record being translated into eye-witness terms.

## V

The wreck of the Wager generated four notable survival narratives. In her book *Imperial Eyes: Travel Writing and Transculturation*, M. L. Pratt is dismissive of survival literature, which she finds a facile genre marked by 'lowbrow sensationalism'. She notes the frequency of the theme of being enslaved by heathens and infidels, but, she goes on, 'The context of survival literature was "safe" for transgressive plots, since the very existence of a text presupposed the imperially correct outcome: the survivor survived, and sought reintegration into the home society. The tale was always told from the viewpoint of the European who returned.'[28] This animus against survivors is perplexing. What would she have the survivors do? Not return? Not write? Not seek reintegration in their own society? The tale was necessarily told from the viewpoint of the European who returned. The literature of experience is more honestly served by being a record of prejudice than by being an attempt to re-create the viewpoint of people of a vastly different culture. It would be very agreeable to find more often a sympathetic attitude to the viewpoint of Indian or Spaniard, but in fact attitudes vary a great deal among our survivors, and it is important to attend to the individuality of each response. One thing is certain. All the survivors were marked by their experience and could not lightly cast it off and resume 'normal life'.

Alexander Campbell was immersed in two separate alien cultures, of the heathen Indians and the Catholic Spaniards, and he came out with a Catholic dye. He was comprehensively rejected as he sought his re-integration in his own society. Isaac Morris uses a time-honoured theme in survival literature when he contrasts the humanity of the Indians with the brutality of the Spaniards. There is little, however, of the 'noble savage' theme. Even while he emphasizes the humane treatment he and his comrades received from their Indian captors, he maintains the tone of European superiority, and is always condescending about their customs and religion; 'I could never observe any Rules of Government among 'em'. He puts behind him his long period of dwelling among Indians without apparent regret, but his acceptance of them in his narrative as

28 Pratt, *Imperial Eyes*, 86–7.

fellow human beings dispossessed by imperialism is a small recognition of the fraudulence of much colonialist justification. John Byron, on the other hand, while forced to accept the reality of the Indians who made menials of them (and saved their lives), allowed his disgust and hatred to translate them into a wholly separate race. He reintegrated himself into home society with a vengeance. Is it possible that the strange astigmatism which made him record in his Dolphin journal the abnormal size of the Indians was some kind of instinctive distancing of those who had formerly humiliated him? A further defence against the claim of kinship from those who had destroyed his understanding of his place in the scale of human superiority?

The Indians are peripheral to the Bulkeley and Cummins narrative. Literally, they come and go. 'A very simple and inoffensive People', they found them, and were amazed at their indifference to cold. They strongly disapproved of the idleness of the men while the women went fishing or diving for 'sea-eggs'. 'Among these People the Order of Nature seems inverted; the Males are exempted from Hardships and Labour, and the Women are meer Slaves and Drudges.'[29] The importance of their narrative is not in their attitude to the Indians, but in their attitude to the naval hierarchy. Basically, their story is of the re-creation of authority after its collapse and disintegration in the wreck of the king's ship. They are very careful to play down their role in challenging established order and discipline, and to shelter behind 'the People' or the wretched Beans when they can; but it is quite clear that they were the leaders in planning and executing the escape from the island. Whether or not their insistence of going south was justified, considering the terrible mortality on board the Speedwell, they were surely right that the makeshift schooner could never have given battle to the Spaniards, and could never have caught up with Anson's fleet (which had left Juan Fernandez at the end of September, 1741, before the Speedwell had left Wager Island). Captain Cheap, so determined not to turn his back upon the enemy, became their prisoner.

In England the grateful lieutenant attempted to re-erect the structure of naval discipline which he had helped Bulkeley to overturn. But the book which the gunner and the carpenter wrote served as a shield against the treachery of Beans, the outrage of the Admiralty and the vengeance of Cheap. Not only that, but it became *the* text of the events on Wager Island, which those who wished them ill could qualify or emend but not destroy. The hack who wrote the *Affecting Narrative* tried to throw their story into their faces; his lack of success may be judged by the need which Byron felt seventeen years later to undermine and denigrate them and their threat to right thinking about conformity and obedience.

[29] Bulkeley, *Voyage to the South-Seas* (1743), 39.

*A Voyage to the South-Seas* may have baffled the authors' enemies, but it did not make their fortunes. No action was taken against Bulkeley and Cummins – except ostracism. They got their pay up to the time the ship was wrecked, but their naval careers were finished.

# 5

# Dr Hawkesworth at sea

## I

Nor will I presume to question the Abilities of Dr. Hawkesworth, who is generally allowed to be an elegant Writer. But why should not Banks, Solander, and Byron, &c be supposed qualified to describe what they saw, felt, and suffered in Terms sufficiently vigorous and proper? Is any Man offended at the plain honest Language of our old Voyagers? Are not Dampier and Wood Rogers still read and understood?

(*Baldwin's London Weekly Journal*, 22 May 1773)

'Why, Sir', said I, 'Hawkesworth has used your narrative as a London Tavern-keeper does wine. He has *brewed* it'.

(Boswell to Captain Cook, April 1776)[1]

If Captain Cook's first round-the-world voyage in the Endeavour, 1768–71, was the start of a new era in English voyages of discovery, it was also a continuation or the culmination of a series of tentative explorations of the South Atlantic and the Pacific, aiming to increase and extend Britain's overseas power and possessions, which followed the conclusion of the Seven Years' War with France in 1763. These explorations were initiated by John Perceval, Earl of Egmont, who was First Lord of the Admiralty from 1763 to 1766. The first voyage was that of John Byron in the Dolphin (see above, pp. 53–5). As soon as the Dolphin returned in 1766, plans were made for her to make a further voyage. Captain McBride had already been sent in the Jason to establish a settlement in the Falklands, following Byron's in-passage communication to Egmont (see p. 54). France and Spain, however, were indignant at encroachments on what they regarded as their own territory. The English Cabinet began to have doubts about international repercussions and to look askance at Egmont's ventures. Egmont resigned in August 1766 because of this

[1] Both these passages may be found in Helen Wallis's invaluable Hakluyt Society edition of *Carteret's Voyage Round the World*, 498 and 510.

opposition, but he made sure before he left that his next expedition was under sail.[2]

The Dolphin was under the command of Captain Samuel Wallis, and he was accompanied by the Swallow, commanded by Philip Carteret, who had been Byron's first lieutenant in the Dolphin. The Swallow was a bad sailor; she was ill-found for a long voyage in the tropics, and Carteret was quite in the dark about the ultimate objectives of the voyage until they were well out to sea. These objectives were to explore 'between Cape Horn and New Zeland' for 'Land or Islands of great extent', and, finding any that 'have not been visited by any European Power', to 'take Possession of such Land or Islands' – 'with the consent of the Inhabitants'.[3] After struggling through the Magellan Straits, always delayed by the slow sailing of the Swallow, whose captain nevertheless knew them as Wallis did not, the two ships lost contact. Carteret was convinced that once his usefulness as pilot through the straits was over, Wallis had no further use for his slow-sailing companion and showed him a clean pair of heels; and it is difficult to think that the separation was an accident.

Wallis, though a sick man, went on to discover Tahiti, which he named King George's Island, where his crew spent five idyllic weeks. Carteret, though not properly equipped for exploration and negotiation with islanders, lumbered on painfully on his own, discovering and naming island after island, including Pitcairn, until with his weary and scurvy-ridden crew he reached Macassar, where he got little help from the Dutch. He had better fortune at the Cape of Good Hope, and was making his way home through the Atlantic when Bougainville, who had been following in his track, caught up with him and spoke with him.

Louis de Bougainville had set out in December 1766 with La Boudeuse and L'Etoile on his great voyage of discovery, his scientific complement including Philibert Commerson. He had been to Tahiti in the wake of Wallis, and had heard at Batavia that the missing Swallow had not in fact been lost. The meeting at sea of the English and French commanders, both of whom had endured so much in the service of their country's imperial aspirations, should have been a romantic and moving encounter. But Carteret was extremely suspicious of Bougainville's overtures (via his lieutenant) and was willing neither to talk nor to accept help.

Wallis reached England on 20 May 1768; Bougainville and Carteret both got home in March 1769. On 26 August 1768, Captain James Cook set sail from Plymouth in the Endeavour. The Royal Society had petitioned King George III in February to defray the expenses of a voyage into southern latitudes, arguing

[2] Helen Wallis in *Carteret's Voyage Round the World*, 10–15.

[3] Robertson, *Discovery of Tahiti*, xxii–xxiii; *Carteret's Voyage Round the World*, 302–4.

that the passage of the Planet Venus over the Disc of the Sun, which will happen on the 3rd of June in the year 1769, is a Phaenomenon that must, if the same be accurately observed in proper places, contribute greatly to the improvement of Astronomy on which navigation so much depends.

Cook I: *Voyage of the Endeavour*, 604.

His Majesty consenting, the Admiralty provided a ship, a Whitby-built collier, and a commander, Lieutenant James Cook, R. N. On the return of Wallis, they also provided a proper place for observation, the newly discovered King George's Island. The Endeavour's scientific team was headed by the young, wealthy, self-confident Joseph Banks.

Cook's instructions were detailed as regards the observation of the transit of Venus on Tahiti. He was 'to endeavour by all proper means to cultivate a friendship with the Natives, presenting them with such Trifles as may be acceptable to them' and 'shewing them every kind of Civility and regard'.[4] Such sentiments were much more emphatically expressed in a list of 'Hints' offered to the 'Gentlemen' on the Endeavour by the President of the Royal Society, James Douglas, Earl of Morton. This is how it begins:

To exercise the utmost patience and forbearance with respect to the Natives of the several Lands where the Ship may touch.

To check the petulance of the Sailors, and restrain the wanton use of Fire Arms.

To have it still in view that sheding the blood of those people is a crime of the highest nature:– They are human creatures, the work of the same omnipotent Author, equally under his care with the most polished European; perhaps being less offensive, more entitled to his favor.

They are the natural, and in the strictest sense of the word, the legal possessors of the several Regions they inhabit.

No European Nation has a right to occupy any part of their country, or settle among them without their voluntary consent.

Conquest over such people can give no just title; because they could never be the Aggressors.

They may naturally and justly attempt to repell intruders, whom they may apprehend are come to disturb them in the quiet possession of their country, whether that apprehension be well or ill founded.

Cook I: *Voyage of the Endeavour*, 514.

Cook was also given a sealed packet of 'Additional Instructions'. These relate chiefly to exploration for the supposed southern continent. If he finds it, he is 'with the Consent of the Natives to take possession of Convenient Situations in the Country in the Name of the King of Great Britain'. If he should come across undiscovered islands, he is to survey and chart them, and, once again, 'take possession for His Majesty'. He is also to

[4] Cook I; *Voyage of the Endeavour*, cclxxx.

make careful observation of New Zealand. Before leaving the vessel on his return he is to collect all logs, books and journals which any of the officers may have kept, and enjoin secrecy about the voyage on the whole ship's company.[5]

The story of Cook's first voyage – his stay on Tahiti, his circumnavigation of New Zealand, his perilous passage up the east coast of Australia, and the toll of fever in Batavia – is too well known to repeat here. The Endeavour returned to England in July, 1771, after a voyage of almost three years. Joseph Banks, apprehensive about the activities of French mariners, was very anxious that an effort should be made 'to publish an account of our voyage as soon as possible after our arrival', so that 'our own countrey shall have the honour of our Discoveries!'[6] First to appear, however, was an anonymous and unauthorized *Journal of a Voyage Round the World in His Majesty's Ship Endeavour*, published in 1771 and rather boldly dedicated by its publisher, Becket, to the Lords of the Admiralty, Mr Banks and Dr Solander. (Banks's copy is in the British Library.) It is a curious work, flat, dull, unimpassioned. Its heavy style moves into the humorous mode over Queen Obrea's pacific policy in Tahiti.

> Obrea, whose feelings were most congenial to the wants of mankind, proposed, in direct opposition to the advice of her counsellors, that a large supply of women and hogs should be instantly sent on board the ship. A proposal so pregnant with benevolent sensibility, that it deserves to be recorded on tables of adamant; for what could have been more acceptable than women and hogs to sailors, who had long been deprived of both?
>
> (p. 65)

The only emotional passage concerns the death of 'Mr Green the astronomer' in Batavia, which 'left the minutes of his observations in a state of disorder which must render several of them unintelligible' (p. 130). This clerkly anxiety is possibly a clue to the identity of the author, who remains unidentified; Beaglehole suggested the midshipman James Magra.

The authorized narrative did not appear until 1773, when Cook was already at sea again on his second voyage, in the Resolution. It was published along with the narratives of the voyages of Byron, Wallis and Carteret, in a redaction by John Hawkesworth. The well-known story given by Fanny Burney is that Lord Sandwich, First Lord of the Admiralty, meeting her father, Charles Burney, at Lord Orford's house in Norfolk in September 1771, and discussing Cook's voyage with him, said that he had 'the papers of it in his possession'. He said 'that they are not arranged, but meer rough Draughts, & that he should be much obliged to any one who could recommend a proper Person to *Write the Voyage*'. Dr Burney suggested Hawkesworth; Garrick confirmed the recommendation,

[5] *Ibid.*, cclxxxii–cclxxxiv. [6] Banks, *The Endeavour Journal of Joseph Banks*, II, 249.

'thinking to put a few hundred pounds into his pocket'. Hawkesworth waited on Lord Sandwich, and that was that.[7]

Neither Burney nor Garrick could have had any other reason for recommending Hawkesworth than the wish to do him a good turn. He had never been at sea and had no experience of this particular task, though, being what they used to call a 'miscellaneous writer', he had tried his hand at many things. Born in 1720, the son of a London watch-chaser, he had been apprenticed as an attorney's clerk.[8] He was entirely self-educated. Sir Joshua Reynolds said disdainfully that 'he had no literature whatever'. Sir John Hawkins said he 'was a man of fine parts, but no learning'.[9] He married Mary Brown, daughter of a Bromley butcher, 'an unassuming woman, of very superior talent'. Together, they rented a mansion in Bromley and set up a girls' boarding school which Mrs Hawkesworth ran while Hawkesworth pursued his literary life, winning for a time the friendship of Dr Johnson and Garrick. Johnson told Mrs Thrale that for information about his early life in London, 'you must all go to Jack Hawkesworth for anecdotes: I lived in great familiarity with him (though I think there was not much affection)'.[10]

Hawkesworth was a major contributor over many years to *The Gentleman's Magazine*, but he became well known because of his popular twice-weekly periodical essay, *The Adventurer* (1752–4). In the final essay he proclaimed himself 'a moral writer',

> determined to mark the first insensible gradation to ill; to caution against those acts which are not generally believed to incur guilt, but of which indubitable vice and hopeless misery are the natural and almost necessary consequences.

For this elevated stance Hawkesworth was rewarded with the Lambeth degree of LL. D. by the Archbishop of Canterbury in 1756. Johnson was contemptuous of the award, saying 'Hawkesworth is grown a coxcomb, and I have done with him'. (He relented later.) Hawkesworth produced a big edition of Swift's works, in which he defended the use of the obscene for moral ends. He spent some time producing texts for revivals of Dryden's *Amphitryon* and Southerne's *Oroonoko*. The real subject of his very successful oriental tale, *Almoran and Hamet*, was, according to his biographer, 'the need to regulate appetite, especially sexual appetite'. A reviewer, contrasting it with *Tristram Shandy*, said the reader would find 'no winding up of Clocks'.[11]

The sixteen-year-old Fanny Burney was disappointed when she met

[7] F. Burney, *Early Journals*, I, 173.
[8] Biographical details are mostly from Abbott's *John Hawkesworth*.
[9] Hill, *Boswell's Life of Johnson*, I, 253; Abbott, *John Hawkesworth*, 6.
[10] Hill, *Johnsonian Miscellanies*, I, 166.
[11] Abbott, *John Hawkesworth*, 116–17.

'the celebrated Dr Hawkesworth' in 1769. He 'does not shine in Conversation so much superior to others. . . . All he says is just, – proper, & better express'd than most *written* language; but he does not appear to me to be at all what is call'd a wit – neither is his conversation sprightly or brilliant.'[12] The truth is he was a prig and a snob. He sedulously courted the company of the well born. In a letter of 1770 he wrote: 'I din'd with the Dowager Lady Shelburne on Sunday was Sev'n night at Twickenham; Lord Kingsborough was so good to give me a place in his carriage'.[13] Johnson thought him 'one of the many whom success in the world had spoiled', and Joshua Reynolds said he was 'an affected, insincere man, and a great coxcomb in his dress'. Goldsmith remarked tersely that he would have made 'a good dancing master'.[14]

'There is nothing about which I would so willingly be employed as the work you mention', wrote Hawkesworth to Charles Burney, and later told him that 'the property of the work will be my own'.[15] He secured from Strahan and Cadell the huge sum of £6,000 for the rights of publication, more than was paid for any other literary work of the century. This staggering figure soon became common knowledge, and indignation and resentment that Hawkesworth should get so much for fashioning the work of other people were a main ingredient in the hostile reception of the work. By the investment of £2,000 Hawkesworth was able to become a director of the East India Company, but he lost the friendship of Garrick, who had used his influence to obtain the work for him and had expected him to deal with the publisher Thomas Becket.

Hawkesworth began his task in the autumn of 1771. He was overjoyed to be allowed the use of Joseph Banks's journal to add to the material which he already had. He finished work in 1773, and the edition was published in June in three volumes:

*An Account of the Voyages Undertaken by the Order of his Present Majesty for Making Discoveries in the Southern Hemisphere. And successively performed by Commodore Byron, Captain Wallis, Captain Carteret, and Captain Cook. In the Dolphin, the Swallow, and the Endeavour. Drawn up from the Journals which were kept by the several Commanders. And from the Papers of Joseph Banks, Esq. By John Hawkesworth, LL.D.*

For the publishers, the work was a success. In spite of being sold at three guineas, a second edition was called for in the same summer. There was a New York edition in 1774, and also French and German translations, and a 'cheap' serial edition was run, of sixty weekly parts, one shilling each (a saving of exactly three shillings on the original price).

But for Hawkesworth, the publication was disastrous. It was 'eagerly

12 F. Burney, *Early Journals*, I, 63.
13 Abbott, *John Hawkesworth*, 132.
14 Hill, *Boswell's Life of Johnson*, I, 253; *Johnsonian Miscellanies*, I, 210.
15 Abbott, *John Hawkesworth*, 144.

read by all European nations', write George Forster, 'but incurred universal censure, I had almost said contempt'. 'Detraction and defamation' was how the loyal Fanny Burney described the response. Mary Hawkesworth said that the *Voyages* delivered 'the *Coup de grace* to all my hopes of happiness on earth'.[16] The attack came on several fronts. The first was the most serious, namely the repudiation of the work by the leaders of the expeditions. As a German visitor put it: 'the respective Commanders, Messrs. Byron, Wallis, Carteret &c, had publicly protested against Dr. H's account of their voyages, as containing misrepresented facts'.[17] (Cook did not see a copy of the book until he got to the Cape of Good Hope on his way home in 1775, and Hawkesworth never knew of his protests.) The second attack was theological, concerning Hawkesworth's refusal to attribute lucky breaks to the operation of providence. The third attack was moral, from those who, like John Wesley, claimed to be shocked at the descriptions of sexual encounters in Tahiti. The fourth was from those such as Horace Walpole who found the book tedious in the extreme. Many of the objections were alluded to in Alexander Dalrymple's published *Letter* (1773), which was chiefly concerned with Hawkesworth's casualness about the existence of a southern continent. The speed and intensity of the attack on the *Voyages* led one of Hawkesworth's defenders to suggest a conspiracy.

> The Torrent of Abuse so illiberally and so industriously propagated against Dr. Hawkesworth seems to have been premeditated, and ready for the News-papers before the Bookseller had Time to publish the Book.
>
> *Carteret's Voyage Round the World*, 500.

Although Hawkesworth wrote a spirited reply to Dalrymple in the preface to the second edition in early August 1773, he was devastated by the reception of the book. In October Fanny Burney said that 'Dr. Hawkesworth looks very ill; he has had very bad Health lately. Indeed I believe that the abuse so illiberally cast on him ... has really affected his Health, by preying upon his mind.' Later she wrote, 'we all agreed that we never saw a man more Altered – thin, livid – harrassed!' He had talked at length about his position: 'that he had had no Education or advantage but what he had given himself: but that he had preserved an unblemished Character & reputation till his last year'.[18] This later entry was written shortly after Hawkesworth's death on 17 November 1773. Fanny Burney said 'he Died of a lingering Fever'. There was a rumour that he had taken his own life. Whatever the precise cause, the 'abuse' certainly hastened his

[16] G. Forster, *A Voyage Round the World*, I, ix; F.Burney, *Early Journals*, I, 326; Abbott, *John Hawkesworth*, 192.

[17] *Carteret's Voyage Round the World*, 468 and 503–4.

[18] F. Burney, *Early Journals*, I, 313 and 325–6.

end. He was a broken man. To understand the depth of his misery, we need to measure the height of the preceding self-esteem, in the overweening self-satisfaction with which he constructed *An Account of the Voyages*.

Hawkesworth's 'General Introduction' shows him as confused as anyone about the purpose of the published voyage-narrative, who its readers were to be and what they required. His lack of faith in the value of historical reports had been ominously demonstrated years before in an early number of *The Adventurer* (number four, 18 November 1752), arguing the superiority of narratives of fiction over narratives of fact. Faced with narratives which just recite events 'the mind is tantalized with an imperfect glimpse of innumerable objects that just appear and vanish'. Events need to follow one another 'in a regular and connected series'. 'Those narratives are most pleasing, which not only excite and gratify curiosity but engage the passions'. Voyages and travels unfortunately excite only the passion of wonder. In any case, 'NATURE is now exhausted; all her wonders have been accumulated, every recess has been explored'. What is left is ART, whose 'infinite variety' can produce whatever effect is to be desired. Centrally the required effect is guidance about thought and conduct (as he propounded in the last number already quoted) through the medium of entertainment. Faithful to this credo, Hawkesworth had specialized in the moral fable; *The Adventurer* is full of them – fanciful, romantic tales deep-laden with warnings and preachment. His problem in 1771–3 was to move the logs and journals of those who had so painfully made their way round the world's oceans towards the kind of literature he approved of, narratives that would entertain and instruct the general reader. It is to this general reader whom he apologizes in case he has 'related the nautical events too minutely'. These, he explains, are for the benefit of 'future navigators'. And he continues, with unnerving candour: 'I was not indeed myself sufficiently apprised of the minuteness that was necessary in this part of the work, so that I was obliged to make many additions to it, after I had prepared my manuscript'.

The tortuous argument at the beginning of the introduction about the authorial voice to be employed can only be understood in the light of Hawkesworth's conviction that events in a narrative must be presented with the accompaniment of their proper moral significance – which he of course was able to supply. 'When I first undertook the work, it was debated, whether it should be written in the first or third person.' The first person had major advantages in the realm of entertainment, 'bringing the Adventurer and the Reader nearer together'. But there was the objection that if the narratives were written in the first-person voices of the individual commanders, 'I could exhibit only a naked narrative, without any opinion or sentiment of my own, however fair the occasion'. It is not, we must understand, so much a question of Hawkesworth's right to impose his sentiments on us – he never doubted that – as of the right of the narrative to be properly clothed. The triumphant solution was that the first-person narration would be preserved, for interest sake, and that the commanders would be asked to approve the sentiments and reflections provided for them by Hawkesworth.

As the manuscript would be submitted to the Gentlemen in whose names it would be written, supposing the narrative to be in the first person, and nothing published without their approbation, it would signify little who conceived the sentiments that should be expressed, and therefore I might still be at liberty to express my own.

These grafted-in sentiments, he said (correctly), would 'be found most frequent in the account of the voyage of the Endeavour'.

It is likely that Hawkesworth honestly believed that this assent by the captains to their new-minted personae would be obtained, and it is possible he believed that it had been obtained. He wrote that the manuscript of each voyage had been read to the appropriate commander at the Admiralty, with Lord Sandwich present 'during much the greatest part of the time'. Cook flatly denied this: 'I never had the perusal of the Manuscript nor did I ever hear the whole of it read in the mode it was written, notwithstanding what Dr Hawkesworth has said to the Contrary'.[19] Cook was choosing his words carefully. He told Boswell that he *had* seen part of the manuscript, and had suggested alterations which Hawkesworth refused to make.[20] This makes it very hard to understand how Hawkesworth could say in the introduction that after the readings to the commanders at the Admiralty, 'such emendations as they suggested were made'. Carteret was furious at the liberties Hawkesworth had taken and the errors he had made in dealing with his journal; it seems that he too saw part of the text before publication and that no notice was taken of his corrections (see p. 96).

It may be that Hawkesworth was misled, accidentally or deliberately, about the readings at the Admiralty, but he is certainly disingenuous or dishonest about revising his work in the light of the commanders' comments. Conceivably the extent of what had been read, and the strength of the hostile reaction, had been kept from him. There was surely a danger, at a late stage, of the whole enterprise being countermanded. Perhaps their realization that this could happen led the Admiralty authorities to be economical with the truth in informing Hawkesworth about the readings.

What was this Hawkesworth persona like, this ghost who accompanies the captains and makes them think what they never thought? In the case of Cook's Endeavour voyage the first-person position is complicated by the presence of Banks (who as a well-born and wealthy gentleman receives

[19] Cook II: *Resolution*, 661. [20] *Carteret's Voyage Round the World*, 509–10.

several pages of adulation to go along with condescension towards Cook, 'an excellent officer, and skilful navigator'). Banks had 'generously over-ruled' Hawkesworth, who felt that Banks's material should not be 'absorbed in a general narrative under another name'. So a curious three-headed monster was created out of Cook, Banks and Hawkesworth (though Mr Banks is often separated off to follow his own activities). One has to grant that the stitching was carried out skilfully. Take as an example Tahiti on 13 May 1769. Hawkesworth takes from Banks the story of Toubarai trying to fire Banks's gun, about which Cook said nothing. Hawkesworth then steps in with the gratuitous sentiment that 'it was of infinite importance to keep the Indians totally ignorant of the management of fire-arms'. He concludes the day with an account of a break-in from Cook, adding Cook's reflection that 'the iron and iron tools . . . were temptations to theft which none of these people could withstand'.

The quality of Hawkesworth's interventions can be judged from an earlier incident which only Banks had talked about, the visit of three Tierra del Fuegans to the ship. Banks, though not above making fun of someone who seemed to be a 'conjurer', wrote simply: 'we conducted them through the greatest part of the ship and they lookd at every thing without any marks of extraordinary admiration'.[21] Hawkesworth turns this into a statement on genetic inferiority.

> Curiosity seems to be one of the few passions which distinguish men from brutes; and of this our guests appeared to have very little. They went from one part of the ship to another, and looked at the vast variety of new objects that every moment presented themselves, without any expression either of wonder or pleasure.
>
> Hawkesworth, *An Account of the Voyages*, II, 45.

It is very surprising that when W. H. Pearson wrote his authoritative study, 'Hawkesworth's alterations', in 1972, his first task was to demolish the 'commonplace' that Hawkesworth's tendency was to 'idealize primitive societies'. Yet this strange misconception persists into the *Oxford Companion to English Literature* of 1985, which says that 'his sympathy with the native inhabitants of the Pacific Islands led Hawkesworth to convey a picture of innocent indulgence which was widely condemned as indecent'. Pearson's grim account of Hawkesworth's omissions and additions in all of his narratives as regards attitudes to the islanders leaves no doubt at all where his sympathies lay.

Something of the complexity of Hawkesworth's re-creation of Cook can be seen in the question of the use of firearms. In Tahiti on Wednesday, 14 June, 'one of the Natives' stole an iron rake out of the British 'fort'. Cook, exasperated by this further addition to a long list of thefts, retaliated by seizing twenty-two canoes, threatening to burn them if the missing things

[21] Banks, *The Endeavour Journal of Joseph Banks*, I, 218.

were not returned. He justified this measure as an alternative to using fire-arms: 'I would not suffer them to be fired upon', because such licence might be misused by sentries 'as I had before experienced'.[22] Like Cook, Hawkesworth was (as we shall soon see more fully) troubled about the ethics of firing upon 'natives', and, weighing up the matter not on the Tahitian beach but in his Bromley home, he thought to give Cook rather more weight in his argument. He began with a class argument about the sentries: 'The common centinels were by no means fit to be entrusted with a power of life and death'. He then attributes the following meditation to Cook, none of which appears in the journal.

> Neither indeed did I think that the thefts which these people committed against us, were, in them, crimes worthy of death: that thieves are hanged in England, I thought no reason why they should be shot in Otaheiti; because with respect to the natives, it would have been an execution by a law *ex post facto*: they had no such law among themselves, and it did not appear to me that we had any right to make such a law for them.
>
> Hawkesworth, *An Account of the Voyages*, II, 149.[23]

The sentiments may be admirable, but they have nothing to do with Cook.

When firing did indeed break out, in the tragic initial confrontation with the Maoris in Poverty Bay in October 1769, Hawkesworth again confidently ventriloquized. This was the day Banks called 'the most disagreable day my life has yet seen, black be the mark for it'.[24] Beaglehole's edition of Cook's journal shows how Cook, who had been desperately anxious to gain the goodwill of the Maori, wrote and rewrote his account of the fracas, explaining rather than justifying his actions, which had caused the death of several Maoris.[25] Cook freely admits that he was responsible for bringing about the confrontation but in the end argues he had to act in self-defence – and in one version added that it would not have done to have given the appearance of Maori bravery alongside his own 'timorousness'. Hawkesworth's Cook argues with himself as follows:

> They certainly did not deserve death for not chusing to confide in my promises; or not consenting to come on board my boat, even if they had apprehended no danger: but the nature of my service required me to obtain a knowledge of their country, which I could no otherwise effect than by forcing my way into it in a hostile manner, or gaining admission through the confidence and good-will of the people.
>
> Hawkesworth, *An Account of the Voyages*, II, 290.

[22] Cook I: *Voyage of the Endeavour*, 100–1.
[23] See the discussion in Pearson, 'Hawkesworth's alterations', 70.
[24] Banks, *The Endeavour Journal of Joseph Banks*, I, 403.
[25] Cook I: *Voyage of the Endeavour*, ccx–ccxii and 170–1.

In desiring to get some of the people on board when the offer of presents had failed, 'my intentions certainly were not criminal', and then 'in such situations, when the command to fire has been given, no man can restrain its excess, or prescribe its effect'.

We give Hawkesworth credit for his anxiety about these confrontations. He wrote at length in the 'General Introduction' about the problem of shooting, expressing 'the regret with which I have recorded the destruction of poor naked savages, by our firearms, in the course of these expeditions'. It was, however, an 'evil' which 'cannot be avoided'. There always will be resistance, and if it is not demonstrated to those who resist that further conflict is hopeless, 'the attempt must be relinquished'. Which is, one must understand, unthinkable; for the following reasons. The conflict on the beaches is a conflict between cultures, a sad but necessary moment in the progress of civilization. Discoveries are undertaken for both the 'gratification of artificial wants', and 'the increase of knowledge'. If civil society, with its 'artificial necessities', could be shown to be 'contrary to the great original principles of morality', then of course we should be in trouble, but it 'must appear extravagant and absurd in the highest degree' that the powers lying latent in mankind should not be developed, and that we should 'continue in a savage state'. The loss of life on the beaches of the Pacific 'is among the partial evils which terminate in general good'.

It is a tortuous, perplexing, evasive and complacent argument. Hawkesworth is trying to show his awareness of commonplaces concerning the corruptness of civilization (he has learned a little from editing Swift), while giving away absolutely nothing to Rousseau and the noble-savage party. Civilization may be accused of artificiality, but naturalness is an abomination and must cease. It is notable that Hawkesworth totally omits Cook's reflections on the aborigines of Australia.

> They may appear to some to be the most wretched people upon Earth, but in reality they are far more happier than we Europeans; being wholy unacquainted not only with the superfluous but the necessary Conveniencies so much sought after in Europe, they are happy in not knowing the use of them. They live in a Tranquillity which is not disturb'd by the Inequality of Condition.
>
> Cook I: *Voyage of the Endeavour*, 399.[26]

What effrontery, to deny Cook his own reflections while being so free in imputing alien ones to him! It is easy enough for us, by comparing editions, to see how Hawkesworth doctored the material he was entrusted with, but it is very disturbing to recollect that in spite of the execration it received, Hawkesworth's *Account of the Voyages* was never withdrawn or replaced. For over a hundred years his laundering of the actual record of the remorseless advance into the Pacific was all that was available. He

26 See also Pearson, 'Hawkesworth's alterations', 48.

bears some of the responsibility for Victorian attitudes to the subject peoples of the British Empire.

From an aesthetic as well as a political view he did great damage. It is the homogenization of the accounts which is so distressing, the smothering of the individuality of the voices of those who were actual witnesses, and the bland substitution of an omnipresent Joseph Surface of the sea. The rest of this chapter seeks to give some indication of the individuality that was lost.

## II

George Robertson was master of the Dolphin under Wallis and his journal of the 1766–8 voyage is one of the most interesting of the Pacific narratives of these times.[27] The journal was used by Hawkesworth in his account of the Wallis expedition,[28] but it is clear that Robertson was hoping for independent publication and had his eye on the general reader; at one point, for example,[29] he proposed an appendix of statistics (which in fact he never provided) 'which I hope will Give More Satisfaction to all that Read it nor any thing of the kind ever did Before'.[30]

Robertson wrote as an experienced and efficient professional seaman whose responsibilities were increased by the long incapacitation of Wallis and his first lieutenant through illness. He has a good deal to say on technical details of the management of the ship, but he was wide awake to everything, on board ship and ashore. He was deeply interested in the political significance of the expedition. At the start he felt badly let down by the late reduction of the status and financial footing of the voyage: 'This is but very poor Encoragement to set out on so Dangerous a Voyage'. But he rallied himself. 'For my part I love the Voyage, and as I am now Imbarkt, its too leat to repine – I hope God will grant us Success, and I make no dout of the Lords of the Admiralty granting us a sutable Reward.'[31] He loved the voyage both as a sailor and as a sturdily loyal Englishman. He was obsessed with the importance of the Falklands as a strategic centre, 'if Great Britain is Determind to propagate her Discovery in the South Sea, in order to Extend her Trade and Commerce'.[32] The importance of the Falklands as a staging post for fleets negotiating Cape Horn was immeasurably increased by the Dolphin's discovery of Tahiti, or King George's Island, 'a Country that will some day turn out to be of the

[27] An edition of the journal was completed by Hugh Carrington just before his death in 1947. It was prepared for publication by the officers of the Hakluyt Society, 1948.

[28] Pearson, 'Hawkesworth's alterations', 61–3.

[29] Robertson, *Discovery of Tahiti*, 53.

[30] In reproducing Robertson's eccentric spelling from Carrington's transcription I have occasionally modified the punctuation for the sake of readability.

[31] Robertson, *Discovery of Tahiti*, 4.

[32] *Ibid.*, 43.

Greatest Concequence to the Island of Great Britain'.[33] He talked of settling the island, and employing the Tahitians as sailors.

Robertson gives an excellent description of the painful three-month passage of the ships through the Magellan Straits, especially of his surveying trips in the cutter, during which the boat's crew ate gargantuan meals of the geese they shot: 'I neaver in my Life saw so mutch Eate by so few men, and non was the worse for it'.[34] He was much impressed by the wild scenery. Of the upper heights of the mountains, 'there is nothing to be seen but bear Barren Rocks Towering up above the Clouds in the most Romantick figures imaginable'.

> The Mountains is immensely high and not one Green Shrub from tope to bottom, the very Valeys that in oyther places has some Trees Shrubs or Grass, here has non, but a Deep Bed of Snow with Rivers of Frost rather than water tumbling down precipices of an Immense hight. It would required the pen of Milton or Shakespeare to Describe this place, therefor I shall give it upp . . .
>
> Robertson, *Discovery of Tahiti*, 54 and 75.

So far as people go, Robertson was extraordinarily benign, except towards the first lieutenant, William Clarke, 'Mr Knowall' or 'Old Groul', with whom he was in constant conflict. Another lieutenant was 'a Gentill Brisk Good Officer'; the surgeon is praised for his 'humain friendly way of treating the Sick; and 'our young Gentlemen' were 'Sober Modest and humain likeways brave Active & Diligent in Learning their Dutys both as Seamen & Officers'. Like many latter-day chief petty officers and sergeant-majors, Robertson was very conscious of his dual relationship with these 'young gentlemen' as both their instructor and their social inferior. He chides the gunner, like him a senior warrant officer, for exceeding his authority in this respect. 'I do not mention this as a reflection on the Gunner, the man was very capable of douing his owen duety as a Gunner, but in my Oppinion, not at all capable of Commanding Gentlemen, who has no oyther vew of comeing in to the Navy, but to be made Officers.'[35]

The greatest part of Robertson's journal relates to contact with the Pacific islanders and particularly the Tahitians. His lively, detailed and valuable accounts never show the least compunction about taking over territory, or any consideration of the rights of the inhabitants to resist. Unless there is a faint recognition in his words describing the onlookers at the slaughter of the islanders in the major confrontation of 24 June 1767: 'to Attempt to say what this poor Ignorant creatures thought of us, would be taking more upon me than I am able to perform'. Before reaching Tahiti, they had touched at Nukutavake, where the entire population took to their boats and left, thus avoiding conflict. Robertson gives a vivid

[33] *Ibid.*, 235. [34] *Ibid.*, 48. [35] *Ibid.*, 33, 41 and 175.

description of wandering through the deserted dwellings musing on the uses and significance of the things he saw: 'we left two handfuls of Nails in the Carpenters work Shope for the things we took away, so that they will be no great Losers by our Visit'.[36] It was a different matter on Tahiti, which with its high mountains and fertile valleys 'hade the most Beautiful appearance its posable to Imagin', and was almost certainly the northern edge of the great southern continent, found at last. Here there was resort to firearms from the start. Robertson in the cutter, surrounded by canoes, 'found it was too leat to treat them with tenderness. . . . I thought myself under a necessity of using violent means, I therefor orderd the serjent and one of the Marins to wound the two most resolute like fellows . . . this orders was Complyed with and the one was killd which the serjent fired at.'[37]

All the time it was a matter of using their guns more in sorrow than in anger against 'the poor unhappy creatures' who were foolish enough to oppose and threaten them. 'We then found lenity would not do, therefor applyed to the Great Guns and gave them a few round and Grape shot.' Later, he hoped the 'poor creatures' would not attack them once more, 'and put us under the disagreeable necessity of killing a few of them'.[38] Wallis and Robertson had no relish for killing, but took it for granted that nobody could be allowed to stand in the way of what they had come across the ocean to do.

They proved their point, and some kind of a *modus vivendi* was struck between the mutually uncomprehending sides. Communication was established by means of nails and sexual intercourse. Robertson described the 'new sort of trade' that began one day, 'but it might be more properly called the old trade', with 'a Dear Irish boy, one of our Marins' in the lead. There is a great deal about these sexual encounters, with Boccaccio-like stories of outwitting jealous husbands, and a new euphemistic vocabulary: 'he tould me the Guard releve one another regularly and got Value for their nail'. The 'old trade' flourished so much that eventually 'the Boatswain informed me that the most of the hammock nails was drawen, and two thirds of the men oblidged to lie on the Deck for want of nails to hang their Hammocks'.[39]

On 9 July Robertson wrote, 'our Liberty men and the Natives is now turnd so freindly that they walk Arm in Arm'. This is the amicable state of affairs that the master of the Dolphin desired. He wanted 'the natives' to recognize the superiority of the visitors, the necessity of their visit and the futility of resisting it; then both sides could join in as companions in common endeavours.

36 *Ibid.*, 124. 37 *Ibid.*, 139 and 145. 38 *Ibid.*, 154 and 177.
39 *Ibid.*, 180, 196 and 207.

I really do beleve their was a vast many of this Country people who would have willingly come home with us, if we could have taken them, and their was some of our Men, who said they would stay at this place, if they were sure of a Ship to come home with[in] a few years.

Robertson, *Discovery of Tahiti*, 229.

There is a curious account of the Dolphin's voyage in *The Dolphin's Journal Epitomized, in a Poetical essay*, by R. Richardson. It was 'Printed for the Author' in 1768, the year of the ship's return, as 'the rude Production of a Sailors Pen ... yet ... free from all romantick Fictions'. It is quite a short account, and both the epistle to the reader and the poem are full of self-deprecation.

Minute Details, I here forbear,
In *Anson's* Voyage, they're better far
Describ'd in Prose, than here I dare
Attempt to write in verse.

The promises of the second stanza are not really fulfilled.

WALLIS I sing, the Hero brave,
Who for his Country, like a Slave
Undaunted, plow'd the Southern wave,
In search of Land unfound.

Richardson is enthusiastically patriotic, and very contemptuous of 'the ambitious thought' of the 'poor simple Men' on Tahiti to attack the Britons.

No safe Retreat they now can find,
For dire Destruction unrestrain'd,
With Balls swift whistling thro' the Wind
O'ertakes th'insulting Band.
But Oh! to paint their vast Surprise,
The Terror sparkling in their Eyes,
Or their confus'd, and hideous Cries,
Requires an abler Hand.

Robertson made almost nothing of the separation of the Dolphin and the Swallow at the western exit from the Magellan Straits. He wrote that 'a very great swell' made them carry sail to avoid rolling, and this got them 'farr ahead of the poor Dull *Swall*'. 'What becam of the *Swallow* after this I know not, as we neather saw nor heard any more of her.'[40] Some years after the event, the commander of the Swallow, Philip Carteret, wrote that he was 'fully convinced ... that Capt. Wallis never intended to be troubled with the Swallow, after he had been safely piloted through the

[40] *Ibid.*, 98.

Streights'.[41] This comes from the narrative that Carteret set about putting together, but never completed, 'in Justice to my own character', following the publication of Hawkesworth's *Account of the Voyages* in 1773.[42] It is a narrative full of bitterness: against John Hawkesworth, against Samuel Wallis, against the Admiralty, against the Dutch. In making notes on Hawkesworth, Carteret at one point wrote, 'that is false, & contrary to what I said in ye Manuscript'.[43] His annoyance was the greater because he had apparently seen at least part of Hawkesworth's manuscript before publication, and his corrections had been ignored.[44] A note clearly intended to form part of the preface of the intended work reads as follows:

When a Man's Voyage is printed not only in his Lifetime but also to his Face & in the place where he is resident, it must certainly be imagined that there is nothing either omitted or added by the publisher that is contrary to the will or desire of the writer, and that the whole is strictly true & well warranted by the original manuscript given into his Hands; But as this is unfortunately not the Case with respect to an account of a voyage I made round the globe in his majesty's Ship the Swallow which has lately been given to the publick by the late Dr. H., I find myself under the disagreeable necessity lest my Silence should be construed into consent & approbation of publishing it myself not only in Justice to my own character that the whole of my voyage should appear together, but for the good of the Service, & the Security of future navigators that they may have all the observations I made, many of which have been omitted.[45]

Carteret's grievances against the Admiralty relate to their failure to fit the Swallow out for a long voyage in distant seas, especially in not providing a forge; against Wallis for not sharing information, not sharing goods intended for peace-offerings and barter, and above all for deserting him; against the Dutch in the East Indies for their unwillingness to help him in distress. He was an embittered man when he wrote, and all one can say is that he had some cause for his resentments, and that bitterness brought out some of his best writing. Of the Dutch authorities at Macassar he wrote:

I have since found that these visits and trifling difficultys where only to amuse and keep me quiet, till they (of y[e] Council) was all agreed in the determining of our fate; Like a parcell (if I may be allowed the comparison) of quack Surgeons on some poor maim'd object some being for Amputation while others were for more lenitive applicatory methods not indeed so much for compassion for y[e] Object as

41 *Carteret's Voyage Round the World*, 120.

42 Helen Wallis assembled a single continuous narrative from the two main elements: the Journal and the Abstract. Quotations are from this Hakluyt Society edition.

43 *Carteret's Voyage Round the World*, 508.

44 See Helen Wallis in *Carteret's Voyage Round the World*, 99–100 and 504–5.

45 *Carteret's Voyage Round the World*, 3, with photograph, 105.

for fear of mischance in so sevear an operation, and the bad Consequence that might insue to their tread & Character, in case it should afterwards be devolged.
*Carteret's Voyage Round the World*, 224.

His indignation against the master of his ship, who, at Egmont Island (Santa Cruz), where he badly needed the friendship of the inhabitants, had disobeyed his orders and provoked an attack, led him into an uncharacteristic empathy for the islanders. The master and his men retreated against a shower of arrows, and in spite of keeping up 'a great fire' with muskets and blunderbusses, they could not 'make these brave fellows give way but like Heroick defenders of their country boldly persued the invaders of their property, as far into the water as they could wade'.[46]

Carteret's later career in the Navy was unsuccessful, and what his editor calls the 'sense of deep disappointment and neglect' was without doubt increased by the fact that the discoveries made in the voyage which he had valiantly continued after the disappearance of the Dolphin, in the face of a poor ship, poor equipment and the ravages of sickness, were eclipsed by the triumph of Cook's first voyage in the Endeavour.

The personalities, achievements and writings of the two main figures on the Endeavour expedition, James Cook and Joseph Banks, have been too extensively and minutely examined and written about, and are too widely known, to require anything more than a tangential description here. The published accounts of the voyage were very few: just the anonymous 1771 publication, then Hawkesworth, then the journal of Sydney Parkinson (the botanical draughtsman who died after leaving Batavia) published by his brother in 1773. But the total inscription of the voyage, its conversion into pen and ink, was substantial. This is not only a matter of logs and journals – by others as well as by Cook and Banks – but the essential surveying record in charts and coastal views, the scientific record in drawings and fauna and flora, and the graphic record of places and peoples (where Parkinson had to stand in for Alexander Buchan, who died at Tahiti).[47] The voyage lived on in two ways. First, in the history of the places visited, irreversibly changed and redirected. Secondly, in the pen-and-ink records, by means of which the voyage was brought home, known and remembered – a partial and imperfect image until very recent times, when so much of the buried record has been brought to light and published. There is a form of inscription which unites these two afterlives, and that is the naming of places; by which a name is given to a territory not only to identify it but to claim it. The name had to be announced and promulgated, sometimes with a ceremony at the place itself, always by

46 *Ibid.*, 164.
47 See *The Charts and Coastal Views of Captain Cook's Voyages*, ed. Andrew David, with R. Joppien and B. Smith, Hakluyt Society (1988 and 1992).

insertion into the written record of the voyage. Beaglehole's edition of Cook's journal demonstrates the continuous concern of Cook with the fashioning of his written record, and in this fashioning the naming of places was a ceremony of some importance.

The journal employs the perfect tense: 'This Bay I have named *Admiralty Bay*'. This is the record of the act of naming in the chart. Naming, and the invention of names, became more necessary as the voyage proceeded along the unknown and uncharted coast lines of New Zealand and eastern Australia. Earlier, the journal shows Cook's hesitation over the proper journal entry. In the Society Islands in July 1769, he had devised a procedure for leaving with the chief a plaque on which was stamped the ship's name, the captain's name and the island's name. At Uliatea (Raiatea), Cook wrote that he had carried out that procedure. 'I then hoisted an English Jack and took posession of the Island & those adjacent in the name of His Britk Majestys, calling them by the same name as the Natives do.' Beaglehole points out that Cook first wrote 'for the Use of' His Majesty, then 'in the name and for the Use of', and finally 'in the name of'.[48] (But the phrase 'for the use of' was certainly not abandoned, as will be seen.)

The full procedure, then, involved a ceremony ashore, an entry on the chart and a record in the journal. Obviously the shore ceremony did not often take place, but there is a remarkable journal-entry about Queen Charlotte's Sound which describes it.

> After I had thus prepare'd the way for seting up the post we took it up to the highest part of the Island and after fixing it fast in the ground hoisted thereon the Union flag and I dignified this Inlet with the name of *Queen Charlottes Sound* and took formal possession of it and the adjacent lands in the name of and for the use of his Majesty, we then drank Her Majestys hilth in a Bottle of wine and gave the empty bottle to the old man (who had attended us up the hill) with which he was highly pleased.
>
> Cook I: *Voyage of the Endeavour*, 243.

Cook's sensitivity to the importance of the act of naming is shown in some ponderous references to Cape Farewell, his point of departure from New Zealand. When he first reached it, it was '*Cape Farewell*, (afterwards so call'd)', and then 'This Point I afterward named *Cape Farewell*, for reasons which will be given in their proper place'. He was not always so scrupulous; the importance of inscribing the name in the journal sometimes outweighed fidelity to the original naming. Oddly, this innocent faking relates to two of the best-known names, Botany Bay and New South Wales. The great quantity of new plants collected in this place, he wrote, 'occasioned my giveing it the name of *Botany Bay*'. But before that it had

[48] Cook I: *Voyage of the Endeavour*, 144.

certainly been Stingray Harbour and Botanist Harbour (with several mutations.)[49] There is quite a solemn and formal entry for New South Wales, recording the hoisting of the English colours, and that in the name of King George III, he 'took posession of the whole Eastern Coast from the above Latitude down to this place by the name of *New South Wales*'. Three volleys of small arms were fired, answered by the same number from the ship. The name of New South Wales is written over a deletion which Beaglehole thinks said 'New Wales', but, he goes on, 'it is clear that the name was not given at once ... and that in fact Cook took possession of the east coast without naming it at all'.[50]

The sources of the names themselves are quite traditional. Native names are sometimes used, but very often they are not known, and when known, they can be overridden. The grandest names carry abroad the very territory of Britain in an act of incorporation, as in New South Wales, or, in names from the monarchy and the government, the authority of the establishment is extended to the antipodes, honouring the place while honouring the person. The peak of a mountain was seen above the clouds on 13 January 1770; it was 'of a prodigious height and its top is cover'd with everlasting snow. ... I have named it *Mount Egmont* in honour of the Earl of Egmont'. But there are also the names of colleagues; both Banks and Solander have capes and islands named after them, and of course the names of those who first sight the places, notably that of Nicholas Young, the surgeon's boy, who first sighted the land of New Zealand, and was rewarded with Young Nick's Head. Sometimes it is the shape of the feature, as with Point Upright, 'on account of its perpendicular clifts', or Mount Dromedary. Having named a headland '*Cape Brett* in honour of Sr Percy', that is, Sir Piercy Brett, he thought that the name Piercy for an adjacent rocky islet 'seem'd very proper', because there was 'a hole perc'd quite thro' it'. Finally there are the 'experience' names, as Cape Tribulation, 'because here began all our troubles', Hope Islands, 'because we were always in hopes of being able to reach these Islands', and Cape Flattery, where they wrongly thought they had the open sea ahead. (All these names belong to the catastrophe and triumph of negotiating the coral reefs in June–August 1770.)

Naming of places was in the forefront of the acquisition of territory. The scientific work of the Endeavour belongs there, too; as a passenger perhaps, like Banks himself. The great Baconian ideal, the Instauratio Magna or great renewal, by which humanity's control over nature, lost by Adam, was to be restored by the systematic investigation, description and classification of the entire phenomenal world, had received tremendous impetus from the Systema Naturae of Linnaeus, providing by the early

49 *Ibid.*, 310 and ccix; see also Paul Carter, *The Road to Botany Bay* (London, 1987), chapter 1.
50 *Ibid.*, 387–8.

1750s a classificatory method for the entire botanical world, known and unknown. In *Imperial Eyes*, Mary Pratt argues that the enthusiastic application of the system by scientists on mid-century voyages of exploration was another form of the 'planetary consciousness' which Europeanized the world, parallel with the circumnavigations and the mapping of the world's coastlines. 'The naturalist naturalizes the bourgeois European's own global presence and authority.' 'One by one the planet's life forms were to be drawn out of the tangled threads of their life surroundings and rewoven into European-based patterns of global unity.'[51] The domestication of the exotic was achieved not only by inscribing it in writings and drawings but by bringing home specimens of creatures to be put in museum cases and plants to be put in botanical gardens (and here we cannot forget the sad careers of Dampier's Prince Jeoly and Banks's Tupaia).

The seas and coasts are charted, territories are claimed for the various European nations, the peoples are encouraged to adopt European clothes, habits and ways of thinking. Those who argue that science is in some ways another form of European appropriation can find, literally, plenty of ammunition in Banks's journal. Banks's colleague, the Swede Daniel Carl Solander, was a pupil and disciple of Linnaeus, and their equipment, intellectual and material, for scientific investigation was a huge advance on what had gone before. Although in many ways one feels in reading Banks's journal that he was only carrying on exactly the same wide-ranging description of just everything that was there to be observed which we can find in Dampier (whose books Banks carried with him and constantly consulted), it is the new scientist who is there on the deck of the Endeavour – with his gun. Any modern reader of Banks must be staggered by his total indifference not merely to ecology but to the creaturely rights of his specimens. I record some examples of his collector's passion as they occur.

Saw a dolphin, and admired the infinite beauty of his colour as he swam in the water, but in vain, he would not give us even a chance of taking him.

I had the good fortune however to see a bird of the shearwater kind which I shot, and it proved to be not describd.

Went out shooting, killd another new procellaria, *æquorea*, and many of the sorts we had seen yesterday. . . . In the evening went out again, killd an albatross *Diomedæa exulans*, who measurd 9ft 1 inch between the tips of his wings, and struck one turtle *testudo caretta*.

Went in the boat and killd *Procellaria velox*, 2 *velificans*, 3 *sordida*, 4 *melanopus*, 5 *lugens*, *agilis* and *Diomedæa exulans*. The Albatross very brown exactly the same as the first I killd. . . . While in the boat among a large quantity of birds I had killd, 69 in all, caught 2 *Hippoboscas* forest flies, both of one species different from any described.

[51] Pratt, *Imperial Eyes*, 24–31.

Very few birds were to be seen, there were however some Albatrosses and a kind of Shearwater quite black which I was not fortunate enough to shoot.

Calm again: at Noon I went out and shot in less than an hour 6 Albatrosses: had the calm continued I beleive I might have shot 60.

Banks, *The Endeavour Journal of Joseph Banks*, I, 173, 174, 207, 235–6, 392 and 468.

What then about human beings? In the course of his long description of the Australian aborigines, the most primitive of all the peoples they came across, Banks offered a meditation on comparative happiness which quite clearly impressed both Cook and Hawkesworth. 'Thus live these I had almost said happy people, content with little nay almost nothing.' Providence, he thought, might wish to counterbalance the pleasure created by the possessions of Europeans by increasing their anxieties. 'Providence seems to act the part of a leveler, doing much towards putting all ranks into an equal state of wants and consequently of real poverty.' This consideration of God as an adjuster of handicaps in the human race comes later than the reflection on the great chain of being which he was led to by evidence of cannibalism among the Maori. In the 'admirable chain of nature', man 'justly claims the highest rank', but within mankind, the Maori is 'a race of beings placd so infinitely below us in the order of Nature'.[52] As regards the ethics of imperialism, Banks was like so many people capable of quite contradictory emotional reactions. Excitedly recording his first impressions of Tahiti, he wrote: 'in short the scene we saw was the truest picture of an arcadia of which we were going to be kings that the imagination can form'. A year and a half later, he refers to the aborigines as 'these poor people, whose territories we had certainly no right to invade either as discoverers or people in real want of provisions'.[53] But emotions like this last were of short duration. For Banks, domination of less advanced races was for their own good. He believed that if the British government took control of West Africa it would make the Africans 'far more happy than they now are under the tyranny of their arbitrary princes'. He opposed the abolition of slavery as a matter of principle.[54] Some of his extraordinary activity in extending the bounds of the British Empire in later years is recorded in Chapter 7.

52 Banks, *The Endeavour Journal of Joseph Banks*, III, 130 and 20.

53 *Ibid.*, I, 252; II, 143.

54 Mackay, *In the Wake of Cook*, 17–18.

# 6

# Cook and the Forsters

## I

On his second voyage, with the Resolution and the Adventure from 1772 to 1775, Cook became Europe's negative Columbus. He discovered that there was after all no great southern continent waiting to be appropriated and exploited. In three deep probes into the ice at 60° south and beyond, west and east of New Zealand and east of Cape Horn, he satisfied himself (in the words of his famous journal-entry) that he 'who had Ambition not only to go farther than any one had done before, but as far as it was possible for man to go'[1] had proved that there was nothing there, except perhaps a land of ice inaccessible and uninhabitable. He used New Zealand as a base, and spent the winters visiting countless Pacific islands, known and unknown, including Tahiti, Easter Island, the Marquesas, Tonga, the New Hebrides and New Caledonia.

In spite of enforcing the Admiralty's injunction to collect all logs and journals at the end of the voyage, and to bind everyone to secrecy, Cook did not get in first with his authoritative, official history. His was in fact the fourth account to be presented to the public. The first was the anonymous *Journal of the Resolution's Voyage*, published in 1775. Cook got wind in September that a bookseller was bringing out a history of the voyage and suspected that the author was Robert Anderson, gunner of the Resolution. In a letter of the greatest interest Anderson cleared himself (protesting that this was the second time he had innocently fallen under Cook's displeasure).[2] At Cook's direction he had gone to every bookseller in St Paul's and, from the shopman's evasive words, discovered that Francis Newbery had a publication in hand. He then went to the lodgings of William Peckover, gunner's mate, who seems to have been another of Cook's suspects. Peckover was not there, but he found John Marra, another gunner's mate, and several of the Resolution's crew. Peckover was fetched, and Anderson told him that 'there would be nothing ever done for

[1] 30 January 1774; Cook II: *Resolution*, 323.
[2] Cook II: *Resolution*, 961–2 (spelling modernized).

him or me' – that is, that their naval careers were over – unless they could discover who was responsible for publishing. This produced information about two journals which had been surreptitiously kept. But finally John Marra said that if Cook would send for him, 'I'll clear every man that is suspected', adding, 'I'm the man that is publishing the voyage'. They took a coach to Newbery's, and Marra, telling him 'his friends was kept out of bread', asked the bookseller, 'What name is my journal of the voyage to come out in?' 'In no name at all', Newbery replied, on which Marra said that he wanted it to appear in his own name. On hearing all this, Cook wrote to the Secretary of the Admiralty, 'If this is the only account of the Voyage that is printing, I do not think it worth regarding; I have taken some measures to find out if there are any more'.

Cook could not have thought Marra a serious rival. He was an Irishman whom Cook had taken on board the Endeavour at Batavia when sickness had decimated his crew, and he liked him well enough to take him on the succeeding voyage. However, he was flogged for insolence to an officer soon after the start of the voyage, and again, for the same offence, on the first visit to Tahiti. When the Resolution was leaving Tahiti at the end of the second visit in May 1774, Marra was caught trying to swim ashore. He was put in irons but given no other punishment, Cook writing a quite friendly note in his journal, remarking that for a person like Marra without a home or connections the prospect of staying in Tahiti must have been alluring. In New Zealand he made another attempt to get ashore – it is not clear whether he was again trying to desert – and this time he was flogged.

Newbery did not respond to Marra's request that his name should appear on the title-page. It looks as though the journal had not been thought publishable as it stood, and that Newbery had called in an editor, David Henry, a writer closely involved with *The Gentleman's Magazine* who had already had experience of editing voyage-narratives.[3] Henry was also given a journal from the Adventure, and, preserving his anonymity, he combined the two journals into a single editorial narrative: for example, 'These however are only conjectural surmises, arising from the courses which the journals before me represent'; 'And here it must be observed that our journalist of the Resolution frequently mentions smoaking the ship with bruised gunpowder and vinegar'; 'But here, if a bye-stander may be permitted to make a remark ...' Marra's journal becomes a kind of suppressed sub-text, surfacing only occasionally, but very frequently making its presence felt.

It surfaces in passages of shipboard experience when the narrator's

[3] It is speculation that Newbery hired Henry, but that Henry did the editing was divulged in his obituary in *The Gentleman's Magazine*, 62 (1792), 578–9.

bland voice-over disappears. 'On the 23d wore ship, and stood in for land. Close reefed fore and main-topsails, and handed them. Blow'd a hurricane, attended with prodigious heavy showers . . .'[4] Marra could be more poetic than that; he had taken part in the game that all the 'journalists' played, of finding comparisons for the ice-islands; 'ruined castles, churches, arches, steeples, wrecks of ships, and a thousand wild and grotesque forms of monsters, dragons, and all the hideous shapes that the most fertile imaginations can possibly conceive'.[5] It would seem that Marra had a great many complaints about the life of the seamen but that Henry was not letting much of them through. This, for example.

> Our journalist . . . particularly enlarges upon the hardships the poor sailors suffer in searching for land where nothing is to be seen but sea and ice, where icicles frequently hang to the noses of the men more than an inch long; where the frost is sometimes so severe as to freeze the very breath upon their cloaths; where he has seen the men cased in frozen snow as if clad in armour; . . . yet under all these hardships, the men chearful over their GROG, and not a man sick but of old fears.
>
> Marra, *Journal of the Resolution's Voyage*, 113–14.

It is presumably Marra dressed in Henry's language who questions the criminality of thieving on the islands, suggesting that, if strangers arrive and 'without ceremony cut down their trees, gather their fruits, seize their animals, and, in short, take whatever they want', it is only natural for the islanders to pay the visitors in their own coin. 'Against whom is the criminality to be charged, the christian or the savage?'[6]

It may well be that the ironical tone used for Marra's attempts to leave the ship belongs to Marra and not to his editor. It was a pity he was discovered swimming ashore at Tahiti because after a few years' stay he could have made available 'a more copious and accurate account of the religion and civil government of these people' than can be expected from the short visits of 'gentlemen who had the language to learn'. As he lay in irons, the narrative says he reflected ruefully on his thoughts of 'being made king of the country, or at least prime minister'.[7] It seems very likely that Henry's redaction of Marra's journal has deprived us of a vivid, witty, irreverent view of the voyage from before the mast.

There was someone else intervening in preparing Marra's journal for publication. It is extraordinary that apart from Cook there is hardly a single person named except the scientist, 'Mr Foster', and he is on the scene a great deal. Whenever the ship touches land, it is noted that Mr Foster goes on expeditions. At Easter Island, for example, 'The Captain . . . attended by his chief officers, and accompanied by Mr. Foster, went on

[4] Marra, *Journal of the Resolution's Voyage*, 74. [5] *Ibid.*, 111. [6] *Ibid.*, 45.
[7] *Ibid.*, 235–6.

shore ...'[8] There can hardly be any other explanation of this singling out of the scientist than that J. R. Forster himself had made sure he was included.[9] If this is the case, it makes the treatment of *Journal of the Resolution's Voyage* by *The Gentleman's Magazine* very interesting. Quite extensive excerpts from the narrative, with a commentary, were printed in four successive monthly numbers of the magazine between December 1775 and March 1776. The reviewer, while remarking that the work 'appears to have been hastily written, and hastily printed', says that there can be no doubt of the authenticity of the journals used. The rather curious remark in the December issue, that 'of the hardships of such a navigation [in the ice] it is impossible to convey to the reader any adequate idea', is illuminated by an even more curious remark in the January number. At Middleburg Island, a native came on board –

> but, say our Journalists, *their languages were totally different*, though this is denied by the Reviewer of this work, who appears to have been a party in the voyage he was employed to review, and who, probably, may himself have some work of the like kind to present to the public
>
> (p. 17).

This sentence seems to be the combined work of the editor of the magazine and the reviewer of the book. And the reviewer can hardly be anyone other than J. R. Forster, who prided himself on being able to discern the similarity which others could not see between the languages of the Society and the Tongan islands.[10] So David Henry, who ran *The Gentleman's Magazine* and had compiled the *Journal*, and J. R. Forster, who had made sure he featured in the *Journal* and whose forthcoming work is here obscurely advertised, were helping themselves and each other to publicity for their own writings.

Forster was indeed busy with writings of his own about the voyage during late 1775 and in 1776. The precise nature and form of these writings, however, was at this time fluid and problematical. There is a long, complicated and painful story to tell, of great importance in the history of the eighteenth-century voyage-narrative, as a necessary prelude to an account of the next major publication to precede Cook's own account of his second voyage.[11]

[8] *Ibid.*, 139. [9] Cf. Hoare, *The Tactless Philosopher*, 159.

[10] J. R. Forster, *The Resolution Journal*, 379; G. Forster, *A Voyage Round the World*, I, 444.

[11] The second publication was the anonymous *Second Voyage Round the World* (1776). Beaglehole was wrong to say that this claimed to be by Cook, and to dismiss it as a 'fake'. The title-page phrase 'by James Cook' refers to the voyage not to the book. The claim is that it is 'drawn from Authentic Papers'. It is high time it was properly examined: it is certainly not a fake. It is heavily edited and padded, but it contains a core of first-hand circumstantial detail. (Paradoxically, Beaglehole admitted this.) A very interesting feature is the editor's disgust with every instance of violence towards indigenous peoples – 'acts of cruelty ... unworthy of Englishmen', he writes at one point (p. 83).

## II

Johann Reinhold Forster was born in 1729 in Dirschau, near Danzig, in West Prussia. He was descended from a Yorkshireman, a Royalist who had emigrated during the Civil War in the 1640s. He was ordained as a minister of the Reformed Church, and served for almost twelve years in a country parish near Danzig. His interests however were scientific rather than religious. His earlier studies in ancient history, Egyptology, geography and so on were augmented by natural science partly because of the curiosity of his son George, the eldest of his eight children and an infant prodigy (born in 1754), who wanted to know all about insects, flowers and birds. In 1765 Forster at last got free of the importunities of his parish and took the eleven-year-old George with him to Russia, on a commission from Catherine the Great to report on the condition of German colonies along the Volga.[12] In his eighteen months in Russia, particularly in St Petersburg, he made advances on a bewilderingly wide range of scientific fronts, from meteorology to ethnology, while his son was precociously establishing himself as a professional botanist. Forster senior then decided that his future as a scientist lay in England, and with his letters of introduction he and his son arrived in London in October 1766, a few weeks before his thirty-seventh birthday.

During the next five years, the progress of Forster's reputation was dramatic. He read papers to the Society of Antiquaries and to the Royal Society, and became a Fellow of both societies. He succeeded Joseph Priestley on the staff of the dissenters' college, Warrington Academy in Lancashire, an enlightened and forward-looking college for those debarred by their creed from Oxford and Cambridge, and for three years he taught science and languages there. (He had now been joined by his wife and other children.) His translation of Louis de Bougainville's *Voyage Round the World* (1772) was important for introducing English readers to the great French voyager, and it declares Forster's belief in the scientific value of the voyage of discovery. It also demonstrates the very sturdy loyalty which Forster felt towards his ancestral homeland; the footnotes constantly emphasize the superiority of the British, who had made the greatest voyages of discovery, and were more accustomed to philosophical enquiry than were the French.

Soon after Banks's return from Cook's first voyage in the summer of 1771, Forster dedicated a Latin work on insects to him, and expressed therein the hope of accompanying him on his next expedition. In January 1772 he managed the insertion in the *Critical Review* of a puff declaring that

[12] Biographical details are from Michael Hoare's book, *The Tactless Philosopher*, supplemented by his introduction to his Hakluyt Society edition of Forster's Journal, 1982.

his translation of Bougainville had proved his qualifications as a colleague for Banks and Solander on their forthcoming voyage. But of course Banks and Solander never made that voyage. They had chosen not Forster but James Lind to accompany them, and obtained a Parliamentary grant of £4,000 for him. However, the elaborate superstructure which Banks insisted on to provide accommodation for his scientific staff and equipment made the Resolution so top-heavy as she sailed down the Thames in May 1772 that Cook got the Admiralty's agreement to demolish the newly built additions. 'Mr Banks came to Sheerness and when he saw the Ship, and the alterations that were made, He swore and stamped upon the Warfe, like a Mad Man, and instantly ordered his Servants and all his things out of the Ship.' So wrote Midshipman John Elliott.[13] When it was clear that Banks was not going to sail, a replacement had to be found in a hurry. Forster was approached, and expressed his willingness to go, provided he could take George (now seventeen years old) with him. Negotiations were carried out through Daines Barrington, who had considerable influence in both government and scientific circles. Forster wanted provision to be made for his wife and children, and for his own future after the voyage. Rights of publication (since Hawkesworth the most lucrative aspect of voyaging) were also discussed. Whatever was agreed, nothing was written down. Barrington may have promised more than he could perform; Forster may have understood more than was promised. The terms of Forster's contract afterwards became an area of bitter dispute, never resolved. But, the council of the Royal Society having certified his fitness, and Parliament having voted him the £4,000 earmarked for Lind, Forster received the royal appointment on 11 June, and after just over a week of frenzied activity obtaining equipment for a three-year voyage, his baggage went on board the Resolution in Sheerness, and in early July he and his son joined the ship at Plymouth.

Forster's biographer, Michael Hoare, has called him 'the best read and most learned of Cook's scientists'. The great Swedish botanist Linnaeus, on hearing of Forster's appointment, wrote that the king 'could not have chosen a more outstanding man'.[14] Until quite recently, however, the achievement of the two Forsters has been belittled and their work ignored, except in Germany, to which country both men returned, bitter and disappointed, three years after the conclusion of the voyage. J. C. Beaglehole, the doyen of Cook studies, was not responsible for the denigration of the Forsters; he inherited a tradition which began on board the Resolution. But there is no excuse for his persistent petty persecution of the two scientists throughout the pages of the second volume of *The Journals of Captain James Cook*. Every mention of them produces some spiteful remark,

[13] Elliott, *Captain Cook's Second Voyage*, 7.

[14] J. R. Forster, *The Resolution Journal*, 64 and 53.

as though they had done him some personal injury which he could not get over. The animus is laughable, but it is incongruous in a great scholar's work. It is because of Beaglehole's persistent sniping that we can read in the pages of Allan Villiers' book, *Captain Cook: the Seamen's Seaman* (1967), that Forster was 'a very bad penny' who heard 'of the soft berth going', and 'in the absence of anybody else . . . was accepted'.

Certainly J. R. Forster was a very difficult man to get on with. Young Elliott called him 'A clever but a litigious quarelsom, fellow'.[15] He was prickly, cantankerous, irascible, obstinate, suspicious of slights to the point of paranoia, resentful, self-important and self-protective. He was his own worst enemy, and he was not a person to be cooped up with in a small ship for three years. But he and his son were two very remarkable men, and their writings richly deserve the closer attention they are beginning to receive. One of the most interesting of these, the candid and self-revealing journal which the older man kept on board the Resolution, lay hidden for two hundred years, and has only been available in print, in the meticulous edition by Michael Hoare for the Hakluyt Society, since 1982.

The substance of the journal is of course a mass of notes on icebergs and volcanoes, birds and beasts, plants and trees, languages and customs, which together with notebooks and drawings compiled by George Forster and Anders Sparrman (engaged as assistant naturalist at the Cape of Good Hope) would be the basis for the publication of the scientific findings of the voyage. But there is also a great deal of diarizing which has little to do with Forster's professional concerns: a private voice complaining of his discomfort, describing his disagreements with Cook and other officers. Then again there is a public voice, a deliberate framing of the proceedings into a heroic mould, which was obviously a preparation for a general history of the voyage. It is this last consideration which answers the question why Forster should have written this shipboard journal in English rather than in his mother-tongue. His German accent, and the mistakes in his English, were a joke on board. But all that was to be published would be, in the first place at least, in the English language. This was a British voyage, conducted by 'the free & spirited Sons of Liberty, who inhabit this Queen of Islands', who, with their 'invincible Navy', and the superiority of their navigators, have been opening up the seas and the hidden places of the globe.[16] A journal so full of tributes to Britain required the tribute of the English language.

To begin, then, with his personal pains and discomforts. During the first Antarctic probe, in March 1773, for example, the problems of a cold and wet cabin were compounded by sheep and goats being placed in the space between the master's cabin and his own.

[15] Elliott, *Captain Cook's Second Voyage*, xxx.

[16] J. R. Forster, *The Resolution Journal*, 239.

The room offered me by Cap[t] Cook, & which the Masters obstinacy deprived me of, was now given to very peacably bleating creatures, who on a stage raised up as high as my bed, shit & pissed on one side, whilst 5 Goats did the same afore on the other side. My poor Cabin was often penetrated by the wet, & all the many chinks in it admitted the air & the cold from all sides freely; so that my Situation became every day more unfavourable, at the increasingly cold weather. I put on a good face, & wanted to shew a mind superior to all these inconveniences & hardships, but had my Shipmates had a Sight into my most private thoughts they would have me found widely different, from what I wanted to appear.

J. R. Forster, *The Resolution Journal*, 233–4.

Each of the three Antarctic probes reduced Forster to misery. There was very little for him and his team to observe, and he had no expectation of finding an undiscovered continent. As his sufferings increased and his health worsened his self-pity grew stronger, and he confided to his diary doubts about the value of what he was doing which are in very startling contrast to the rhapsodies written in warmer waters. Following the passage just quoted, he wrote that he would not do the voyage again if twice the £4,000 were offered him, and regretted that he had given up the prospect of a comfortable post in the British Museum. He reached the nadir of his depression during the second, deepest probe in December 1773 to February 1774. 'I do not live, not even vegetate, I wither, I dwindle away.' 'The charm is gone.' The sea was rough, his cabin cold and wet.

Every thing I touch is moist & mouldy & looks more like a subterraneous mansion for the dead than a habitation for the living. In the Captain's Cabin there are broken panes, the apartment full of currents & smoke, a parcel of damp Sails spread, & a couple of Sailmakers at work, now & then discharging the mephitic Air from the pease & Sower-krout they have eaten.

Having toiled for more than 18 Months, we have seen nothing which has not been seen before. ... The profits I reap are but small, for more than half of the Sum granted, must go to equip & support myself. The satisfaction in making usefull Discoveries is still less satisfied, & the reputation I might gain by publishing even these little Discoveries is very precarious.

Quite remarkably, he ends this despairing entry with a therapeutic move into his public voice.

The great Impartiality & Justice of the English nation is so well known & so well attested by eternal Monuments, that she no doubt will reward one way or another Her brave Sons, who navigated these inhospitable Seas. ... Britannia's glorious son's will stand unrivalled in this arduous task: The Track of the Resolution will remain for ever an eternal & only monument of the power & greatness of the Nation, of the wisdom & attention of the Men, who are at the head of the Affairs & of the Conduct, bravery & perseverance of the people who went on this perilous & difficult Expedition.

J. R. Forster, *The Resolution Journal*, 447, 450 and 438–9.

It is quite clear that the elder Forster did not share his son's strong concern about the violation of the life of the islands by the intrusions of the Resolution and by the use of firearms which always attended them. Forster's worst conflict with Cook was over what Forster considered the condign punishment of misdemeanours. On Huahine in the Society Islands (September 1773) Sparrman was mugged, stripped and robbed. Cook's failure to punish the thieves or recover the stolen goods, Forster wrote, would 'encourage the natives to all manner of acts of Violence, & is therefore a very dangerous tendency'. A week later, on Uliatea (Raiatea), George's gun was wrested from him. His father shot at the robber and wounded him in the back. 'I had resolved in default of proper protection ... to stand to the last drop of my blood in defence of my property & to punish the robbers in a manner proportionate to the act of violence.' Cook objected to Forster's conduct. Forster insisted on his independence of Cook's authority. An angry quarrel followed. 'Some hot & unguarded Expressions came out on both sides & he sent me by Force out of his Cabin.' Three days later Cook sent word indicating regret for his violence. Forster asked for a formal reintroduction to the cabin from which he had been expelled. Cook 'came next morning to my Cabin, & desired me to come into the great Cabin, where after several Discourses, we both yielded without giving any thing up of honour, & then shook hands'.[17] Cook's journals contain no mention of this whole dispute. There were many other clashes.[18] It is from Forster we hear that before the start of his third voyage, Cook replied to Lieutenant King's enquiry about scientific participation, 'Curse the scientists, and all science into the bargain!'[19]

The public voice of Forster's journal is most apparent in the patriotic rhapsodies already illustrated, and also in a curious Virgilian vein in which the labours of the Resolution are seen as the building of a new empire or a new order. This vein is very much in evidence in his description of the first visit to New Zealand (when he actually quotes Virgil). The statements of both Forsters throughout their written works in their English period as regards the relationship between savage and civilized life are a kind of extended commentary on and dispute with Rousseau's hugely influential *Discourse on Inequality*, printed in 1755 and translated into English in 1761. Their experiential knowledge of what Rousseau theorizes about did not offer any escape from the main datum of natural innocence and civilized viciousness, and George Forster was much more worried than his father about the results of the commerce between the two. But the older man repudiated the idea (as did Hawkesworth) that the development of humankind in social organization, knowledge and technical command was necessarily a deplorable descent into wickedness and

[17] *ibid.*, 355, 363, 365 and 369. [18] E.g., *ibid.*, 509. [19] Cook II: *Resolution*, xlvi.

misery. Forster's Dusky Bay notes are, as we shall see, the beginning of a very long campaign.

'I made some reflexions', he wrote, 'over the superiority & advantages, which the use of Sciences, arts & mechanical improved trades, & the use of convenient tools give to civilized Nations over those that live in a pure state of Nature'. Looking around him, he saw an observatory erected with men busily observing the motions of the celestial bodies and calculating latitude and longitude. A vast number of plants and animals were being examined and described. He then gave a long lyrical description of the bustling activity around him – the anvil resounding, the brewery making spruce-beer, the cooper making casks, and so on, ending as follows.

> The brow on the larboard side of the Ship, which a few days ago was an impenetrable forest, is now clear & airy, & contains an Observatory, a forge, a green hut for the woodcutters & a pen for our Sheep; & more than an acre of ground is cleared of the woods; a thing which 500 natives of New Zeeland could not have brought about with their stone-hatchets in more than 3 months.
>
> J. R. Forster, *The Resolution Journal*, 265–6.

When he is in this enthusiastic vein, Forster employs a perspective which like a Claude-glass casts a mellow light on people whom individually, when he was in his private mode, he usually wrote about with disgust and rancour. The description of the 'marooning party' – a kind of camping trip – is a good example. They show the skills of their culture by creating fire with gunpowder and oakum, building a tent, catching, dressing and cooking their food (all skills, it is understood, that the savage should excel them in). Then the feast, at which the sailors 'give way to mirth & jollity & crack jokes, wherein you observe a good deal of genius, & goodnature, blended with roughness, bluntness, hearty curses, oaths & baudy expressions'.[20]

Tahiti, 'this happy Island', was as everyone agreed the showpiece for the advantages of the natural or pre-civilized state, and it occupied a central place in Forster's later theories on the development of civilization in his major work of 1778, *Observations Made during a Voyage Round the World*. But the Tongan islands also made him weigh carefully the loss and gain of western advancement. Their hospitality and unselfishness 'to us, who were utter strangers to them' overwhelmed him. 'Their Charity is preferable & more warm, more sanguine than that of the professors of Christianity. . . . We think ourselves much superior to these Nations in regard to Arts & Trades . . . & the use of letters . . . but let us only give them their due. . . . They have more civilization than we at first outset think.'[21]

And of course, the astonishing spread of venereal disease – that reality which was also such a potent symbol of the corruption of innocence – was

[20] J. R. Forster, *The Resolution Journal*, 271. [21] *Ibid.*, 395–6.

always an obstacle to welcoming the spread of civilization. Writing of New Zealand, Forster said that if the man who first brought the infection had 'immediately after fulfilling his brutal lust, stabbed the object of his temporary passion', it would have been a lesser crime than that of poisoning from their very infancy 'a harmless brave & numerous Nation'.[22]

Forster's journal was one of many being kept on board the Resolution, several of which are extant, or extant in part: for example, those of Clerke, Elliott, Pickersgill and the astronomer William Wales. Wales played a very important part in attacking the Forsters in the publication warfare; his journal is more attractive than his later polemic, especially in his anxiety to prove that the cannibalism of the Maori was only a supposition based on prejudice and hearsay, until the evidence became too horribly real. Cook himself spent a great amount of time writing and rewriting his own account.[23] All this recording activity, including the surreptitious journals of Marra and other seamen (one of them interlined in a Bible), is not in any way remarkable. But it does seem very strange that during three years close company on board the Resolution neither of the two main 'journalists', Cook and Forster, discussed the vitally important matter of who was to be responsible for the official authoritative history of the voyage. Once the Resolution docked, the issue erupted into violent controversy.

George Forster's explanation is that before they sailed his father received the Admiralty's agreement, through Barrington, that he should write the history of the voyage and receive the emoluments of publication, with a pension besides. When they reached the Cape of Good Hope, however, towards the end of their voyage, and Cook got his copy of Hawkesworth and found what the doctor had done to his journals of the first voyage, and got besides 'the news of the prodigious profits of the compiler', he decided that he would be responsible for publishing his own account.[24] There can be no doubt that there *was* an agreement, though it was verbal and no doubt vague, that Forster should have responsibility for writing the history of the voyage and take or partake of the profits. Forster made a sworn affidavit in the King's Bench that this undertaking was given, and the succeeding negotiations make no sense unless some such contract was understood to exist; it took the king's personal agreement to break it.[25] As for Cook making a late decision to come into the publishing business himself despite his lack of formal education, it is certainly possible. Earlier on he may well have continued to assume that, though his own journals would be the basis of any official history, arrangements for

22 *Ibid.*, 308. 23 Cook II: *Resolution*, cxxxi–cxliii, and Appendices IV and V.
24 G. Forster, *A Letter to the Right Honourable the Earl of Sandwich*, 12.
25 Hoare, *The Tactless Philosopher*, 161.

publication were the Admiralty's responsibility, not his. At the Cape, however, as well as resolving never again to submit his work to such doctoring as Hawkesworth had given it, he may well have felt that if there was a sum of £6,000 in the offing, it might as well come in *his* direction, particularly if he was aware that his unloved scientist was eyeing it.

Forster and his team were busy preparing their scientific findings for early publication well before the ship anchored at Plymouth on 30 July 1775. The first volume to appear was a sumptuous large folio, *Characteres generum plantarum*, under the names of both Johann Reinhold and George Forster, which was personally presented to the king in November 1775 (the presentation copy is in the British Library). Well before this, however, the First Lord of the Admiralty, John Montagu, Earl of Sandwich (who had appointed Forster), was trying to make terms for writing the history of the voyage which would allow Cook a share of the profits. Forster would submit a specimen section and if it were approved he would prepare the history and share the profits equally with Cook (whose journals would of course be used). This proposal was known to Solander and Banks by 5 September.[26] It seems to have been accepted by Forster, who set to work on his history in English, French and German. Ominously, however, Sandwich wrote to Barrington in October that 'I begin to fear that there is no possibility of doing any thing with Mr. Forster; I am almost convinced that he is what has been represented to me to be, an utterly impracticable man'.[27] At this time, the word 'impracticable' meant impossible to deal with, or get on with, intractable, stubborn. Who had been representing Forster to Sandwich in these terms? At the same time, Sandwich was being urged by 'several of the principal literary people in England' not to allow Forster the privilege of writing Cook's voyage. By the end of October, Sandwich had forbidden Forster to continue with his foreign-language versions, on the ground that his expenses had been paid by an English public.[28]

It is clear that Sandwich did not think much of the specimen submitted by Forster, and before the end of the year he approached Dr John Douglas, Canon of Windsor, and asked him, 'on condition of secrecy', to edit Cook's journals. In ignorance of this, Forster was going ahead with his version. On 13 April 1776, Sandwich brought Cook and Forster together at a formal meeting at the Admiralty, and in the presence of witnesses a wholly new agreement was made and signed. Two volumes were to be written, one by Forster and one by Cook. Forster's would be the second volume, and it would contain observations on natural history, with his 'philosophical remarks [i.e., scientific notes] in the course of the voyage', and a general introduction. Both men were to aid and assist each other.

[26] *Ibid.*, 154. [27] *Ibid.*, 151. [28] *Ibid.*, 156.

The net profits would be equally divided between them. The Admiralty would bear the expense of the plates, which would afterwards become the property of the two men.[29]

Presumably at Sandwich's request, Forster submitted to him at once a long opening section of his narrative. Sandwich found this unacceptable, and it is easy to understand why. The section submitted has been printed in volume 4 of the modern German edition of George Forster's works, pp. 446–65. It is wordy, sententious, sentimental. Two particular incidents are quite unnecessarily elaborated. The first is the loss overboard of the carpenter's mate on 20 August 1772; Forster repeats from his journal his musings on what the feelings of his mother and other relations will be when they hear the news. The second is the fate of the swallow which for a time made a home on board. After the long description of 'our little friendly guest', Forster hoped that his readers would 'pardon the author this tribute of humanity he thought due to a little gentle Creature which seemed to be so sensible of the kindness and hospitality we shewed him'.

Sandwich's response was to get Barrington to tell Forster that his manuscript was to be subject to correction, and a new redactor was brought in – Richard Owen Cambridge. Forster absolutely refused to agree to the alterations proposed. As his son put it, he 'could not submit to the indignity of having his manuscript corrected in a manner which totally deprived it of common sense'.[30] But Forster was desperate for money, and his biographer Michael Hoare shows that he was prepared to sell his manuscripts to the Admiralty for £200, let them write them up as they wished (but not under *his* name), and he would forgo all his profits for a lump sum of £1,200. Cook was in favour of acceptance, but not Sandwich, who went to the king and got his permission that they should 'proceed with Capt. Cook's Narrative solely unless he [Forster] submitted to have his narrative corrected'.[31] A meeting was arranged at the Admiralty for 10 June 1776, but Forster refused to attend, sending instead a letter to Cook in which he claimed that Sandwich was manoeuvring to exclude him 'from all participation of the Admiralty's assistance', and it was therefore pointless to have a meeting. Cook wrote to Canon Douglas (with whom he had been in communication some months about the editing of his journals) telling him of the letter, and continuing thus:

What steps my Lord sandwich will now take I cannot say, but I apprehend I shall have to Publish alone. . . . What M$^{r}$. Forster intends to do I have not heard, but suppose he will publish as soon as possible and if so he will get the start of me. He has quite deceived me, I never though*t* he would have separated him self from the

[29] G. Forster, *A Letter to the Right Honourable the Earl of Sandwich*, Appendix, 5–6. [30] *Ibid.*, 14.
[31] Hoare, *The Tactless Philosopher*, 161.

Admiralty, but it cannot hurt me & I am only sorry my Lord Sandwich has taken so much trouble to serve an undeserving man[32]

It is difficult to take the force of that 'he has quite deceived me', with its implication that Forster was manipulating events in order to publish first. It is in any case impossible to suppose that Cook felt much regret at Forster's withdrawal, though he did make an effort to get him to change his mind. In a letter to Douglas of 23 June, he wrote with what seems like relief, 'It is now Settled that I am to Publish without M$^{r}$. Forster, and I have taken my measures accordingly'. He was off to join his ship at the Nore, and he thanked Douglas for all he had done and was going to do. On 12 July he took the Resolution out of Plymouth at the start of his third voyage. He did not live to see either Forster's history of the second voyage, or his own.

Sandwich's own response to Forster's withdrawal does not suggest the villain of Johann's letter or George's later *Letter to the Earl of Sandwich*. 'I am truly concerned', he wrote to Barrington, 'that Dr Forster does not know his real friends, and that he is not a judge of his own interests or of his talents as an English writer'.[33] Cook had correctly judged that Forster would go ahead on his own. But the Forster history was to appear not as the father's work but as the son's. In July 1776 George Forster, not yet twenty-one, sat down to several months' work that exhausted him and damaged his health, creating a comprehensive narrative out of his father's journals and his own notes, recollections and reflections. The manuscript was vetted by Thomas Hornby, the Oxford astronomer whom Cook had introduced to the Forsters in 1772. *A Voyage Round the World* was published in two volumes, without plates, in March 1777, six weeks before Cook's official version, with its sixty plus engravings (some of them taken from George Forster's botanical drawings), entitled *A Voyage Towards the South Pole and Round the World*.

## III

The Forster *Voyage Round the World* is a major document in the history of voyage-narratives, but who is the author? The basis of it is the older man's journals, very tactfully and prudently edited by the son, but there is a great deal of detail not to be found in the journals, the most striking of which show the extreme sensitivity of this very gifted youth, who for much of the voyage was still in his teens. It is George who notices the piles of stinking human faeces in the pathways of the pastoral paradise of Tahiti,

32 11 June 1776. London, British Library, Egerton MS 2180, f. 13 (r and v). See also Beaglehole, *The Life of Captain James Cook*, 468–9.

33 Hoare, *The Tactless Philosopher*, 182.

George who enlarges on the drunkenness and foul language of the seamen, George who sees the lice in the Maori woman's hair as she couples with a sailor – and George, equally, who remarks on the *délicatesse* of the Tahitian maiden who, about to grant the last favour, discovers that her sailorman has only one eye and fetches a one-eyed girl-friend to take her place. But whose are the sentiments and ideas that make *A Voyage Round the World* so powerful and different? Even in those sentiments where *A Voyage Round the World* is most markedly different from Johann's journals, the attitude to British prowess and achievement, we cannot say that here, unequivocally, is the voice of George. It is certainly a surprise to find in place of all those patriotic rhapsodies a cool disenchanted voice noting Cook 'performing the idle ceremony of taking possession', or, at another such ceremony in the South Atlantic, speaking of the barren rocks re-echoing with the sound of the volley of muskets, 'to the utter amazement of the seals and pinguins, the inhabitants of these newly discovered dominions'. And, instead of hymns to our navigators, we hear of 'the prejudices of a naval education, which inclined him to look upon all the natives of the South Sea with contempt'.[34] Of course this is the voice of the young radical who died penniless in Paris, thirty-eight years of age, with a price on his head for having espoused the cause of the French Revolution in Mainz. But by the time George wrote those words, Johann was himself utterly disenchanted with Britain and all her works, had lost all hope of royal patronage, and would have seen no reason for altering his son's words. *A Voyage* is a collaborative, consensual work; a single author has been created out of the two minds involved in the composition. The extremes of both have been modified or repressed. Generally, whatever the content, the intellectual initiative is with the younger man, but sometimes it is patently with the older. Some of what seem to be contradictions in attitudes to primitive life, or to the sharpness of the encounter between cultures, or to the validity of the enterprise as a whole, may originate in the different emphases of father and son, but they genuinely reflect the uncertainty and indecision of both men about this critical moment in the history of the human race they knew they were witnessing. What I discern to be George Forster's mind seems to me to be more interesting than that of his father, but I am never confident that I can clearly distinguish the two. They make up a kind of continuum. After all it was the older man who taught his son to love the ideals of the enlightenment, and it was the younger who ten years afterwards, in his extraordinary essay, 'Cook, der Entdecker', revered Cook as a furtherer of the moral development of mankind.[35]

We should begin with the strange epigraphs chosen for the two volumes.

[34] G. Forster, *A Voyage Round the World*, II, 165, 529 and 458.
[35] See Saine, *Georg Forster*, 46–53.

The title-page of the first has a quatrain from a forgotten poet, César de Missy, minister at Huguenot churches in London, whose *Paraboles ou fables* had just been reissued. It makes the optimistic statement that you cannot silently conceal the truth and if you try you will be shamed in the end. So the Forster history will show up its rivals, who are attempting to hide or alter the facts. The epigraph of the second volume is from Seneca: *Mobilis enim et inquieta mens homini data est; nunquam se tenet; spargitur, et cogitationes suas in omnia nota atque ignota dimittit; vaga et quietis impatiens, et novitate rerum lætissima.*[36] The mind of man is changeable and restless; it never holds itself firm: it dissipates itself, sending its thoughts in pursuit of everything known and unknown: it is unsettled and impatient of rest, happiest with novelty. What has this to do with Cook's voyage, and is it a proper confession of faith from two empirical scientists? The answer may be found in the classics which provide the quotation, but first in the conclusion to Rousseau's *Discourse on Equality* (always lurking in the background). The essential difference between the savage and the civilized person, wrote Rousseau, is that the savage desires only to live and be idle, with an indifference to every other consideration that surpasses the serenity of the stoics. Civilized people, on the contrary, live in a ferment of restless activity, tormenting themselves to find new labours, killing themselves in order to live.[37] This last point is a version of a well-known tag by Juvenal about living in a way that destroys the meaning of life, *Propter vitam vivendi perdere causas*, and Johann Reinhold quoted this very tag in his journal at his moment of great depression during the second sweep for the non-existent southern continent (see above, p. 109).

Cook's voyage (we are to understand) is an illustration of the restless, self-destructive inquisitiveness of modern man, the direct antithesis of the tranquillity of the primitive peoples whose lives they were breaking into. Rousseau's distinction between primitive and advanced peoples was a commonplace deriving from the great beginning of Ovid's *Metamorphoses*, which describes the different ages of mankind. In the Golden Age, the weather was always warm and there was no need for agriculture. There were no laws and no crimes. And there was no travel either. As Dryden's translation put it, it was a time –

> Ere sails were spread, new oceans to explore;
> And happy mortals, unconcerned for more,
> Confined their wishes to their native shore.

Travel came in with the Iron Age, which followed the Ages of Silver and Bronze. The very first token of this new age of criminality, of deceit and

36 From the *Ad Helviam matrem de Consolatione*.

37 Rousseau, *Discours sur l'origine et les fondements de l'inégalité, Œuvres complètes* (Pléïade), vol. 3 (1964), 192. See the Penguin Classics edition by M. Cranston (1984), p. 136.

treachery, was that trees were made into ships and 'sails were spread to every wind that blows'. After that, land which had been held in common was divided up, men started digging for gold, and wars broke out. It is a strange literal realization of the ancient myth that initially what western man most wanted in the New World it sailed to was gold, and that in these later Pacific travels, the contact between sailors and islanders was most evident in the sexual coupling for which payment was made in iron nails.

The very heart of the Forster *Voyage Round the World* is a continuing meditation in the face of the actual experience of the two men, first on the differences between cultures; secondly, on how far these differences represented stages in the evolution of mankind; thirdly, how far in this evolution technical advance necessarily brought about moral decline; and fourthly, what the likely effects were, immediately and in the long term, of the violent interruption of natural change by the confrontations of the voyage. It is a straggly, confused meditation, but it grew into the formidable evolutionary theory of J. R. Forster's *Observations* of 1778, to which George undoubtedly contributed.

When the Resolution was in Queen Charlotte Sound in New Zealand in June 1773, Cook reflected on the alteration in behaviour since the visit of the Endeavour three years earlier. He was disturbed as others were by the way that this time the men were offering their wives and daughters for prostitution – with nails as the immoral earnings. This second visit, he wrote ruefully in his journal, 'hath not mended the morals of the Natives', and went on:

> Such are the concequences of a commerce with Europeans and what is still more to our Shame civilized Christians, we debauch their Morals already too prone to vice and we interduce among them wants and perhaps diseases which they never before knew and which serves only to disturb that happy tranquillity they and their fore Fathers had injoy'd. If any one denies the truth of this assertion let him tell me what the Natives of the whole extent of America have gained by the commerce they have had with Europeans.
>
> Cook II: *Resolution*, 175.

This candid reflection Canon Douglas must have thought far too subversive for the British public to read so he cut it out. In the shortened printed version, Cook's use of *litotes*, that they had 'not mended' the morals of the natives (in other words that they had as the Irish say disimproved them), now deprived of its context, becomes a prim regret that the higher moral standards of the English had failed to stem the self-corruption of the natives.

Similar reflections occur at the same point in the Forster history. George (is it?) notices that it is the women who are the victims, caught between brutally importunate sailors on the one hand and their own greedy menfolk on the other. And which party of men is the more guilty, he asks, those who make the demand or those who provide the supply? The harm being done to the Maori community he thought 'irretrievable'. If there were some tangible benefit to set against the damage they were doing, they could take some comfort. 'But I fear that hitherto our intercourse has been wholly disadvantageous to the nations of the South Seas; and that those communities have been the least injured, who have always kept aloof from us.'[38] Maori cannibalism might seem reason to restore the westerners' confidence in their moral superiority, 'but though we are too much polished to be canibals, we do not find it unnaturally and savagely cruel to take the field, and to cut one another's throats by thousands'.[39]

The matter of benefits conferred (in which they wanted to believe) absorbed the Forsters, and is prominent in a remarkable Tahitian passage which is exclusively George's. It is a long lyrical account of an outing with Richard Grindal and the painter William Hodges, during which they were entertained by an elderly couple at 'a small but cleanly cottage'. 'We ... might have believed ourselves feasted by the hospitable Baucis and Philemon, if our inability to reward them had not reminded us of mortality.' Baucis and Philemon were poor peasants who entertained the disguised gods Jupiter and Mercury, and were rewarded with untold riches. All George and his two colleagues could offer was 'beads and nails'.[40] Shortly after this, we have the following:

> It were indeed sincerely to be wished, that the intercourse which has lately subsisted between Europeans and the natives of the South Sea islands may be broken off in time, before the corruption of manners which unhappily characterizes civilized regions, may reach that innocent race of men who live here fortunate in their ignorance and simplicity. But it is a melancholy truth, that the dictates of philanthropy do not harmonize with the political systems of Europe!
>
> G. Forster, *A Voyage Round the World*, I, 303.

George Forster understood his own society by observing another. He was particularly attentive to the reactions of Mahine from Bora Bora who had come on board with them (he was sometimes called Hitihiti or Oediddee), particularly his horror at everyday instances of inhumanity and racism. Finding the moral superiority of Europeans so tenuous, George was angered by the repeated instances of the use of firearms (and in this he must be distinguished from his father). It was his lack of loyalty to his shipmates and to his adopted country in describing these incidents that particularly incensed Wales and fuelled the vituperative pages of *Remarks on Mr. Forster's Account*. Mahine was deeply affected by the shooting of a Marquesan islander in April 1774. The islander had stolen a large iron stanchion from the gangway, and an officer, coming up on deck, obeyed Cook's order to open fire but (wrote Cook) 'took better aim than I

[38] G. Forster, *A Voyage Round the World*, I, 212–13. [39] *Ibid.*, I, 517. [40] *Ibid.*, I, 299.

ever intend*ed* and killed him'.[41] Forster claimed that the officer who fired the shot was not even aware of what the offender was supposed to have done, and thought the shooting was yet another example of the 'prejudice and rashness' which had led to so many fatalities, and which put the people of 'our enlightened age' in the same category as the *conquistadores* who shot 'for diversion'. He thought that his shipmates showed too often 'a disposition for cruelty', and a 'horrid eagerness to fire upon the natives on the slightest pretences'.[42]

A shooting on Tana in the New Hebrides seemed to George Forster especially unfortunate, a 'dark and detestable action'. They had spent a fortnight winning the affection of the islanders and George had been active in musical get-togethers, in which both sides showed intense interest in the other's music. Then, coming from an expedition, Forster and Sparrman found 'two natives seated on the grass, holding one of their brethren dead in their arms'. One of the marines, William Wedgeborough, had shot him for crossing a forbidden area. Cook was furious, and had the marine brought to the gangway to be flogged but the officers dissuaded him on the grounds that he was only obeying the orders of the Lieutenant of Marines, John Edgecombe. Thus, wrote George, 'the officer's right to dispose of the lives of the natives remained uncontroverted'.[43]

The different levels of technical advancement, social organization – and happiness – from island to island, were closely observed and analysed. Tahiti came out on top in every count, and the inhabitants of Tierra del Fuego bottom. In between were the Maori. The wretched Tierra del Fuegans seemed to dispose of the idea of the noble savage, and later Johann Reinhold formed the theory that they were in fact degenerate rather than undeveloped human beings. The islanders of Malekula in the New Hebrides puzzled the Forsters about their point in the evolutionary graph.

> Their ugly features, and their black colour, often provoked us to make an ill-natured comparison between them and monkies. We should be sorry, however, to supply Rousseau, or the superficial philosophers who re-echo his maxims, with the shadow of an argument in favour of the Orang-outang system.[44]

This sounds very much like Johann Reinhold, who was an ordained minister of a Christian church. In a long note in his *Discourse on Inequality*, Rousseau had discussed the possibility of mankind being descended from orang-outangs, but, while clearly inclined to accept the theory, he had

41 Cook II: *Resolution*, 365.

42 G. Forster, *A Voyage Round the World*, I, 465 and 536.

43 *Ibid.*, II, 353; cf. Cook II: *Resolution*, 499–500.

44 G. Forster, *A Voyage Round the World*, II, 207; cf. J. R. Forster, *Observations Made during a Voyage Round the World*, 242.

abandoned it as not proven. Among the 'superficial philosophers' is presumably Lord Mondobbo, whose views on man's descent from monkeys was derided by Dr Johnson. Rousseau's discussion was itself a challenge to 'the authority of revealed religion', and Johann Reinhold argued in *Observations* that in spite of the great variety of races, mankind is of one species and *could* be 'descended from one couple'.[45]

More in tune with another aspect of Rousseau's treatise, his ideas on the development of civilized society, is George's comment on Tahitian society. He noted that there was very little class-distinction in Tahitian society, but that it was beginning to manifest itself. He had already been struck by the existence of fat and idle chiefs whose appetites were ministered to by inferiors, and he argues that these inferiors will eventually become genetically distinct from the leisured class. This inferior class will in time come to a proper sense of 'the general rights of mankind' and there will be a revolution. 'This is the natural circle of human affairs.' The whole process of moving towards the inequality of a class-based society was however being speeded up by 'the introduction of foreign luxuries'.

> If the knowledge of a few individuals can only be acquired at such a price as the happiness of nations, it were better for the discoverers, and the discovered, that the South Sea had still remained unknown to Europe and its restless inhabitants.
>
> G. Forster, *A Voyage Round the World*, I, 367–8.

The young botanist condemns his own calling as a symptom of the disease of the Age of Iron, whose intellectual restlessness Seneca knew about; to pursue the calling was only to spread the infection.

It is scarcely possible to imagine that this disillusioned view of British endeavour could have gone unanswered. The astronomer William Wales rode up like a knight on a white charger to reassert proper values. He refused, in his *Remarks on Mr Forster's Account* (1778), to accept George as the real author; there was too much 'arrogance, self-consequence, and asperity' in it to be the work of anyone but the disgruntled senior scientist. The Forster book was full of 'ill-natured misrepresentation', and in particular 'ill-natured invectives against the poor seamen'. 'The Doctor is always so eager to blame the Europeans.'[46] Wales gives alternative versions of a host of incidents to show that the blame lay elsewhere. George Forster published a *Reply to Mr Wales's Remarks*, 'a foreigner ... appealing to a free people'. It is a much more temperate and witty piece than Wales's, who is vitriolic in his attack. He defends himself against the charge of abusing his own people by insisting that there is only one judgement of the morality of actions and it is not dependent on national allegiance. He criticizes in turn those travellers who will always blame 'the

[45] J. R. Forster, *Observations Made during a Voyage Round the World*, 257.

[46] Wales, *Remarks on Mr. Forster's Account of Captain Cook's Last Voyage*, 71, 24 and 27.

inhabitants of distant regions' rather than their own countrymen. The controversy hinges on very important questions of principle, but the detailed refutations and rebuttals and counterclaims are tedious, and the debate often turns into a slanging match. Wales disputed J. R. Forster's status as a linguist because he 'pronounces the English language very imperfectly', and George retorts that 'he that speaks a broad Yorkshire dialect must be allowed to be a very competent judge indeed!'

*A Voyage Round the World* was published on 17 March 1777. After only six weeks it was eclipsed by *A Voyage Towards the South Pole and Round the World*, which, being the official history by the leader of the expedition and a great bargain at two guineas,[47] sold very rapidly and went into a second edition. Its handsome engravings (see plates 6 and 7) had been published in February and were *referred to* by the Forsters, sometimes critically (see plate 6), but they could not reproduce them. Sales of the earlier book hung fire; in the autumn 570 copies were still unsold.[48] The work has never been reprinted in England. (It was reissued in an edition by R. L. Kahn as the first volume of the East-German collected edition of George Forster's works in 1968.) Johann Reinhold Forster lived from hand to mouth in the succeeding months. He sold George's botanical drawings to Banks (400 guineas), he sold his books to Banks (£350), he borrowed from Banks (£200).[49] George went to Germany in 1778 to seek a post for his father and was himself offered a professorship at Cassel. He eventually engineered a chair of natural history at Halle for Johann. So ended the elder Forster's dream of fame, wealth and financial security in 'the Queen of Islands'.

## IV

*A Voyage towards the South Pole* is Cook's work; his only published work, though he never saw it. The account of the first voyage was Hawkesworth's; his journals for the third voyage, brought back after his death in Hawaii, were written up by Canon Douglas. But Douglas did comparatively little to Cook's account of the second voyage. His delicacy circumvented all direct mention of penis-wrappers, and political wariness blotted out not only Cook's troubled conscience about the effect of the exploration on the life of Pacific islanders, but also quite casual remarks unhelpful to feelings of European superiority. Cook wrote of the Tahitians: 'The more one is acquainted with these people the better one likes them, to give them their due I must say they are the most obligeing and benevolent people I ever met with'.[50] This sentence does not appear in the printed

[47] A subsidized price, as George Forster complained in his *Letter to the Right Honourable the Earl of Sandwich*.

[48] Hoare, *The Tactless Philosopher*, 169.

[49] *Ibid.*, 164 and 170–2.

[50] Cook II: *Resolution*, 236.

volume. But Douglas was not shadowing Cook and ventriloquizing for him in the manner of Hawkesworth. What one reads is Cook, trimmed a little and tidied.

In the General Introduction, Cook asked for his readers' indulgence for the lack of literary ornament, in that he had 'not had the advantage of much school education' and had been constantly at sea since his youth. What was being provided was the work of 'a plain man, zealously exerting himself in the service of his Country, and determined to give the best account he is able of his proceedings'. Even a superficial acquaintance with the different versions of incidents in the various texts of the journals collected by Beaglehole shows that the plain man was not above putting things in their best light, but the claim is well founded. *A Voyage to the South Pole* is a story of zeal and exertion and service. It is not self-serving; indeed the story is not about Cook, though the narrator is seen as Cook would wish the public to see him. What comes through without any special striving is the hugeness of Cook's responsibilities – all of which he insisted on shouldering. The day-to-day routine of the Resolution, what the men ate, the cleanness of their linen, their health and the orderliness of their behaviour were as much his concern as the management of the ship in storm and calm, setting and reefing sails as he worked it in uncharted waters through ice and fog and between coral reefs; as was the task of reconciling the two chronometers, and his own and Wales's calculations, in ascertaining longitude, or reconciling what past voyagers had written with what they themselves could see. Overarching these were the major strategic decisions about their course and their objectives, within the scope of the Admiralty's remit. And even more exacting than all of these was the responsibility for all major and minor political decisions about relations with the inhabitants of every territory they touched on. Although, as we have seen, every person had his own idea about how 'the natives' should be treated, it was Cook alone who drew up the general terms of relationship within which everyone had to operate, and Cook who oversaw the observance of those terms by all parties. If there is tedium in Cook's history, it is in the account of his unending attempt in island after island to counter and punish thieving without excessive force. He could never understand why people just went on pilfering, and he reads at times like an exasperated headmaster having to deal with wayward and unruly children.

They nosed their way through the Pacific, warily approaching island after island to see how the inhabitants would accept their presence, hoping for a welcome, but prepared for the intimidation of firearms if they did not get it. There is a well-known passage in Cook's journal relating to the reception of the Europeans on Tana (or Tanna) in the New Hebrides (see above, p. 120). Douglas reproduced it more or less as it stood. A slightly

Plate 1 The Racehorse and the Carcass in the Ice. From C. J. Phipps, *A Voyage Towards the North Pole*, 1774. The voyage was 'undertaken by His Majesty's Command', and this illustration is taken from the royal presentation copy, now in the British Library.

South side is a pretty large Iland where is good (G) anchoring

From the Gulfe of Dulce 12 Leagues N W is the Iland (H) Caneo where is a very good riding

Within the Iland Caneo near the maine is another small Iland betweene which Iland and the maine Sr Francis Drake carreened when he left the Coast of Perrue

Foure Leagues to the northward of the Iland Caneo lives a sort of Indians who are not subject to the (*) Spaniards the Land being low and drowned three months in the year only some ridges excepted

From the Iland Caneo to the river Stella is five Leagues and from thence to the Iturredura the Coast runs N W and S E betweene these two places is a large sandy (A) Bay at the southermost end of this bay is the Iland Quipo which is halfe a league broad

Betweene the Iland Caneo and Cape Blanco is a deep inlett which is called the Gulfe of Nicoya and in this Gulfe are many Ilands viz.t the Iland St Lucas (B) Chira and the middle Ilands on the N W side of this Bay is a small Town of (*) mixt people yett called by the (D) Spaniards a Town of Spaniards

The Iland St Lucas is a small Iland lying on the N W side of the Gulfe being nine Leagues from the Cape Blanco bearing from the Cape N E by N

Cape Blanco is in latitude 9d 56m it hath a

(G) there is good anchoring all over the gulf but at this Island ships may ride out of the strength of the tide which setts out very swift especially in the wett season

(H) on this Iland are wild hogs but commonly there is no want of fresh water on this Coast

(*) I believe the Spaniards doe not think it worth their while to trouble themselves about them there being nothing to be gott

[illegible] all this Coast is good riding & in [illegible] ground & good landing but noe trade

(A) this sandy bay is 18 Leagues from Cape Blanko:

(B) Chira is a small Island at the mouth of the river Nicoya where ships use to lye that Lade here

(*) Spaniards Indians mulattos & mustesees

(D) but there are but 20 or 3 Spaniards in a town & the rest Indians they call it a Spanish town

Cape Blanko in Latt 9d 56 no:

Plate 2 Manuscript of the early version of Dampier's *New Voyage Round the World*. The fair copy is on the right-hand side, with letters marking the points where Dampier wanted to add fresh material. The additions, in Dampier's hand, are in the left-hand margin. (Sloane MS 3236, f. 121v.)

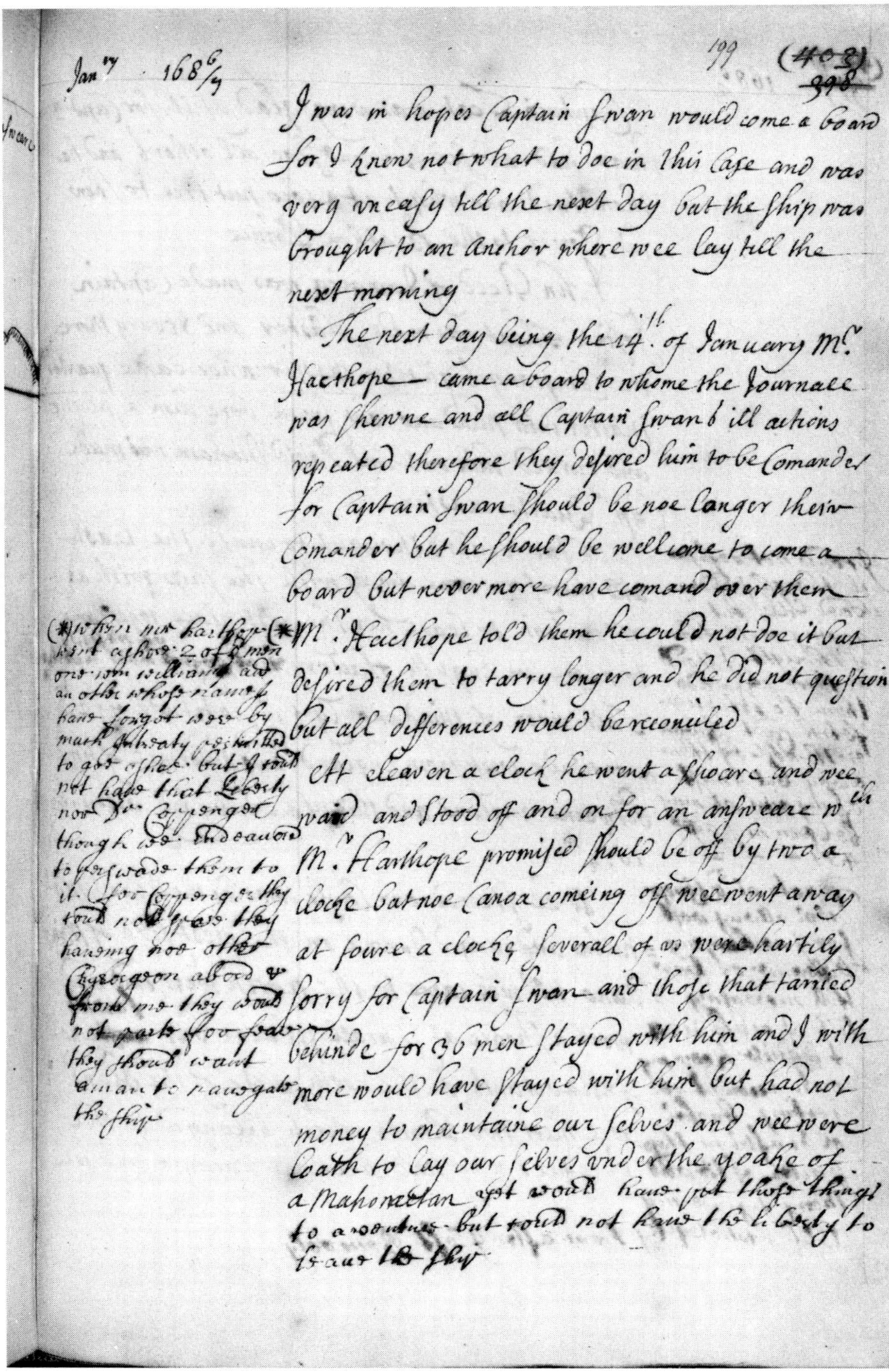

I was in hopes Captain Swan would come a board for I knew not what to doe in this case and was very uneasy till the next day but the ship was brought to an Anchor where wee lay till the next morning

The next day being the 14th of January Mr. Harthope came a board to whome the Journall was shewne and all Captain Swans ill actions repeated therefore they desired him to be Comander for Captain Swan should be noe longer their Comander but he should be wellcome to come a board but never more have comand over them

(*Mr. Harthope told them he could not doe it but desired them to tarry longer and he did not question but all differences would be reconciled

At eleaven a clock he went a shoare and wee waid and stood off and on for an answeare wch Mr. Harthope promised should be off by two a clocke but noe Canoa coming off wee went away at foure a clock severall of us were hartily sorry for Captain Swan and those that tarried behinde for 36 men stayed with him and I with more would have stayed with him but had not money to maintaine our selves and wee were loath to lay our selves under the yoake of a Mahometan est would have put those things to a venture but could not have the liberty to leave the ship

(*when mr harthope went ashore 2 of our men one John williams and an other whose name I have forgot were by much intreaty permitted to goe ashore but I could not have that Liberty nor Mr Coppinger though wee endeavored to perswade them to it. for Coppinger they could not spare they having noe other Chyrurgeon abord & from me they would not part for fear they should want a man to navigate the ship

Plate 3 Dampier's manuscript, f. 199. This page relates the abandoning of Captain Swan at Mindanao. Dampier's attempts to improve the account of his own involvement are in the left-hand margin and at the foot of the page.)

Plate 4 William Dampier. Portrait by Thomas Murray.

Plate 5 The Wreck of the Wager. The scene as imagined by Samuel Wale, R.A., used as the frontispiece to *The Narrative of the Honourable John Byron*, 1768.

Plate 6 The Landing at Middleburgh, one of the Friendly Isles (Eua, in the Tonga Group), October 1773. Engraving by J. K. Sherwin from William Hodges's painting (now lost), appearing in Cook's *Voyage Towards the South Pole*, 1777. See Joppien and Smith, *The Art of Captain Cook's Voyages*, 70–2. George Forster criticized the 'Greek contours and features, which have never existed in the South Sea.' He kindly suggested that perhaps Hodges had lost his original sketches (*Voyage Round the World*, I, 427–8).

Plate 7 The Landing at Tanna in the New Hebrides, August 1774. Engraving by J. K. Sherwin from the painting by William Hodges now in the National Maritime Museum, appearing in Cook, 1777 (see Plate 6). See Joppien and Smith, *The Art of Captain Cook's Voyages*, 94–8.

*Wynee, a Native of Owyhee,*

*One of the Sandwich Iſlands.*

Plate 8 Wynee, a Native of Owyhee (Hawaii). She died being returned to her native land. From John Meares, *Voyages Made in the Years 1788 and 1789*, 1790.

Plate 9 Henry Fielding and his Landlady on the Isle of Wight. Illustration by Michael 'Angelo' Rooker from Fielding's *Works* (1784), vol. 10.

Plate 10 Engraved title-page of William Spavens, *The Seaman's Narrative, 1796.*

rougher version than the one Douglas had before him is given by Beaglehole.

> Thus we found these people Civil and good Natured when not prompted by jealousy to a contrary conduct, a conduct one cannot blame them for when one considers the light in which they must look upon us in, its impossible for them to know our real design, we enter their Ports without their daring to make opposition, we attempt to land in a peaceable manner, if this succeeds its well, if not we land nevertheless and mentain the footing we thus got by the Superiority of our fire arms, in what other light can they th*e*n at first look upon us but as invaders of their Country; time and some acquaintance with us can only convince them of their mistake.
>
> Cook II: *Resolution*, 493.

Cook was writing in all sincerity and honesty. He had no hidden agenda. But he surely shows great innocence about the import of his mission, which carried explicit instructions to take possession of territory wherever possible. The later unhappy history of these islands shows that the islanders were not in fact mistaken. It is Cook who is showing ignorance of 'our real design', and in this respect young George Forster was the wiser man.

# 7

# The silence of Fletcher Christian

## I

Cook died a violent death in Kealakekua Bay, Hawaii, in February 1779. He had set out on his third voyage in the summer of 1776 in the Resolution, accompanied by the Discovery under the command of Charles Clerke. From New Zealand he had gone to Tonga and Tahiti, and then, pushing north for the main objective (neglected by Byron) of searching for the north-west passage, he discovered the Sandwich or Hawaiian Islands. He explored the north-west coast of America, visiting Nootka Sound (Vancouver Island), and moving in to the Russian fur-trading territory of Alaska and the Aleutian Islands. He went through the Bering Strait to the Arctic Ocean, and being turned back by the ice, retreated to Hawaii with the intention of returning next summer. After Cook's death, Clerke took the ships back to the far north-west and gave his letters and Cook's journal to the Russians for despatch overland to the Admiralty. He tried the Bering Strait again and then he himself died, of tuberculosis; James King and Charles Gore brought the two ships home via China, reaching Britain in the late summer of 1780, after a voyage of over four years. The official history of the voyage did not appear until 1784. Cook's journals were again edited and prepared for publication by Canon Douglas, with a final volume by King, under the general guidance of Joseph Banks. A number of others published their own accounts: John Rickman, William Ellis, Heinrich Zimmermann, John Ledyard and the irrepressible David Samwell.[1]

For the remaining twenty years of the century the Pacific Ocean was busy with English ships. In the south-west there was the establishment of the penal colony of New South Wales, in the north-east there was further search for the north-west passage, and much fur-trading; in the south-east there was whaling, and in Tahiti, there was the collection of breadfruit plants for the West Indies.[2] At the centre of all these activities was the

[1] There is a good account of the progress of the authorized history in Lynne Withey's *Voyages of Discovery*, 402–5.

[2] David Mackay's *In the Wake of Cook* is a helpful and concise account of these operations.

immensely influential figure of Sir Joseph Banks, President of the Royal Society from 1778 until his death in 1820, created a baronet in 1781 and a Privy Councillor in 1797. He advised the government on colonial affairs in all parts of the world, and his patronage was indispensable for the furtherance of careers or of projects. James King wrote to him on returning to England in 1780: 'It is with real pleasure & satisfaction that I look up to you as the common Centre of we discoverers'.[3] Cook too influenced the Pacific ventures which followed his death: a number of those most active had been his own officers, George Dixon, Nathaniel Portlock, James Colnett, William Bligh, George Vancouver.

Almost as important for the success of a Pacific venture as Banks's patronage and support was the subsequent publication. A disappointing voyage could be turned into a triumph or at least treated as a prelude to future riches by a sufficiently impressive account. A very good example of this is James Colnett's book, *A Voyage to the South Atlantic and ... into the Pacific Ocean* (1798), concerned with the voyage of the Rattler in 1793–4. The British Library's copy is George III's copy, presumably presented to him, magnificently bound in tooled red morocco. The book is beautifully printed, with handsome charts; it was 'printed for the Author'. Colnett was a naval officer, but he had been engaged in commercial voyages in the north-western fur-trade. His very interesting preface recounts both his own history and the occasion of the Rattler expedition. Colnett had been nominated by the Admiralty on what was originally to have been a naval survey for suitable South American bases for the whaling industry. The government was worried about offending Spain, and the protracted negotiations exasperated the leading merchants, Messrs. Enderby and Sons. The Rattler was a naval sloop, and to avoid political problems, Enderby bought the ship, converted it into a whaler, and put Colnett in command. Colnett says that he purchased a half-share in the ship, and contributed many fittings. 'I also purchased the various voyages of former navigators, and such books on the subject of natural history, as might assist me in my pursuits.'[4] Colnett's situation was ambiguous, serving both a commercial firm, and the Navy; the objectives of the voyage were ambiguous, being directed towards both surveying and whaling; and Colnett's expectations were ambiguous, depending on what profits the whaling might achieve, and what the Navy might provide in the way of promotion. The sumptuousness of his book seems wholly out of proportion to the results of the voyage. Whales were hard to find, and hard to catch when found, and as for future bases, all Colnett could do was come up with James's Island in the Galapagos group and Chatham Island (north of the Magellan Straits) as 'very convenient places for refitting and refreshment'.[5] Of his activities

[3] *Ibid.*, 21. [4] Colnett, *A Voyage to the South Atlantic*, xiii. [5] *Ibid.*, 159.

just previous to the Rattler voyage, Colnett wrote: 'I never ceased to blend the zeal of my naval character with the spirit of commercial enterprize'. It very much looks as though his book, 'printed for the Author', and published a year or two after his return, was a bid for further commissions in either of the two maritime spheres.

As we saw with Betagh's angry riposte to Shelvocke's account, a book which tried to stamp a high valuation on a voyage was not safe from challenge. This is the case with another handsome publication, this time by John Meares, *Voyages made in 1788 and 1789, from China to the North West Coast of America*, 'Printed at the Logographic Press', 1790. There is a long list of subscribers, a fine portrait of Meares as frontispiece, and many maps, charts and engravings. This work followed closely on the heels of two books published in 1789, each called *A Voyage Round the World*, by George Dixon and Nathaniel Portlock. Both these books relate to the expedition of the King George and Queen Charlotte, 1785–8; Dixon's book is dedicated to Banks, Portlock's to the king. The narrator of the account in Dixon's book is William Beresford, the 'Assistant Trader', a person 'who has been totally unused to literary pursuits, and equally so to a sea-faring life'. Beresford sometimes puts Dixon's words in quotation marks, but I imagine that he is at all times Dixon's mouthpiece.

In 1785, George Dixon had been discussing with Banks the possibility of a commercial sponsor to exploit the 'new and inexhaustible mine of wealth' opened up by Cook's last voyage; namely, trading for furs in north-west America.[6] They got the interest of Richard Cadman Etches, and the King George's Sound Company was founded, with the quite illusory expectations of opening up the Japanese market to sea-otter skins.[7] But expectations were far too high about the fur-trade generally: about the availability of furs from the Indians, and about the market for them in China. Portlock and Dixon found other expeditions busy on the American coast, and in Prince William Sound (the Gulf of Alaska), they were astonished, following word from local Indians, to come across 'a snow, called the *Nootka*, from Bengal, commanded by a Captain *Meares*, under English colours'.[8] She had been locked in the ice all winter and was in urgent need of assistance. The sufferings of the crew, said Dixon, had been worsened by 'a free and unrestrained use of spirits'. They generously helped Meares with food and the assistance of two seamen, but the Dixon–Beresford voice is very scornful of Meares's contradictory reports about the state of the fur-trade, and of his handling of his ship and his crew. Portlock's account is fuller, he having had the closest dealings with Meares. He gives full details of all the assistance he gave to this unlicensed

6 Dixon, *A Voyage Round the World*, x.

7 Mackay, *In the Wake of Cook*, 62–3.

8 Dixon, *A Voyage Round the World*, 152.

interloper, who had been ruining the trade by paying the Indians too much for furs.

Meares's book gives his version of what went on between the trading rivals – all three of them former British naval officers – on the coast of Alaska. He had set out with two ships, but the Sea Otter under William Tipping (another naval lieutenant) became separated and was never heard of again. He had had a very bad winter in the ice, with scurvy and many deaths. Though it is quite impossible to sort out the truth of what happened when the King George and the Queen Charlotte turned up, and though Meares was, like the Hon. John Byron, a congenital exaggerator, it is clear that the smug and self-righteous accounts of Dixon and Portlock conceal the fact that all the help they gave Meares was on strict condition that he cleared off and left the fur-trading to them. 'You have made a good purchase, – I have mine to make', Portlock wrote to him, and demanded that Meares should sign a bond agreeing to leave the coast as soon as his ship was seaworthy.[9]

Meares's account of his voyage in the Nootka in 1786–7 is only a prelude to the main subject of his book, an account of his subsequent trading voyage in the Felice and Iphigenia, sponsored by merchants in India. Meares was experimenting with mixed crews of Europeans and Chinese; the Chinese were 'hardy and industrious', lived on fish and rice, and required 'but low wages'. On his way, Meares was taking home two islanders, Tianna, a prince from Atui in the Cook Islands, and the beautiful Wynee (see Plate 8), brought from Hawaii by the indefatigable Mrs Barclay, wife of the captain of the Imperial Eagle. Mrs Barclay intended to take her to Europe, but since she was 'in a deep decline' she left her in China. She died on the way home.

Meares makes much of the settlement he created on Vancouver Island (later to become a matter of international controversy) and of the first ship built in north-west American waters. (He has a bold engraving of it being launched, flying the Union Jack.) His book was written to boost British trade, and Meares was closely concerned with the dispute which broke out with Spain over the right of the British to operate in these waters.

> From the encouragement given by wise ministers, and the enterprising spirit of opulent merchants, every corner of the earth where the winds blow and the sea rolls its waves, will, sooner or later, be explored, to encrease the wealth, the power, and the prosperity of the British Empire.
>
> Meares, *Voyages Made in the Years 1788 and 1789*, lxvii.

(Meares is supposed to have had someone helping him with his narrative,[10] but even if this florid language is not his the sentiments are.) In this

[9] Meares, *Voyages Made in the Years 1788 and 1789*, xxvii–xxx.
[10] W. Kaye Lamb , in Vancouver, *A Voyage of Discovery*, 229.

expansion of British mercantile activity, voyage-narratives have a special place.

> If histories of navigation were written merely to amuse the leisure hours of the rich, or to satisfy the eager enquiries of the philosopher, much of the minute parts of such a work as this would be necessarily omitted, as unentertaining to the one, or beneath the notice of the other; but narratives of voyages are applicable to other purposes; and, if they should not prove instructive to future navigators – if they should not tend to aid and facilitate the progress of commercial enterprize, the difficulties and dangers of such voyages must have been encountered in vain, and the time employed in writing an account of them be added to the waste of life.
>
> Meares, *Voyages Made in the Years 1788 and 1789*, 117.

No story, no voyage! However, the right of Meares to take this lofty stand, and to use such a narrative as his in order to promote national trade, was hotly disputed by George Dixon, who regarded Meares as a romancing gatecrasher. He published *Remarks on the Voyages of John Meares, Esq.*, – 'Guess then, Sir, my surprise, when I found your pompous publication scarcely anything more than a confused heap of contradictions and misrepresentations'. To this Meares replied with *An Answer to Mr. George Dixon* (1791), and Dixon came back with *Further Remarks*. In this last, the interminable contention over fact gives way to what was for Dixon the fundamental issue, namely Meares's right to be trading at all, and the flag he was trading under.

> When I first went on board your vessel in Prince William's Sound, I inquired by what authority you was trading on that coast under English colours; at the same time I informed you that no vessels under such colours had any right there, unless they had a license from the South Sea Company, this you declared you had not.
>
> Dixon, *Further Remarks*, 34.

The century's activity off the north-west coast of America concluded with the major voyage of George Vancouver, 1791–5, which was originally intended to assert by force the trading rights of the British, but which became more pacific and exploratory following the signing of the Nootka Sound Convention with Spain. However important the voyage, the history of it, written laboriously by Vancouver himself in the two years before he died, was described by Robert Barrie, one of the midshipmen in the Discovery, as 'one of the most tedious books I ever read'.[11] It is hard not to agree; Vancouver's style is stilted, pompous, periphrastic, ponderous, and above all humourless. It is not always the case that the seaman is best left to tell his own tale.

11 Vancouver, *A Voyage of Discovery*, 243.

## II

Having bought his slaves, the West Indian planter had a supply of free labour, but they had to be fed. The idea of free food growing on trees and needing only to be plucked had obvious attractions. Whether or not it was Banks who first thought of the breadfruit tree, which he had seen growing in Tahiti on Cook's first voyage, he was a strong advocate of the scheme to introduce the tree to the West Indies. Dampier had first noted the tree in 1697, and for Banks the ready availability of this food was a feature of the pre-adamite Tahitian idyll. As early as 1772 the planters were in touch with him about the project, and in 1775 John Ellis published a pamphlet recommending the bringing in of the breadfruit tree to the West Indies to provide food for slaves. The French were first off the mark, and they transplanted the tree first to Mauritius and then to the West Indies. [12] The American War of Independence, and then independence itself, made supplies from America for the plantations more difficult and more costly, and the project grew more desirable as time went on.

Banks had the idea of combining two of his favourite schemes, and suggested that a ship having taken convicts to Botany Bay should proceed to Tahiti to pick up the breadfruit trees.[13] But in the spring of 1787 he was convinced that a separate ship and a separate expedition were needed, and he persuaded the government to advise the king to instruct the Admiralty to provide a vessel. Such was Banks's power. Banks advised on the purchase of the ship, which was renamed the Bounty, and he personally recommended that William Bligh, aged thirty-three, and the sailing master of the Resolution on Cook's last voyage, should be commander and purser. Bligh wrote to Banks thanking him for bringing about his appointment, but when Banks visited the Bounty at Deptford he found that Bligh had not been told the object of the voyage. When Banks enlightened him he said that he was 'delighted with the Idea of rendering such service to his Country & mankind'.[14]

There seems to be no end to retelling the tale of the mutiny in the Bounty, with each new author choosing sides as in the children's game of Oranges and Lemons. It is an endlessly fascinating subject, inviting explanations as forcefully as it rejects them. My concern is entirely with the nature of the written record, and I assume the reader is familiar with the main features of the story – and is aware in particular that Bligh was not a flogging captain and that his record in that respect was far superior to that of Cook or Vancouver.[15]

Following the wreck of the Wager and the consequent collapse of

[12] Mackay, *In the Wake of Cook*, 127–30. [13] *Ibid.*, 131. [14] Kennedy, *Bligh*, 19–20.
[15] Facts and figures are available in Dening, *Mr Bligh's Bad Language*, especially 113–30.

authority there were a great number of publications but silence from the captain (see Chapter 4). With the Bounty there were few publications and most of them came from the captain. Some oral testimony from other participants was printed by Edward Christian in 1794, and George Hamilton, who was surgeon in the Pandora, sent to round up the mutineers, published his *Voyage Round the World* in 1793. For an affair that has been so hotly and vociferously debated and disputed ever since it happened, the contemporary printed record is thin and one-sided. Of course, a great deal of manuscript material has come to light, but it is illuminating to focus on what was available to the public at the time. Bligh published his *Narrative of the Mutiny* as soon as he got back to England in 1790. His wider account, *A Voyage to the South Sea*, which included a slightly revised version of his *Narrative*, was edited for him by James Burney and Banks and published in 1792, while he was at sea in the Providence on his second (and successful) attempt to collect the breadfruit plants. Then in 1794 Bligh published his *Answer to Certain Assertions*, challenging the argument of Edward Christian that it was his own behaviour that caused the mutiny. And that is all that was printed from those who sailed in the Bounty.

Bligh knew the importance of monopolizing the published record, or at least the importance of getting in first, establishing an official version and investing it with authority. His own vituperative disagreements with the official version of Cook's last voyage, especially what James King recorded, remained quite literally marginalized.[16] Such disagreements did not lead him (apparently) to accept the subjectivity and relativity of all record. With himself in command, he was intolerant of alternative views. His first lieutenant in the Providence wrote: 'Among many circumstances of envy and jealousy, he used to deride my keeping a private journal, and would often ironically say he supposed I meant to publish'.[17] In the open-boat journey, he kept writing materials strictly to himself. It is not just a rhetorical way of putting things to say that the moment Bligh was forced into the Bounty's launch, on 28 April 1789, with his eighteen companions, he entered on a long voyage of self-exoneration, self-justification and self-congratulation. His clerk, John Samuel, had rescued the Bounty's log and brought it into the launch. Bligh appropriated a notebook of Midshipman Hayward's which, he said, 'was kept in my bosom' during the whole of the hazardous journey to Timor, over three thousand miles in forty-one days. What he jotted down in the notebook was written up in the journal as conditions permitted.[18] When they parted from the Bounty, Bligh took the launch to the nearby island of Tofua. They had an unpromising reception, and they feared an attack (which eventually

16 Mackaness, *The Life of Vice-Admiral William Bligh*, I, 25–33.

17 Bligh, *A Book of the Bounty*, xv.

18 Bligh, *The Bligh Notebook*, 5.

came). Nevertheless – 'I had my journal on shore with me, writing the occurrences in the cave, and sending it down to the boat it was nearly snatched away, but for the timely assistance of the gunner' (1 May).

What he was writing there may have been the germ of the long entry which in the fair copy made by Samuel appears under the date of the mutiny itself (28 April).

> Here we may observe to what a height the baseness of human Nature may arrive at, not only ingratitude in its blackest die, but eternal criminality against their Country and connections.
>
> I had scarcely got a furlong on my way when I began to reflect on the vicissitudes of human affairs; but in the midst of all I felt an inward happiness which prevented any depression of my spirits, conscious of my own integrity and anxious solicitude for the good of the Service I was on. I found my mind most wonderfully Supported, and began to conceive hopes notwithstanding so heavy a Calamity, to be able to recount to my King and Country my misfortune.
>
> Bligh, *The Log of the Bounty*, II, 122.

This passage is curtailed in the printed *Narrative*, but consciousness of his own integrity remains, and so does the last sentence, with the interesting change from 'recount ... my misfortune' to 'account ... for the misfortune'. The need to justify himself rather than simply tell his story has perhaps unintentionally come to the surface.

It is not in the least to take an anti-Bligh stance to say that on his long journey from Tofua to England, via the Australian coast, Timor and Batavia – ten and a half months – he was preoccupied with fashioning the story of the voyage in the way that would reflect most credit on himself. He would not have been human had he not done so. This book shows over and over again that all published voyage-narratives are exercises in public relations. The unrelenting self-protection which they evince is no doubt instinctive, but a good deal of calculation goes on in the manipulation, accommodation and adaptation of reality. Fabrication and lying, which were second nature to Shelvocke, play no part in Bligh's presentation of himself. But he was adept at suppression: whether of the fact that Fletcher Christian gave him his own sextant to help him in the launch voyage,[19] or of the punishments meted out to Churchill, Muspratt and Millward for deserting on Tahiti, and to Midshipman Hayward for sleeping on watch at the time they got away.[20] As regards the latter, it is commonly said that in omitting portions of his log from his printed *Voyage* and *Narrative* Bligh was protecting others rather than himself, as they were often accounts of insurbordination or inefficiency, or adverse comments on the conduct of

[19] *Ibid.*, 30, 38, 128 and 132.

[20] Cf. Bligh, *The Log of the Bounty*, II, 11, 12, 22–3 and 30, with Bligh, *A Voyage to the South Sea*, 120. See also Morrison, *The Journal of James Morrison*, 33–4.

his officers.[21] But it was clearly in Bligh's interest to record a voyage as trouble-free as possible until the disaster, and this frequently meant suppressing incidents and comments which indicated friction or could imply grounds for resentment or revenge.

Bligh's log of the open-boat voyage is vivid, dramatic, enthralling. The starkness of the entries in the notebook and the log, which is their power, is softened in the more literary presentation in the *Narrative*; here, for example, are entries for 16 May (maritime reckoning):

*Log*: The Night was dark and dismal. Not a Star to be seen to Steer by and the Sea breaking constantly over us.
*Narrative*: The night was very dark, not a star could be seen to steer by, and the sea broke continually over us.

The Log entry for 21 May reads: 'Sleep, altho we long for it, is horrible'. In the *Narrative* this becomes: 'Sleep, though we longed for it, afforded no comfort'. The most powerful sentence, in the entry for 20 May, is quite lamed by being made 'clearer'. 'Our appearances were horrible, and I could look no way but I caught the Eye of some one.' In the *Narrative*, this becomes the patronizing 'caught the eye of some one in distress'.

Nevertheless, the log and the narrative are accounts which centre on Bligh, on his skill in the navigation which (he claimed) only he in the boat could undertake, on his care and firmness in rationing and dividing the food, and on his superior endurance. There is another account of the open-boat voyage, by John Fryer the Bounty's master (who was in almost continual conflict with Bligh), which presents a very unflattering account of Bligh. Fryer's journal may have been written in part on the voyage home from Batavia, but it was also composed as a rebuttal of Bligh's 1790 *Narrative*.[22] It was not published, and first saw the light in a limited private press edition by Owen Rutter in 1934. I want to spend some time comparing the two accounts of one particular incident as they rested on an island off the Australian coast, the incident of the carpenter and the oysters. It is not a question of saying who was right and wrong about what was actually done and said, but of contrasting the two modes of narration: the one heroic, the other subversive; one epic, the other burlesque; a contest in presentation between *alazon* and *eiron*, Ajax and Thersites. No doubt Fryer was, as Gavin Kennedy constantly calls him, a troublemaker; but we do not have to believe all Fryer says to appreciate how much he reveals about the figure Bligh wished to create for himself.

Bligh's account of the incident in the published *Narrative* is much briefer than in the manuscript log. This is how it goes:

[21] E.g., Mackaness, *Life of Vice-Admiral William Bligh*, I, 108.

[22] Kennedy, *Bligh*, 90n.

I sent two parties out, one to the northward and the other to the southward, to seek for supplies, and others I ordered to stay by the boat. On this occasion their fatigue and weakness so far got the better of their sense of duty, that some of them began to mutter who had done most, and declared they would rather be without their dinner than go in search of it. One person, in particular, went so far as to tell me, with a mutinous look, that he was as good a man as myself. It was not possible for me to judge where this might have an end, if not stopped in time; I therefore determined to strike a final blow at it, and either to preserve my command, or die in the attempt: and, seizing a cutlass, I ordered him to take hold of another and defend himself; on which he called out I was going to kill him, and began to make concessions. I did not allow this to interfere further with the harmony of the boat's crew, and every thing soon became quiet.

Bligh *A Narrative of the Mutiny*, 55.

This account makes reasonable sense, though it is rather puzzling that Bligh should see this incident as the ultimate challenge to his authority. The passage (which was subjected to quite a lot of rephrasing for the 1792 edition) is in fact a scissors-and-paste job, but Bligh's fuller account in his MS log (as printed by Rutter in 1937) still leaves it vague where the provocation precisely lay. The 'person' referred to above is now designated the carpenter, William Purcell, another warrant officer who with Fryer was in constant conflict with Bligh.

I now sent two parties out, one to the Northward and the other to the Southward, to see what could be got, and others I ordered to Stay by the Boat. A muttering now began who had done the Most, and some declared they would rather go without their Dinner than go out. In short I found I had but little Command among a few if they had not feared I was yet able to enforce it by more than laying simply my Command.

The carpenter began to be insolent to a high degree, and at last told me with a mutinous aspect he was as good a Man as I was. I did not just now see where this was to end, I therefore determined to strike a final blow at it, and either to preserve my Command or die in the attempt, and taking hold of a Cutlass I ordered the Rascal to take hold of another and defend himself, when he called out that I was going to kill him, and began to make concessions. I was now only assisted by Mr. Nelson, and the Master very deliberately called out to the Boatswain to put me under an Arrest, and was stirring up a greater disturbance, when I declared if he interfered when I was in the execution of my duty to preserve Order and regularity, and that in consequence any tumult arose, I would certainly put him to death the first person. This had a proper effect on this Man, and he now assured me that on the contrary I might rely on him to support my Orders and directions for the future.

This is the outlines of a tumult which lasted about a quarter of an hour. I saw that there was no carrying Command with any certainty or Order but by power, for some had totally forgot every degree of obedience.

Bligh, *The Log of the Bounty*, II, 192.

Here now is Fryer's account. It will be seen that according to him the site of the conflict was the carpenter's *double entendre* about Bligh's responsibility for their situation (safety/misery), and not a refusal to go searching for food.

Mr Purcel had got to the Boat a little before me but when I was upon the Rocks with the oysters at my back I heard a great noise in the boat, Captain Bligh calling someone a damn scoundrel &c what have I brought you here when if I had not been with you, you would have all aperished, yes Sir the carpenter said, if it had not been for you we should not have been here – you damn'd scoundrel what do you mean – I am not a scoundrel Sir the carpenter said. I am as good a man as you in that respect – when Captain Bligh snatch up a cutless and went forward in the Boat and told the carpenter to take another the carpenter said no Sir you are my officer[.] By this time I had got into the Boat when I could not help laughing to see Captin Bligh swaggering with [a] cutless over the carpenter's head – when I said no fighting here – I put you both under arrest – Captain Bligh turn his conversation on me. By God Sir if you offerd to tuch me I would cut you down – I said Sir this is a very wrong time to talk of fighting – Captain Bligh said that man pointing to the carpenter – told me that he was as good a man as I am – the carpenter made answer when you called me a scoundrel I told you that I was not – but as good a man as you in that respect and [when] you said that you had brought us here I told you that had it not been for you we should not have been here – well then Captain Bligh said if you had not any meaning in what you [said] I ask your pardon and the matter rested. This Quarrel happen in consequence of Captain Bligh ordering the carpenter to hand in his oysters aft and the carpenter told him they belongd to his party – as agreed before they went out the Boat.

Fryer, *The Voyage of the Bounty's Launch*, 70–2.

It is lamentable that the prolonged privations shared by the boat-party did nothing to cement their fellowship. There was very serious conflict between Bligh, Fryer and Purcell after they had reached the safety of Dutch territory and before they split up and took ship for England from Batavia. When he reached safety, Bligh sent long explanatory letters to the Admiralty and Sir Joseph Banks, and also to his wife: 'Know then, my own Dear Betsy, I have lost the *Bounty* . . .' He went on:

I know how shocked you will be at this affair, but I request of you, my dear Betsy, to think nothing of it; all is now past and we will again look forward to future happiness; nothing but true consciousness as an officer that I have done well could support me. I cannot write to your uncle or any one, but my public letters, therefore tell them all that they will find my character respectable and honour untarnished. I have saved my pursery books so that all my profits hitherto will take place and all will be well.

Bligh, *Book of the Bounty*, 305.

Soon after Bligh reached England, the Admiralty despatched the Pandora under Captain Edward Edwards to search the Pacific for the Bounty mutineers. Captain Edwards is a disgrace to his name and to the human race, and in all the vast debate about the Bounty most commentators have united in condemning the viciousness with which he carried out his manhunt. He did not find Fletcher Christian and the Bounty, but he had no difficulty in rounding up those who had chosen to remain on Tahiti, partly because some, like the young midshipman Peter Heywood (still in his teens), considered that they had not assented to or cooperated with the mutiny, and went aboard of their own accord. All were treated alike, however, manacled in irons and put in a specially built suffocating prison on the Pandora's deck, which they called Pandora's Box, and in which Edwards left them to drown when he wrecked his ship on the Great Barrier Reef. Ten of the fourteen survived, however, and among them was James Morrison, boatswain's mate of the Bounty. Morrison, together with Heywood, Tom Ellison, John Millward, William Muspratt and Thomas Burkitt, was found guilty at the court martial in Portsmouth in August 1792. All were sentenced to death, but Morrison and Heywood were recommended for pardon and Muspratt was freed on a technical legal point. Ellison, Burkitt and Millward were hanged. The court-martial was held in the absence at sea of the chief witness for the prosecution, Captain Bligh.

In the months that followed, using whatever material he had previously prepared, Morrison was busy writing his own account of the voyage of the Bounty, of the mutiny, of his time on Tahiti (with a full description of the island and its inhabitants), and of his treatment by Edwards. His account is so circumstantial that many have thought he must have managed to keep a journal or notes secreted during all his vicissitudes. Gavin Kennedy has argued that this was humanly impossible, and has gone on to claim that therefore Morrison's narrative 'is of absolutely no use as eye-witness evidence against Bligh'.[23] This is a *non sequitur*. Eye-witnesses do not cease to be eye-witnesses by not writing down their testimony on the spot. Morrison's account is intensely valuable eye-witness evidence. Like Bligh's, it is not by any means wholly trustworthy.

Kennedy has good evidence that Morrison was writing his narrative for publication. It certainly would have been a best-seller. In November 1792, the Rev. William Howell, a young Portsmouth parson friendly with Morrison, wrote to Captain Molesworth Phillips, 'Morrison is getting very forward with his publication which will be ready for the press in about six or seven Weeks'. Morrison's journal was not in fact published until 1935 (again by Owen Rutter in a limited edition, 315 copies). Kennedy argues that Joseph Banks was instrumental in suppressing it. Molesworth Phillips (one of Cook's officers) was associated with Banks and sent him Morrison's abbreviated 'Memorandum' of his journal. 'Not much pressure would

[23] *Ibid.*, 150.

have been needed', writes Kennedy, 'to convince young Howell of the indiscretion of publishing a damaging attack on a senior naval officer who was serving his country at the other end of the earth'. Banks sent the 'Memorandum' to Bligh when he returned from the voyage in the Providence, and Bligh gave him his written comments on it.[24]

The most significant addition to the Bounty story which both Fryer and Morrison make is their account of the flaming row over the coconuts which immediately preceded the mutiny and which Bligh does not even mention in his *Narrative*. Just before this (they are at Annamooka island) there had been a clash between Bligh and Christian which Bligh alludes to without mentioning Christian – the stealing of an axe and an adze from a shore watering party led by Christian. When Christian told Bligh of the theft, Morrison writes that Bligh 'dam'd him for a Cowardly rascal, asking him if he was afraid of a set of Naked Savages while He had arms; to which Mr Christian answerd 'the Arms are no use while your orders prevent them from being used'.[25] As for the coconuts, Bligh had had a pile of them stored between the guns, and when he came on deck on 27 April, the day before the mutiny, Bligh thought the pile had gone down. According to Morrison, Bligh called all the officers together. They said they had seen no one taking coconuts. 'Then you must have taken them yourselves', said Bligh and ordered that every coconut in the ship should be collected. He then asked each officer in turn how many coconuts he had bought for himself. When he came to Christian, Christian said, 'I hope you don't think me so mean as to be Guilty of Stealing yours'. To which Bligh retorted, 'Yes you dam'd Hound I do – You must have stolen them or you could give a better account of them – God damn you you Scoundrels you are all thieves alike, and combine with the Men to rob me'.[26] (Bligh's argument is that if a person said he did not know exactly how many coconuts he had he must be lying.) Fryer's account is very similar, but it does not single out Christian for Bligh's special abuse.

In 1794 Stephen Barney published an account of the proceedings of the Bounty court-martial, and to it Edward Christian, brother of Fletcher and professor of law at Cambridge, added his Appendix, seeking to prove that it was Bligh's conduct and not desire for Tahitian women which was the cause of the mutiny. Edward Christian knew about the coconuts, and included the incident, though the details differ from Morrison's account. In his answer, Bligh makes no direct mention himself of the row about the coconuts, but prints affidavits from those of the Bounty company who had given information to Edward Christian, all playing down the importance of the coconut incident. But Bligh did write an unpublished comment, in

24 *Ibid.*, 201, 203 and 209. 25 Morrison, *The Journal of James Morrison*, 37.
26 *Ibid.*, 41.

his notes on Morrison's Memorandum. The charge as he saw it was that he 'called the officers thieves and villains, &c'. He wrote that he had given orders no one should touch the coconuts. The officers of the watch claimed they had been stolen by stealth. 'Here was a publick theft', wrote Bligh, 'a contumacy, and direct disobedience of orders – the particular offenders could not be found out . . .; could therefore either the epithet thief or villain, had it been used, have justified their taking the ship the next day[?]'[27] I infer that the argument of Bligh's note is: (a) there was theft, and it could not have been clandestine; (b) the officers either knew of the theft, and connived at it, or they stole the nuts themselves; (c) someone merited being called a thief; (d) if I applied the term generally [he does not deny it], it would not have been reason enough for mutiny.

There is another manuscript note of Bligh's, also in the Mitchell Library in Sydney, in which he is again answering, in the third person, Edward Christian's charges:

> The Facts made Publick in the *Narrative* are not of a nature to be concealed or altered. . . . Captain Bligh declares every thing in his *Narrative* to be sacred truths, & defies the utmost Malice to pervert them.
>
> Kennedy, *Bligh*, 240.

Besides all these words, all these asseverations, these accusations, self-justifications, assertions and counter assertions, there is the almost total silence of Fletcher Christian. He told Morrison, 'I have been used like a Dog all this voyage'. Bligh asked him to have supper with him, on that last night before he took the ship, and he declined, pleading illness. What three witnesses agree on, Bligh, Fryer and Morrison, is that he said 'I am in hell'. (They report it in different ways.) Peter Heywood claimed that when the two said goodbye on Tahiti, Christian communicated to him 'other circumstances connected with that unfortunate disaster' which, after the deaths of his relatives, 'may or may not be laid before the public'. They could implicate none but himself, and might extenuate though not justify his crime.[28] Plenty of opportunity for speculation here, but all we really have is silence except for, 'I am in hell'.

Did he just mean that he was suffering a lot, or did he mean that he felt himself to be a lost soul, really damned? Taking the ship was surely an act of total despair: a meaningless deed, bound to end in ruination. Christian had apparently conceived the idea of slipping over the side with an improvised raft that night. That certainly was an act of perdition, an act of no-hope, of self-destruction; there was no conceivable chance of a fortunate outcome. Why he changed or was persuaded to change his plan to that of seizing the ship, and thus involve so many other lives, is hard to

[27] Mackaness, *Life of Vice-Admiral William Bligh*, 159.
[28] Barrow, *The Mutiny and Piratical Seizure of H. M. S. Bounty*, 99.

know. The faint possibility of finding somewhere like Pitcairn and making a success of a life there? Or was it the need to make more public his gesture of denial, of refusal, of defiance, and renunciation? It was not the loss of the true God that made him declare 'I am in hell', but a disavowal of the Father of All as invented by society, to whom just about this time William Blake was giving the name of Nobodaddy. This is the god who perhaps licensed Bligh to call his massaged record of events 'sacred truths'. It is certainly the god who licensed the social structure which sent petty thieves and political dissenters to Australia and made naval discipline what it was. And to deny that god was indeed to enter a living hell.

William Bligh was an excellent seaman, navigator and surveyor. He was very responsible in carrying out his orders and he was a very careful and solicitous commander as regards the physical health and welfare of his men. But he was also exacting, unreasonable, petty, abusive and vindictive. He appears to me to be small-souled and little-minded; utterly deficient in real warmth, generosity and understanding. These failings, however, might never have come to the surface in some other arena. He had the command of a naval ship, and it brought out the worst in him. He was immensely conscious of his position and what he felt was due to him in this position. That he carried out the responsibilities of this position very conscientiously is certain, but that he should demand so much credit for doing so is pitiful. That he was genuinely concerned for the advancement of his young gentlemen, perhaps Fletcher Christian especially, is certain, but it is lamentable that they should have to grovel before him to obtain his favour, and must never fail to show their gratitude to him. (His great success here was Thomas Hayward, whom he had in an armlock because of his having twice been discovered asleep on watch during a crisis, and who behaved like a spaniel to him.) It is significant that the context of Fletcher Christian's cry was a demand for gratitude.

> I asked him, if this treatment was a proper return for the many instances he had received of my friendship? he appeared disturbed at my question, and answered, with much emotion, 'That, – captain Bligh, – that is the thing; – I am in hell – I am in hell'.
>
> Bligh, *A Narrative of the Mutiny*, 8.

Bligh showed his littleness by sheltering behind the terrifying edifice of eighteenth-century naval discipline. He was no flogger, but he never ceased tormenting everyone about him with abuse, belittlement, revilement. He was doing more than destroying his men's pride in themselves and their work. He was enjoying their humiliation as more crudely sadistic captains enjoyed floggings. Greg Dening appropriately entitled his latest work on Bligh, *Mr. Bligh's Bad Language*. His abusiveness was central to the loss of his ship.

Bligh could only behave in this way because those whom he loved to torment could not answer back. He was shielded and protected from retaliation by the whole grim terror-structure of naval discipline, which made him inviolable and invulnerable. When Fryer refused to countersign some accounts in October 1788, Bligh summoned the ship's company and read out the Articles of War. Captains were indeed court-martialled and broken for cruelty, but not for contemptuous abuse. Fryer claimed that Bligh was always trying to provoke him to go over the edge and make him 'say something that he could take hold of'.[29] Bligh was living very dangerously at the edge where somebody might *do* something as well as say something, and it looks as though Fletcher Christian finally snapped. It is characteristic of the safety within which Bligh imagined himself that, having called Christian a thief, he invited him to dinner.

No one should underestimate the difficulty of command at sea, the importance of maintaining authority, and the need for a well-disciplined and obedient crew. But I see Bligh exploiting the unnecessarily severe penal codes which were meant to back up his authority in order to break the spirit of those he worked with, and force them into servility and acknowledged dependence on him. He dared them to say, 'I am as good a man as you'. So far as I can see, Christian put up with it for a long time and in the end was not prepared to surrender his right to his own identity and individuality. But even as he defied Bligh's right to make him his creature, all his upbringing told him that this action was in fact damnation, a wilful self-exclusion from society: 'I am in hell'.

Fletcher Christian does not appear in the least as a saintly man, as we watch the subsequent states of his attempt to set up an alternative life, but I must say I honour him for not being prepared to put up with Bligh's persistent humiliating abuse. However, there was no way of demonstrating his non-compliance that was not a dead-end, blocked off in advance by the Admiralty. The act of mutiny was an act of madness.

[29] Fryer, *The Voyage of the Bounty's Launch*, 74.

# Part III

# 8

# The slave-trade

## I

In the huge body of writings generated by the long-drawn-out atrocity of the transatlantic slave-trade, there are very few narratives directly about the 'middle passage' between the West African coast and the West Indies, the sea-voyage which was literally and figuratively the centre of the trade for the slave-ships from Liverpool or Bristol or London. The slavers had little motive for writing, the slaves no means. Nevertheless, the slave-trade was so substantial an element in English shipping life during the century that in one way or another it features in a great many voyage-accounts which may not be centrally concerned with the issue of slavery or conditions on the middle passage. This chapter chooses for discussion a number of these narratives in order to illustrate the wide range of attitudes and perspectives to be found. At the centre are the writings of John Newton, captain of a slave-ship and later vicar of Olney, Buckinghamshire, about what he called 'that unhappy and disgraceful brand of commerce'.

An early observer was Nathaniel Uring, whose autobiography is discussed in Chapter 10. In 1701 he was second mate of the Martha, setting out from the Downs for the Guinea coast and the West Indies; on the death of the captain in the Canaries he became chief mate. They fixed on Loango in Portuguese Angola as their centre for trade.[1] The new captain had to treat with the African authorities, the 'Mucundy', who was 'the Queen or Chief Governess' and the 'Mafucca' who was governor of the town.

The Captain hired a House in the Town, which we made our Factory, and the Governor of the Town imposed upon us six Servants, which we were obliged to pay a certain Rate *per* Month; the First of these was our Linguist, who was also an Officer of the State, by the Title of *Mafucca Mallimbo*; One was to cook, and One to fetch Water, Another Wood, and Two to take Care of the Slaves, and conduct

[1] At a later point, Uring wrote of Portugal's African possessions: 'the Portuguese may be compared to Setting Dogs or Pointers, who have taken great Pains to spring the Game, while others reap the Benefit'.

them to the Sea-Side, and deliver them safe to the Ship's Boat, which they were answerable for Body for Body. When this Factory was settled, we began our Trade, and the Captain fix'd another about Forty Miles to the Southward, at a Place call'd *Sammon*, on the Sea-Coast; and leaving a young Man that was an Accomptant at *Loango* to do Business there, he went and resided at the Factory at *Sammon*, and purchased Slaves at that Place. ... The Accomptant at *Loango* fell sick, and came on board; I went thither in his Room to purchase Slaves, and left the Second Mate to take Care of the Ship and those on Board.

The Manner of purchasing Slaves in this Town, is thus: As soon as they are brought into Town, the Person whose they are applies to one of the Towns-People to sell them to some *European* there, and pays him for so doing; the Townsman is in the Nature of a Factor, which they call *Marcadore*; he undertakes to sell them, and treats with the *European* in a Language the Countryman does not understand; by which he has an Opportunity of cheating him as much as he thinks fit.

Uring, *A History of the Voyages and Travels*, 37–8.

Uring gives a great deal of information about his bargaining, and about the habits of the free Africans, to whom his attitude at this stage of his narrative is uniformly condescending. But there is almost nothing about the slaves themselves, except that 'I was informed, that the greatest Part of their Slaves were brought Eight or Nine Hundred Miles out of the Country, which they call *Poamboe*; I take this to be *Ethiopia*'. Some came from nearer at hand, people whom they seized 'and drove 'em before 'em, as other People do Cattle, till they bring them to a Trading Town, where they are sold for Slaves; and this is as much a Trade among them, as selling Horses, Cows, Sheep, or the like, in other Countries'. 'It seldom happens that any of the Towns-People are sold for Slaves, except in Cases of Adultery, or when their Great Men sell some of their Servants for Disobedience.'[2]

Uring does not transfer to the European slave-buyers his criticism of the callousness of the African slave-suppliers. His account of the conclusion of the voyage shows little interest in the ship's human cargo.

We remained at *Loango* about Four Months in purchasing Slaves; in which Time we disposed of all our Cargo, and had bought about Two hundred Slaves, Men, Women, Boys and Girls, and laid in for them a good Quantity of *Indian* Corn and *Calavances*, having also good store of Horse Beans on Board to feed them with during the Passage to the *West-Indies*. ... I went on board in order to prepare the Ship for the Sea; and having wooded and watered her, and made everything ready for our Departure, the Captain returned from *Sammon*; he and the Accomptant, with the rest of our People, came on board, and being provided with all Things necessary for our Voyage, in *October* we set sail for the *West-Indies*. ... We had fresh Gales of Wind after we left the Coast of *Angola*, which occasioned a favourable Passage to *Nevis*, where we arrived the latter End of *November*; but in the Passage we buried

[2] Uring, *A History of the Voyages and Travels*, 49–50.

about Twenty Slaves. Soon after our Arrival at *Nevis*, our Slaves were sold to the Planters; and when the Crop came in, we laded Sugars; and in *April* 1702, set sail for *England*.

Uring, *A History of the Voyages and Travels*, 68–9.

In 1709 Uring was pondering on his future, and thinking of setting up in trading between Jamaica and New Spain; in order to get to Jamaica he accepted an invitation to join in a slaving voyage with Captain Forster in the Joseph. Once again, Uring talks in great detail about the Africans ashore, but hardly mentions the slaves, who are simply a commodity. 'Canows came from several of the Towns to trade with us, of whom we bought Gold, Slaves, and Teeth, but paid dearer for our Slaves than on the *Quaqua* Coast.'

We visited several of the Chief Men of the Place at their Houses, who are called *Cabocers*; they all entertained us with Palm Wine, after the Manner of their Country. The People were very courteous, and treated us very civilly; they live mostly upon Fish, Plantins, Bannanoes, and Roots; they have some *Indian* Corn and Calavances. The Commodities we purchase of them are Gold, Elephants Teeth, and Slaves, most of which are brought several Hundred Miles out of the County.

Uring, *A History of the Voyages and Travels*, 136–7 and 140.

When they had anchored at Pompanea Point, near the Dutch fort at Butteroe (Boutrou) on the Gold Coast, they bought slaves as well as corn and gold from canoes, and Uring went ashore 'being willing to acquaint my self with as much of the Country and Trade of the Inhabitants as I could'. He met 'Capt. *Ben*, who is the Chief of the Place', 'and the Natives were very civel, courteous and tractable'. In less than three hours, however, he was horrified to see his ship under sail, making out to sea. Forster owed Captain Ben for three slaves and a quantity of corn, and Uring was detained as a pledge for the debt. Uring tried not to show his uneasiness, and was very well treated.

I spent the Afternoon in talking with the Natives; and when it grew towards Night, Capt. *Ben* ordered Supper to be provided for me, and entertained me very kingly. I lik'd every Part of his Behaviour, but his detaining of me. When it was Bed-Time, he shewed me to one of his Houses, where he had provided some Matts and Carpets laid upon each other: I laid down but could get but little Rest, for reflecting how unhandsomely I had been used by Captain *Forster*, and what Capt. *Ben* intended to do with me.

Uring, *A History of the Voyages and Travels*, 146–7 and 149.

Uring was released by the intervention of the captain of a London ship who paid Forster's debt. He caught up with Forster further along the coast and refused to accept his excuses, but he refrained 'from taking Satisfaction of him for the Affront he had put on me' because of 'his pretended Sickness'. He got to Jamaica in another ship.

Uring now set up in trading between Jamaica and the Spanish Main, and slaves were his main cargo; it appears the need for slaves overcame considerations of Spain and England being at war. In 1711 he was sailing from Bluefields along the Mosquito Coast (Nicaragua) under the guidance of a pilot when his sloop was caught in a storm, driven ashore and wrecked on False Cape, north of Cape Gracias a Dios. Uring suffered from mosquitoes, sunburn, hunger and (he claims) the treachery of his crew. Early on, some of the crew found a cow which they shot. They had eaten the beef before 'a Native of the Country . . . who spoke broken *English*' told them the cow belonged to 'Capt. *Hobby*, one of the Chief Men on that Side of the Country', who would 'be much displeased when he heard of it'. Their wrecked ship had drifted some way along the coast, and they came up with it near an Indian habitation, where they found most of the Indians hopelessly drunk on rum from the wreck. Captain Hobby arrived, and though he made 'a heavy Complaint' about his cow, Uring pacified him. He 'behaved very civilly'. His mother 'drank so much Rum, that she lay speechless for three Days: He asked me what he should do to save his Mother's Life? I told him, Time would throw it off'.[3] Who were Captain Hobby and his mother? Uring was later among some Indians who told him that a slave-ship had been wrecked on the coast, 'and those who escaped drowning mixed among the Native *Muscheto* People, who intermarried with them, and begot a race of *Mulattoes*'. 'Capt. *Hobby* . . . was of that Race, his Mother being a Negroe.'[4] Uring's informants told him that they had broken away from their own people because these 'new Upstarts were got into the Government'.[5]

Some time later, now with only a couple of companions, Uring was attempting to get to Cape Camerone to the west. They were lost and exhausted when they found 'the Print of a Man's Footing'. Next day, 'we discovered a Path which led into the Woods, the Sight of which gave us All inexpressible Joy; we followed it, and in about half a Mile farther we saw a Hutt, and soon after to our great Comfort a White Man appeared. I need not paint the Joy that circled round my Heart at this Sight.' They told him their story, and the white man said he had known Uring when he was in the packet-boat service.

[3] *Ibid.*, 176 and 178. [4] *Ibid.*, 227.

[5] There are many reports of this shipwreck, with widely varying dates. If it ever happened it was not the only source of interbreeding with the Sumu tribes. The Sambo–Miskito tribe, firmly associated with English settlements on the Atlantic coast, contained strong African elements. They were English-speaking; hence Uring's ability to converse with Captain Hobby. See Newson, *The Cost of Conquest*, 32; Floyd, *Anglo-Spanish Struggle*, 22; Hale and Gordon, 'Costeno demography', 17.

This Person's Name was *Luke Haughton*, whose family consisted of two Women and an *Indian* Boy of above fifteen Years of Age; the Boy was his Slave, as was one of the Women, who used to sleep with him and dress his Provisions, which he kept as his Wife; the other Woman was Slave to a White Man who was absent ... *Luke Haughton* had been Master of a Boat at *Jamaica*. ... He being in Debt, and having an Intreigue with a marry'd Woman, persuaded her to leave her Husband and go with him, which she did to this Place: But they disagreeing sometime after, she went away with a Logwood Cutter to the Bay of *Honduras*, and his *Indian* Woman supply'd her Place.

Uring, *A History of the Voyages and Travels*, 207, 208 and 209–100.

Much later we are told more about this Indian woman. Uring related in considerable detail how the '*Musqueto Indians*' carry out raids on 'the wild *Indians*', who have fled from Spanish cruelty and live in the recesses of the forest.[6] When they reach the settlements, they try to surprise them and capture all the inhabitants. If the alarm is given, and there is a fight, 'few are made Prisoners, except Women and Children, who are generally sent to *Jamaica*, and sold for Slaves. I have seen many of those poor Wretches sold there, which have had so pitiable a Look it would soften the most obdurate Heart. My *Padrone's* Wife was one of those People, and some other White Men kept these Women as their Wives, which live tolerably well.'[7]

Uring stayed some months with his 'Padrone', and eventually made his way back to Jamaica.

## II

John Atkins was a naval surgeon in ships which went out in 1731 to patrol the Guinea coast and protect 'our Trade and Factories' from pirates. In 1735 he published his meditations on his experiences. He accepted the widespread view, though he thought it might be 'a little Heterodox', that 'the black and white Race have, *ab origine*, sprung from different-coloured first Parents'.[8] His book gives a very detailed account of 'the Guinea Trade', its practices and personalities. The 'private Traders' of Bense Island, Sierra Leone, as opposed to the officials of the Royal African Company, he calls 'loose privateering Blades', prepared to rob and cheat the Africans if necessary. They keep 'Gromettas' (or gromettoes), black servants who 'are obedient to any Prostitution their Masters command'. Of these traders, '*John Leadstine*, commonly called *old Cracker*, is reckoned the most thriving'. Atkins would go and watch the transactions. Most of the slaves looked 'very dejected'. But there was an exception.

[6] These slaving-raids are well documented. See Hale and Gordon, 'Costeno demography', 17, and Floyd, *Anglo-Spanish Struggle*, 65, as well as John Roach's testimony (below, pp. 201–2).

[7] Uring, *A History of the Voyages and Travels*, 231.

[8] Atkins, *A Voyage to Guinea*, 39.

I could not help taking notice of one Fellow among the rest, of a tall, strong Make, and bold, stern aspect. ... He seemed to disdain his Fellow-Slaves for their Readiness to be examined, and as it were scorned looking at us, refusing to rise or stretch out his Limbs, as the Master commanded; which got him an unmerciful Whipping from *Cracker's* own Hand, with a cutting *Manatea Strap*, and had certainly killed him but for the loss he himself must sustain by it; all which the *Negro* bore with Magnanimity, shrinking very little, and shedding a Tear or two, which he endeavoured to hide as tho' asham'd of. All the Company grew curious at his Courage.

Atkins, *A Voyage to Guinea*, 41–2.

Atkins's sympathies may be in the right place but it is not pleasant to see him as one of a group of spectators of this scene, and his language is clearly moving the victim into a conventional frame. Cracker told them that this obdurate slave was Captain Tomba, 'a Leader of some Country Villages that opposed them, and their Trade, at the River *Nunes*; killing our Friends there, and firing their Cottages'. They surprised him at night, and although he killed two of the raiders, they bound him, and 'he was brought hither and made my Property'.

Captain Tomba was bought by Captain Harding, of the Robert of Bristol. He refused to accept his situation, and conspired to kill the crew; his main accomplice was a woman slave. The rising was unsuccessful; Tomba killed three sailors with a hammer but was overpowered. Atkins's account of the punishment of the rebels is very well known; its veracity cannot be confirmed.

The Reader may be curious to know their Punishment: Why, Captain *Harding* weighing the Stoutness and Worth of the two Slaves, did, as in other Countries they do by Rogues of Dignity, whip and scarify them only; while three others, Abettors, but not Actors ... he sentenced to cruel Deaths: making them first eat the Heart and Liver of one of them killed. The Woman he hoisted up by the thumbs, whipp'd and slashed her with Knives, before the other Slaves till she died.

Atkins, *A Voyage to Guinea*, 71–3.

Atkins is concerned in his book to repudiate some of the extreme views to be found in Captain William Snelgrave's *New Account of Some Parts of Guinea, and the Slave-Trade*, published in the previous year, 1734. Snelgrave realizes that his account may shock those who are not acquainted with 'the Manners and Customs of several barbarous brutish Nations, that have been and are still on the Globe'. He has lurid stories of human sacrifice and cannibalism among the African tribes, and of the sufferings endured by Europeans in the King of Dahomey's conquest of Whydah. His personal interest in the slave-trade was strong, being the captain of a slave-ship as his father had been before him. He tells us he carried over 600 negroes on one voyage which took seventeen weeks. They eventually reached Antigua 'where the Cargo of *Negroes* (who had stood very well) came to a good Market'.[9]

Snelgrave is certainly conscious of concern about slaves. 'I have always charged my white People to treat them with Humanity and Tenderness.'

> Several Objections have been raised against the Lawfulness of this Trade, which I shall not here undertake to refute. I shall only observe in general, That tho' to traffick in human Creatures, may at first sight appear barbarous, inhuman, and unnatural; yet the Traders herein have as much to plead in their own Excuse, as can be said for some other Branches of Trade, namely, the *Advantage* of it; and that not only in regard of the Merchants, but also of the Slaves themselves.
>
> Snelgrave, *A New Account*, 160.

For the slaves have been made slaves by their own people, and if there were no market for them they would be killed. So because of the slave-trade 'great numbers of useful Persons [are] kept in being'. And they live better in their new country than they could do in their old. Their owners, having paid money for them, look after them. They are fitter to cultivate the land than white people. 'By this means the *English* Plantations have been so much improved, that 'tis almost incredible, what great Advantages have accrued to the Nation thereby.'

Atkins is impressed by none of this. He is totally sceptical of the stories of cannibalism, and he regards the King of Dahomey as a selfless hero rather than a brute, for he had relinquished his own financial interest in order to redeem his countrymen from being sold as slaves. For Atkins, the slave-trade is 'highly offending against the Laws of natural Justice and Humanity'.[10] As for Snelgrave's argument that the slaves are better off in the plantations, he has this to say:

> When the Nakedness, Poverty, and Ignorance of these Species of Men are considered, it would incline one to think it a bettering their Condition, to transport them to the worst of Christian Slavery; but as we find them little mended in these respects at the *West-Indies*, their Patrons respecting them only as Beasts of Burthen; there is rather Inhumanity in removing them from their Countries and Families. ... They are fed, it's true, but with the same Diet and Design we do Horses; and what is an aggravating Circumstance, they have a Property in nothing, not even in their Wives and Children.
>
> Atkins, *A Voyage to Guinea*, 61.

A curious insight into the life of a white slave-dealer (though he was not in Cracker's class) is provided by the journal of Nicholas Owen, first printed from manuscript in 1930. It is clear that Owen would have tried to publish his journal had he lived. He writes at the start, 'I should think my time lost in obsecurity if I sh'd neglect giveing a short discription of my

9 Snelgrave, *A New Account*, 109. 10 Atkins, *A Voyage to Guinea*, 178.

past life and lay open to the world the many dangers atending a seafareing life'. He came of an Anglo-Irish family but his father was a spendthrift who got through a large fortune and left his dependants destitute. Nicholas went to sea and in 1750 he and his brother Blayney joined a slave-ship in Liverpool. There was discord after a failed attempt to capture a French ship that had been taken over by slaves. Owen and four others commandeered the long-boat and for a long time (seemingly a year and a half) wandered up and down the West African coast. Their favourite resort was the Turtle Islands.

> These islands was not inhabated when we ware there by any thing but munkays and wild creatures of difrt. sorts, well stored with oisters and other fish. . . . Here flourishes Nature in its first bravery without the help of man, beasts, birds and freut has thier full swing of groath and drops each in his season. Here we lived like hermits, sometimes on board and the rest on shoar; our chief diet was oisters and rice.
>
> Owen, *The Journal of a Slave-Dealer*, 28.

A bout of fever forced them to Sierra Leone, and Owen joined an American slave-ship. However, he went with a shore-party who were captured by Africans. These, he claims, were acting in retaliation for the violence they had suffered from the crew of a Dutch slave-ship. They were bound and robbed, but were rescued by Richard Hall, a white man who had once been a doctor, and, being stranded on the coast, had lived with the Africans for four years without seeing another white man and had taken an African wife.

> This gentleman was one who has, like a great many others, spent his estate at home, therefore obliged to go abroad in search of a new one, one of those who goes by the name of a good fellow, that dispizes all who shrinks his shoulders at that generous spirit of liberality, one who said in his heart 'let tomorow provide for itself' and to conclude he had a good many principles of honour, yet mix't with some stains that made his charecter jubus.
>
> Owen, *The Journal of a Slave-Dealer*, 38.

Hall gave them employment, and later Owen became a resident slaver at Sherbro (Sierra Leone), not without scruples of conscience. Up to this point his narrative has been retrospective; now it becomes a journal. He is often very unhappy. He loathes the inhabitants, keeping 'as far from these people as we can'. He meditates on his future, toys with the idea of going to sea again, but rejects it as he reflects on the misery of a sailor's life. Sometimes he whistles to keep his spirits up and counts his blessings. More often he deplores the tedium of searching for slaves. He is in a very small way of trade; generally it is only one or two slaves he has to sell. He is making no profit. In the eight years since he left England he has had no letters from home. 'If it weren't for my woman, and 4 or 5 people, I might very well pass for an hermit.'[11] Then he falls ill.

> In this manner we spend the prime of youth among negroes, scrapeing the world for money, the uneversal God of man kind, untill death overtakes us.
>
> Owen, *The Journal of a Slave-Dealer*, 105.

Then the journal is continued by his brother Blayney, who writes that Nicholas died on 26 March 1758, and 'left me to struggle with the world a little longer, disconsolate & alone amidst negroes'.

The uncertainty of the testimony in these narratives is well illustrated by a small incident in *The Surprizing Adventures* of John Roach (see Chapter 10). In the original edition of 1783/4, speaking of his early voyages, Roach wrote that in 1769 he went to Bristol 'and shipped myself on board the Jane, Captain Clarke, for the slave trade on the coast of Guinea. We soon arrived there, and took in five hundred slaves: after which we proceeded to Jamaica.' But in an edition of 1810, rewritten for him by sympathizers, the Gladders brothers, who taught in Workington in Cumberland, the account of the slave-voyage is significantly amplified. It says that Captain Clarke was a vicious man, given to 'wild excesses and ungovernable fury', violent towards both his crew and the slaves.

> Under the conduct of such a ruffian, the sufferings of the wretched negroes, thus torn from their kindred and their country by the infamous agents of the most infamous traffic that ever disgraced the commerce of a civilized people, were insupportable. Above a hundred of them died and were thrown over board during the passage. The remainder, less fortunate than their deceased brethren, survived to endure a few years of unutterable misery and despair. No one possessed of any degree of commiseration for the sufferings of his fellow-creatures, who has witnessed the dreadful effects of the slave trade, will ever cease to deplore the havoc it made of the human race, or to execrate the unhumanity of its barbarous and atrocious abettors. Happily for the credit of the present generation, the government of Great Britain, amongst the few measures it has adopted for the benefit of mankind, has interdicted its subjects from continuing so scandalous a trade. May the salutary measure be the fore-runner of liberty to all the inhabitants of the earth, and the happy precursor of every species of oppression both abroad and at home.
>
> Roach, *Surprizing Adventures* (1810), 13–14.

'Disgusted with the scenes he had witnessed', Roach left the Jane in Jamaica. Clarke got back to Bristol with only six of the thirty-six crew he started out with. All this may well be true; the narrators claim that every fact is from Roach himself. But if the amplified story of the Jane is not *their* story, it is their way of telling it, and no doubt Roach needed some prompting to produce the extra information. The left-handed compliment

[11] Owen, *The Journal of a Slave-Dealer*, 85.

to the government refers to the 1807 act suppressing the slave-trade (not yet abolishing slavery).

One may well wonder whether there is another side to the story of life in a Bristol slave-ship as told by Robert Barker in *The Unfortunate Shipwright, or Cruel Captain*, but if only half of what he wrote is true it is grim evidence of the brutality and cruelty in the slave-ships among the whites, let alone towards the blacks. This little pamphlet was poorly printed on inferior grey paper, and 'Printed for, and sold by the Sufferer, for his own Benefit; and by no one else'. The date is 1759 or 1760.[12] Barker, born near Wigan in 1722 and apprenticed to a Liverpool shipwright, had helped to build the Thetis at Bristol and decided to ship in her as carpenter. When they reached the African coast, there was nothing but disagreement and feuding aboard ship. Barker claims he was the target of the persecution of the chief mate, Robert Wabshutt, and the ship's doctor, John Roberts. Captain Fitzherbert, residing ashore at the factory to negotiate purchases, generally sided with Barker until Wabshutt and Roberts accused him of mutiny. He was put in irons. Then the captain died very suddenly; in Barker's opinion poisoned. Wabshutt assumed command, and Barker spent the entire voyage to the West Indies chained to the deck of the Thetis, ill and starved, and he went blind. Notwithstanding, Wabshutt hauled him before the justices and charged him with mutiny. As the case seemed to be failing for lack of evidence, Wabshutt told the court that Barker 'had been in the rebellion in the North of England' (i.e. the '45). This was enough to ensure his imprisonment. He eventually got back to England, and spent years vainly attempting to get legal redress.

As for the slaves, it is so far only in Atkins's narrative that they come alive as individuals. There is, however, the invaluable testimony of one of the slaves, Olaudah Equiano, who, in 1789 at the age of about forty-four, published *The Interesting Narrative of the Life of Olaudah Equiano, or Gustavus Vasa, the African, written by himself*. Olaudah, a boy-slave in Virginia, had become the personal servant of an English naval officer who named him Gustavus Vasa. Ten years later, in 1766, after many adventures, he bought his freedom. Olaudah was an Ibo from Nigeria, and at the age of eleven he and his sister were kidnapped. He was in the hands of several masters and though unhappy was not maltreated until in 1756 he was brought to the sea-coast and sold to English slavers.

Olaudah's narrative brilliantly conveys his terrified disorientation at the sight of the sea, the huge ships, and his treatment at the hands of 'those white men with horrible looks, red faces, and loose hair'.[13] On board the ship he found 'a multitude of black people of every description chained

[12] E. G. Cox's date of 1755 (in the *Reference Guide to the Literature of Travel*, II, 460) is not possible.
[13] Olaudah Equiano, *The Interesting Narrative*, 72.

together, every one of their countenances expressing dejection and sorrow'. He could not eat the food given him, and for that he was held down and flogged. Some were 'hourly whipped for not eating'. 'I had never seen among any people such instances of brutal cruelty; and this not only shewn towards us blacks, but also to some of the whites themselves.'[14] Below deck the conditions were simply intolerable. In the suffocating stench and heat, many of the slaves fell ill and died,

> thus falling victims to the improvident avarice, as I may call it, of their purchasers. This wretched situation was again aggravated by the galling of the chains, now become insupportable, and the filth of the necesary tubs, into which the children often fell and were almost suffocated. The shrieks of the women and the groans of the dying, rendered the whole a scene of horror almost inconceivable. Happily perhaps for myself I was soon reduced so low that it was thought necessary to keep me almost always on deck; and from my extreme youth I was not put in fetters.
>
> Olaudah Equiano, *The Interesting Narrative*, 79–80.

Two slaves, chained together, 'preferring death to such a life of misery, somehow made through the nettings and jumped into the sea.'

It may well be that Olaudah, looking back on his childhood in his opening chapter, gave a rather coloured picture of the serenity and stability of conditions in his homeland. But there can be no gainsaying that (because of the acts of his own fellow-countrymen) in coming into European hands he fell among savages, and this movement from civil society into the barbaric conditions of the slave-ships makes the more shameful the constant refrain of the apologists that they were rescuing savages from the anarchy and viciousness of a godless life.

## III

John Newton, born in 1725, the son of a sea-captain, was brought up to the sea. Press-ganged into the Navy in 1744, his experience and contacts raised him to the rank of midshipman. He had, however, fallen so deeply in love with Mary Catlett that just before a long voyage he impulsively deserted. He was brought back, put in irons, flogged and deprived of his rank. Off Madeira, he managed an exchange into a slave-ship, and from that, in West Africa, into the employ of a slave-trader, Clow. He was thoroughly wretched, persecuted by Clow's African wife, and forced into the hardest menial labour in the trade. His consolation was his only book, Euclid. Eventually he was rescued through his father's efforts. The ship that picked him up was caught in a violent storm as it was making its way back to England in March 1748, and seemed to be in immediate danger of sinking. Newton involuntarily prayed, though for years he had been an

[14] *Ibid.*, 75.

out-and-out free-thinker. The recovery of the ship he took as divine intervention, an inexplicable singling out of himself for mercy, and his life was changed from that moment. He was now 'a serious professor', and engaged himself 'to be the Lord's for ever'.

Newton then sailed as mate in a Liverpool slave-ship, the Brownlow, and after marriage to his Mary in 1750, was captain on three long slaving-voyages. Illness forestalled a fourth voyage and in 1755 he left the sea and became tide-surveyor at Liverpool. It was some years before he was successful in being ordained; in 1764 he became curate of Olney in Buckinghamshire, where he remained for fifteen years, the close associate of William Cowper and co-author of *The Olney Hymns* ('Glorious things of Thee are spoken', etc.). In 1779 he became rector of St Mary Woolnoth in London, where he died in 1807.

The main source of information about Newton's life is his own autobiographical work, *An Authentic Narrative of Some Remarkable and Interesting Particulars in the Life of * * * * * * * [John Newton], communicated in a Series of Letters, to the Rev. Haweis* (1764). Actually, the first draft of this had been finished in 1762 and brought to the attention of Thomas Haweis, of Christ Church, Oxford, who had suggested it should be rewritten and enlarged. The work led directly to his ordination.[15] This is a spiritual testimony, a record which emphasizes if it does not exaggerate the violent godlessness of the author's unregenerate days and which concentrates after his conversion on his personal relationship with a God who took a particular interest in his welfare. It is alarmingly blinkered, frighteningly egotistical. It could be argued that the subject being the state of his soul, Newton is simply excluding from the text his relationships with those around him (except for his wife). But the impression that the reader gains is that the nature of his religion is purely a matter of the state of his soul and has nothing to do with his relationships with those around him. There is not the slightest indication that his discovery of belief made any alteration to his values, opinions, attitudes and actions as regards the African slaves whom he was forcibly conducting to the West Indies.

Regarding his first slaving-voyage, as mate in the Brownlow, he describes how God protected him during many hardships, misadventures and difficulties on the African coast, including 'the temper of the natives, who are, in many places, cruel, treacherous, and watching opportunities for mischief'.[16] He makes no mention of the middle passage but comments on his problem in finding the 'serious people' in Charleston among those who attended public worship. His account of the first slaving-voyage in command is even more extraordinary. He never mentions the slaves, though he does speak of his crew.

[15] Martin, *John Newton: A Biography*, 195–6.

[16] Newton, *An Authentic Narrative*, 151–2.

I had now the command and care of thirty persons; I endeavoured to treat them with humanity, and to set them a good example. I likewise established public worship, according to the liturgy, twice every Lord's day, officiating myself . . .

Having now much leisure, I prosecuted the study of *Latin* with good success . . .

. . . My first voyage was fourteen months, through various scenes of danger and difficulty, but nothing very remarkable. . . . I was preserved from every harm; and having seen many fall on my right hand and on my left, I was brought home in peace . . .

Newton, *An Authentic Narrative*, 164–9.

His account of his next voyage speaks of the opportunities which the command of a ship offers for meditation and reflection on spiritual matters. Of the seafaring life, he writes:

I know not any calling that seems more favourable, or affords greater advantages to an awakened mind, for promoting the life of God in the soul, especially to a person who has the command of a ship . . . and still more so in *African* voyages, as these ships carry a double proportion of men and officers to most others, which made my department very easy; and, excepting the hurry of trade, &c. upon the coast, which is rather occasional than constant, afforded me abundance of leisure.

Newton, *An Authentic Narrative*, 172–3.

'Evident interpositions of Divine Providence', he goes on, 'in answer to prayer, occur almost every day; these are helps to quicken and confirm the life of faith'. Among the perils he was saved from was 'a conspiracy among my own people to turn pirates, and to take the ship from me'. 'The slaves on board were likewise frequently plotting insurrections, and were sometimes on the very brink of mischief; but it was always disclosed in due time.'

*An Authentic Narrative* was written seven or eight years after Newton left the sea. There are two other writings giving a closer view of these three voyages as captain of a slave-ship. One is his journal, not published until 1962, and the other is *Letters to a Wife*, published in 1793. The edition of the journal by Bernard Martin and Mark Spurrell usefully correlates the two testimonies. The journal of the first voyage, in the Duke of Argyll (1750–51), bleakly records the tedious hanging around off the African coast, engaging in sordid transactions with the traders – white, black and 'mulatto' – for two or three slaves here or there, rejecting a woman with fallen breasts because she won't sell, and feeling uncomfortable about one deal involving slaves who it was suspected had been taken from a French ship whose crew were murdered: 'am obliged to dissemble at present and say little, or hurt my own business without any advantage to the sufferers' (the sufferers are the Frenchmen).[17] There were constant deaths to record, among his own crew and among the slaves he was spending so much time

17 Newton, *The Journal of a Slave-Trader*, 40.

in seeking. The ship's cats too had died, and the rats were gnawing the sails and the cables and biting sleepers. As the ship filled up and the rains commenced, he wrote to his wife, 'Two hundred people confined in a small vessel, in bad weather, occasion noise, dirt, and trouble enough'.[18]

That this voyage was not a financial success we learn from a letter written to his wife when he had been 'near seven months upon the coast' in his second voyage, 1752–3. 'I . . . must expect to make a losing voyage, at last.'

> How far two unsuccessful voyages may affect my interest, or diminish my expected profits, I am tolerably easy. I have placed my dependence higher: I consider my friends and employers, as instruments in the hand of God, for my good.
>
> Newton, *Letters to a Wife*, 162–3.

While still on the coast during this second voyage the slaves made two attempts to break out.

> *Monday 11th December* . . . By the favour of Divine Providence made a timely discovery to day that the slaves were forming a plot for an insurrection. Surprized 2 of them attempting to get off their irons, and upon farther search in their rooms, upon the information of 3 of the boys, found some knives, stones, shot, etc., and a cold chissel. Upon enquiry there appeared 8 principally concerned to move in projecting the mischeif and 4 boys in supplying them with the above instruments. Put the boys in irons and slightly in the thumbscrews to urge them to a full confession . . .
>
> *Tuesday 12th December* . . . In the morning examined the men slaves and punished 6 of the principal, put 4 of them in collars.
>
> Newton, *The Journal of a Slave-Trader*, 71.

These 'collars' were iron contraptions, often with long spikes which made it impossible to rest the head in any position. On 23 February Newton had information from the boys that there was another 'intention to rise upon us. Found 4 principally concerned, punished them with the thumb screws and afterwards put them in neck yokes . . .'[19] Martin and Spurrell quote a passage from an unpublished diary of Newton's written during the Atlantic voyage, noting that the men slaves seem 'to have entirely changed their tempers'. 'From about the end of February they have behaved more like children in one family, than slaves in chains and irons.' He attributed this alteration to 'the helping of the god of peace'.[20]

During the third voyage, 1753–4, Newton had an unhappy time on the coast. Slaves were scarce and expensive, and there were several reports of successful risings on board slave-ships. He wrote to his wife of 'this distasteful climate and employment'.[21] Finding the trade unpleasant is not

[18] Newton, *Letters to a Wife*, 67.

[19] Newton, *The Journal of a Slave-Trader*, 77.

[20] *Ibid.*, 80.

[21] *Ibid.*, xii.

the same as finding it immoral. In *An Authentic Narrative* Newton gave this account of giving up the trade, and the sea, because of an illness which seemed to him providential, just before his fourth voyage.

I was again ready for the sea: but the Lord saw fit to over-rule my design. During the time I was engaged in the slave trade, I never had the least scruple as to its lawfulness. I was upon the whole satisfied with it, as the appointment Providence had marked out for me; yet it was, in many respects, far from eligible. It is indeed accounted a genteel employment, and is usually very profitable, though to me it did not prove so, the Lord seeing that a large increase in wealth would not be good for me. However, I considered myself as a sort of *Gaoler* or *Turnkey*; and I was sometimes shocked with an employment that was perpetually conversant with chains, bolts, and shackles. In this view I had often petitioned in my prayers, that the Lord in his own time would be pleased to fix me in a more humane calling.

Newton, *An Authentic Narrative*, 191–2.

Newton was twenty-nine at the time of this illness. He was thirty-nine when he wrote the account quoted above. In 1788, when he was sixty-two, the renowned evangelical preacher of St Mary Woolnoth, a man who influenced Cowper to write his anti-slavery poetry, the confidant and guide of the young William Wilberforce, friend of Hannah More, Newton gave great impetus to the abolitionist movement by writing his pamphlet, *Thoughts upon the African Slave Trade*. It is a fine document, dignified in its exposition and horrifying in its details. It is also an act of contrition.

I am bound, in conscience, to take shame to myself by a public confession, which, however sincere, comes too late to prevent, or repair, the misery and mischief to which I have, formerly, been accessary.

I hope it will always be a subject of humiliating reflection to me, that I was, once, an active instrument in a business at which my heart now shudders.

Newton, *Thoughts upon the African Slave Trade*, 2.

It was Newton's purpose not so much to demand pity for the slaves as to puncture the indefeasible sense of superiority among Europeans, and to demonstrate that of the two parties in this dreadful transaction it was the whites who were the inferior. Cowper had written of the whites' contempt for blacks, 'He finds his fellow guilty of a skin / Not colour'd like his own'. Newton argues that it is in the nature of the slave-trade to corrupt those who engage in it. 'I know of no method of getting money ... which has more direct a tendency to efface the moral sense.'[22] It was accepted as proper conduct to swindle the free Africans, rape the slave-women, and inflict extreme pain on the men. Details of the suffering quite normally imposed are sickening: slaves chained together in pairs for many months together so that they can neither move nor rest without difficulty, 'unmerciful whippings', 'the torture of the thumb-screws; a dreadful engine,

[22] Newton, *Thoughts upon the African Slave Trade*, 14.

which, if the screw be turned by an unrelenting hand, can give intolerable anguish', the conditions in the hold where the five-foot height is divided in two, 'for the Slaves lie in two rows, one above the other, on each side of the ship, close to each other, like books upon a shelf'.[23]

In trying to portray the feelings of the Africans, it is clear that Newton must have seen a manuscript copy of Olaudah Equiano's narrative (not yet published) because he models his picture of an African slave going aboard the white man's ship very closely on Olaudah's account. His experience of Africans was that their standards in sexual morality and business ethics were much higher than those of the Europeans on the coast. 'What! do you think I am a white man?' said one black when he was accused of dishonest dealing. Newton acknowledges that the slaves whom the Europeans bought had first been enslaved by their fellow-Africans. But as regards those captured in tribal wars, he argues that 'the far greater part of the wars' would cease if Europeans ceased to provide the market for the captives. The slave-trade degraded both Africans and Europeans. And on both sides it was responsible for a dreadful wastage of human lives.

Newton made no attempt to rewrite his part in the slave-trade, nor to palliate his responsibility. 'I never had a scruple upon this head, at the time.' But perhaps he does not sufficiently engage with what disturbs the reader of his earlier accounts so much, his confidence that God was directing him, and his satisfaction at the continuous improvement of his spiritual state at the very time he was directly causing the wretchedness and despair of those in the hold.

> What I did, I did ignorantly; considering it as the line of life which Divine Providence had allotted me, and having no concern, in point of conscience, but to treat the Slaves, while under my care, with as much humanity, as a regard to my own safety would admit.
>
> Newton, *Thoughts upon the African Slave Trade*, 4.

It was not the experience of the slave-trade that brought Newton to see the slaves as his fellow-creatures, and it was not his discovery of God either, or not in the first place. The very image he uses to express his revulsion – that of being a kind of gaoler – suggests that in 1754 he still saw the slaves as convicts or criminals. His indifference to the injustice of their position is a very strong criticism of the kind of religion he had made for himself. Whenever it was that he began to understand how impercipient he had been, *Thoughts upon the African Slave Trade* is a noble recantation of belief in a false God.

[23] *Ibid.*, 17 and 33.

## IV

Very extraordinary testimony direct from a slave-ship by one who became an abolitionist soon after the ship left port is provided by James Field Stanfield, an Irishman who had been trained for the priesthood but found himself in some unexplained crisis in Liverpool which concluded by his making a will in favour of his landlady and joining the crew of a slaver. He wrote about his experiences in two forms: first, a series of letters addressed to Thomas Clarkson, and secondly a poem, *The Guinea Voyage*. He wanted the two to be published together, but apparently the publishers did not want the poem. So the letters, *Observations on a Guinea Voyage*, came out in 1788, and the poem in 1789. The two came out together in 1807, however, to mark the suppression of the trade; the poem was extensively revised.

The prose letters tend to dwell on the sufferings of the crew more than on those of the slaves. The cruelty of the captain was hideous; even though we make considerable allowance for exaggeration, he must have been a sadistic psychopath. Stanfield writes that when the captain was ill, he would have his victim, crewman or slave, trussed to the high bunk in his cabin so that he could watch their faces as they were flogged. The poem gives a much wider view of slavery, but it still goes into detail about the constant floggings, with 'quiv'ring morsels' of flesh flying off as the lash is plied.

However worthy the sentiments, the verse is terrible.

> Help me to paint the melancholy view,
> The dismal track of ocean to pursue,
> And with the Eagle-eye of Truth pervade
> All the dark mazes of th'*inhuman Trade.*

We begin with 'the harden'd merchants' who conspire 'th'insatiate thirst of avarice to supply', and the various stratagems to get a crew together. There is a good deal about poor 'Russel', 'lov'd companion, faithful friend', who seems to have taken passage because of a broken heart:

> Far from fair freedom's blisful regions thrown,
> The mournful seamen heave th'unheeded groan.

In the second book, the spirit of Africa calls for vengeance on 'these traffickers in human blood', and because of this curse disease and death afflict the European crews and traders. The poet pleads with the 'Senatorian band' to join their sympathetic aid and 'blast the horrors of th'infernal trade'. In the third book, the middle passage is described in quite revolting detail. There is special attention to the sufferings of the women slaves, with a description of childbirth on board in these awful surroundings. He appeals to British women:

O rise auspicious, lead the lib'ral train,
That aims to shake oppression's iron reign.

Finally, he looks forward to a free Africa, prosperously trading with the rest of the world.

Of course, he had not the talent to do what he was trying to do. The slave-trade never had its Wilfred Owen. The design, of an interlinked twin literary representation in prose and verse, was ambitious and interesting, but the double publication presumably failed because the publisher of the letters did not think much of the verse. According to the *Dictionary of National Biography*, Stanfield turned his attention to the theatre, and became director of a touring company in the north of England. He died in 1824. His son, Clarkson Stanfield, became a marine and landscape painter.

## V

My last narrative touching on the slave-trade takes us back to the troubled early history of the state of Sierra Leone. In the mid-1780s there was a considerable black population in England – several thousand strong, most of them youngish men. They were a fall-out from the slave-trade, many having been taken on as personal servants by ships' captains, or brought back to England for use as servants, but many of them former American slaves who had fought for the British, especially in the Navy, in the American war. Since the celebrated ruling by Judge Mansfield in 1772 in the cause originated by Granville Sharp, slavery did not exist in England. But the black people, congregating in towns and especially London, were living in poverty and remained the object of social concern. The Committee for the Relief of the Black Poor was started in 1786, with Granville Sharp as a leading light.

One Henry Smeathman undertook to lead a resettlement in Sierra Leone, a land which he sometimes but not always painted in glowing colours. His death did not damp enthusiasm for the project, which initially had the support of the writers Ottobah Cuguano and Olaudah Equiano. Eventually, with Government approval and support, over 500 passengers sailed in a man-of-war to Sierra Leone, mostly black men, with a number of white wives. They arrived in May 1787, their complement depleted by fifty deaths *en route*. Captain Thompson negotiated a grant of land from King Naimbana and the subsidiary chief King Tom, but everything went wrong. They had arrived at the beginning of the rainy season, and fever and dysentery took a heavy toll. Many in disillusionment found occupation in the slave-trade. Early in the new year only 130 of the colony remained. Sharp sent out reinforcements but the rot continued. King Tom was succeeded by King Jemmy, who refused to accept the grant of the settlers' land. A visiting warship burned his village down and when the ship left the new king burned down the settlers' village, Granville Town.

Meanwhile, in London, the St George's Company had been formed to promote the colony. Its directors included Sharp, Wilberforce, Thomas Clarkson, Samuel Whitbread the brewer, and Henry Thornton, banker and member of Parliament. Despite blocking from slaving interests they won Parliamentary authorization and soon became the Sierra Leone Company. Having got the news of the dispossession of the settlers at Granville Town, they sent out early in 1791 Alexander Falconbridge, a former ship's surgeon in the slave-trade whose experiences had made him a convinced abolitionist. He took with him his new wife, Anna Maria, of Bristol.[24] His rescue mission was reasonably successful and he was back in London to report later in the same year. When he went back to the colony, still accompanied by his wife, things were on an entirely different footing. Falconbridge was now Commercial Agent. Clarkson's brother John brought out from Nova Scotia a thousand blacks, loyalists who had fought for the British in the American war and were unhappy with the climate and the terms of their resettlement. Clarkson worked heroically to re-establish the colony in what was now called Freetown, while Falconbridge, a chronic alcoholic, faded out and died. In 1794 his widow, already remarried, published her *Narrative of Two Voyages to the River Sierra Leone.*

The narrative is framed as a series of letters, to 'My dear Friend', unnamed, but it is very unlikely that the letters are real, in spite of the detail ('Mr. Gilbert, our clergyman, returns to England in the vessel I write by ...'). Real or not, she says in the preface that she wrote the letters with publication in mind. The basis would seem to be a journal, and it looks as though it has, in the end, been carefully fashioned to reveal a sensibility being shaped by sad experience. The end to which it moves, quite unsuspected in the innocent opening and coming as a considerable surprise, is seen to obey the logic of all that has been described. If there is a good deal of artistry in this, she makes one big mistake. Her rule, quite properly, is never to allow the final text to indicate any awareness of what followed the original moment of writing. But this rule is quite inappropriate for the narrative course of a single letter. At the start of the letter which records her husband's death, she gives no hint of what has happened, although he died nine days before the point at which the letter begins. 'Within ten or twelve days after the date of my last, arrived the two ships that were expected.' It is some time before we reach her husband,

[24] The preceding account is drawn from Fyfe, *A History of Sierra Leone*; West, *Back to Africa*; and Braidwood, 'Initiatives and organisations of the Black poor, 1786–1787'.

and the company's unfair treatment of him, and then the bombshell, 'he spun out his life in anguish and misery till the 19th instant, when without a groan he gasp'd his last!!!'[25] Even though, as she goes on immediately to say, she does not regret his death, after two years of unkindness '(not to give a harsher term)', it would have taken very little to provide the verisimilitude of telling her correspondent at the outset that there were important things to relate.

The attitude to the husband is a delicate matter of considerable importance. On the one hand her growing sense of his shortcomings has to be seen as one of the reasons for her growing disillusion with the cause (abolition) which he espoused. On the other hand, she needs to show sympathy with him as the victim of the heartless London directors in order to fuel her denunciation of those directors for keeping from her the money they owe to Falconbridge. In the account of the first tour, the balance is anti-husband. In his arguments with the slaving-captain he is bigoted and inebriated. He forces her to sleep in dirty and offensive conditions in the cutter Lapwing rather than on shore. She refuses to accompany him on the second day of the great palaver with Naimbana and enjoys the company of a polite Frenchman on shore.

But she establishes her ready sympathy for the oppressed and despised. As they are leaving Portsmouth they see the convict fleet bound for Botany Bay, and she is afflicted by 'the sight of those unfortunate beings, and the thoughts of what they are to endure'.[26] She is horrified by her first sight of a slave-yard. Of the free Africans, she writes:

> Cleanliness is universally observed; their simple furniture, consisting generally of a few mats, wooden trenchers and spoons made by themselves, are always tidy, and their homely habitations constantly clean swept, and free from filth of any kind: nor do I think nature has been so unkind to endow these people with capacities less susceptible of improvement and cultivation than any other part of the human race.
>
> Falconbridge, *Narrative of Two Voyages*, 79.

Her most famous emotional shock was the discovery of the white women among the distressed and dispossessed settlers.

> I never did, and God grant I never may again, witness so much misery as I was forced to be a spectator of here: Among the outcasts were seven of our country women, decrepid with disease, and so disguised with filth and dirt, that I should never have supposed they were born white; add to this, almost naked from head to foot; in short, their appearance was such as I think would extort compassion from the most callous heart . . .
>
> I always supposed these people had been transported as convicts, but some conversation I lately had with one of the women, has partly undeceived me: She

[25] Falconbridge, *Narrative of Two Voyages*, 169. [26] *Ibid.*, 16.

said, the women were mostly of that description of persons who walk the streets of London, and support themselves by the earnings of prostitution; that men were employed to collect and conduct them to Wapping, where they were intoxicated with liquor, then inveigled on board of ship, and married to *Black men*, whom they had never seen before; that the morning after she was married, she really did not remember a syllable of what had happened over night, and when informed, was obliged to inquire *who was her husband?*

Falconbridge, *Narrative of Two Voyages*, 64–5.

This charge, that the white women who accompanied the black settlers were street-women who had been abducted and drugged, has been widely discussed over the years and is generally discredited. That the directors would countenance it, that the women would put up with it (it was a long time before the ship left the English shore), that the men themselves would want it or accept it, is extremely improbable. It is quite possible that some of the wives had been prostitutes, possible that some had been fuddled with drink when they went aboard, but that this was a scheme to provide the male-settlers with partners seems to arise from Anna Falconbridge's enthusiasm to blacken the sponsors of the enterprise. She describes the settlers as 'the unhappy people sent out by government', and the government has been misled by the do-gooders.

Anna returned to England with her husband for his report on the outcome of his negotiations. Her vigilance apparently saved the Lapwing from wreck on the Cape Verde Islands.

The first thing I saw, upon lifting my head out of the cabin, was those lofty perpendicular rocks pending almost directly over us, and not a man upon deck but King Naimbana's son, and him fast asleep.

'Good God!' cried I, 'Falconbridge, we are on shore!'

Falconbridge, *Narrative of Two Voyages*, 108–9.

Although Anna Falconbridge thought that the plan to bring a large contingent of blacks from Nova Scotia was 'a premature, hair-brained [*sic*] and ill-digested scheme', when she was back in Sierra Leone and the new settlers arrived she found them 'in general, a religious temperate, good set of people' and she was particularly enthusiastic about the efforts of Lieutenant Clarkson to produce some semblance of order and purpose into the colony's life.

In her account of this second tour, she views her husband as a man betrayed by the Directors' unwarranted lack of confidence in him and balked at every turn by the self-important local officers who are also obstructing Clarkson. Between them, they drive him more deeply into drink and towards his death. The neighbouring slaving factories and the masters of the slave-ships view the confusion of the colony with glee, 'highly gratified with the anarchy and chagrin that prevails'. The many deaths during the rainy season gave her more sombre thoughts. 'I am surprised our boasted Philanthropists, the Directors of the Company, should have subjected themselves to the censure they must meet, for sporting with the lives of such numbers of their fellow-creatures.'[27] These directors are 'a parcel of hypocritical puritans', a 'pack of canting parasites'. She wishes the colony could be run by people without 'religious tenets' but with actual knowledge of commerce and the coast of Africa. The supreme example of their lack of judgement was the replacement of Clarkson by the 'austere, reserved' Mr Dawes.

> It may not be *mal-a-propos* to mention here, that Mr. Dawes is a subaltern of Marines; that the prejudices of a rigid military education has been heightened by his having served some time at Botany Bay, where, no doubt, it is necessary for gentlemen to observe an awful severity in their looks and actions; but such behaviour, however suitable for a Colony formed wholly of Convicts, and governed by the iron rod of despotism, should be scrupulously guarded against in one like this, whose *basis is Liberty and Equality*, and whose Police is dependant, in great measure, if not altogether, on the whimsical disposition of an ignorant populace, which can only be advantageously tempered by placidness and moderation.
>
> Falconbridge, *Narrative of Two Voyages*, 178–9.[28]

Anna Falconbridge left Sierra Leone with her new husband, Isaac DuBois. He was an American, and a recent recruit to the colony, but as he was of Clarkson's party he fell with Clarkson. They went to England via Jamaica, in a slave-ship. Anna Falconbridge was 'agreeably disappointed' in her expectations. The slaves were well treated, allowed to stay on deck all day, 'their provisions were excellent', and 'great attention was paid to the sick'. She admits the ship had only two-thirds of its full complement, but the experience overthrew her previous beliefs.

> For a length of time I viewed the Slave Trade with abhorrence – considering it a blemish on every civilized nation that countenanced or supported it . . . but I am not ashamed to confess, those sentiments were the effect of ignorance, and the prejudice of opinion, imbibed by associating with a circle of acquaintances, *bigoted for the abolition*, before I had acquired information enough to form any independent thoughts upon the subject. . . . I now think it in no shape objectionable either to morality or religion, but on the contrary consistent with both, while neither are to be found in unhappy Africa; and while three fourths of that populous country come into the world, like hogs or sheep, subject, at any moment, to be rob'd of their lives by the other fourth.
>
> Falconbridge, *Narrative of Two Voyages*, 235.

Slavery, she argues, saves the lives of the slaves, and their 'future existence is rendered comfortable, by the cherishing hands of Christian masters'.

[27] *Ibid.*, 150 (printing errors corrected). [28] Printing errors corrected.

The slaves whom she saw in Jamaica seemed 'vastly well satisfied', far better off than the labouring poor in England. When education can overcome the 'innate prejudices, ignorance, superstition, and savageness' which overspread Africa, it will be the time to abolish slavery, for 'I wish freedom to every creature formed by God, who knows its value'.

The book culminates in a vigorous onslaught on the directors of the Sierra Leone Company, particularly Henry Thornton, for hazarding the happiness of the settlers, who were 'mostly comfortably settled' before, for their humiliating and unjust treatment of the black deputies who had arrived in London to plead for the implementation of their promised rights, and in particular for keeping from 'a Woman, aggravated by insults and injury' the money owing to her former husband. Indeed, the final letter is an open letter to Thornton, summing up the Directors' injustice to Falconbridge and denouncing him personally. The value of the book as an impartial record is compromised by her animus against the Directors for cheating her out of money that she considered due to her. All that issues from them is wrong, and that includes the entire Sierra Leone project. These people, she argues, have no idea what misery the remorseless application of their high-minded compassion is having on its victims. But if her testimony is warped so is the testimony of everyone else in this book. Her bias is easily identified. Her rancour and cynicism are wittily and intelligently deployed, and though she is a hostile witness, she is a witness. As for what happened afterwards, apparently she succeeded in getting her money, and went off with her husband to the West Indies.[29]

[29] West, *Back to Africa*, 51 (without sources).

# 9

# Passengers

During the whole of the eighteenth century, men, women, and children were travelling by sea to all parts of the globe. They were emigrants, or soldiers, or soldiers' wives, or merchants, or officials, or the brides of officials, or convicts, or indentured servants, or visitors, or absconding debtors[1] – or they were even travelling for their health.[2] Passengers in ships who wrote about their travels naturally tended to concentrate on the places they visited rather than on their experiences at sea. What they wrote about their sea-journeying was usually brief, being in their eyes of secondary importance. But the passenger's perspective is important in the story of the voyage, and the passengers themselves are interesting. In what follows I have included something from two major writers, Henry Fielding and Mary Wollstonecraft, and from a talented amateur, Janet Schaw; from one of the leading evangelists of the century, George Whitefield; from one of his disciples, a methodist physician travelling to the West Indies; and from a woman in financial distress going to Russia to be a governess. But I begin with a boy whose very existence has been disputed.

### Robert Drury

*Madagascar: or Robert Drury's Journal, During Fifteen Years Captivity on that Island* was published in 1729. It was 'Written by Himself, digested into Order, and publish'd at the Request of his Friends'. It was to be sold by the three booksellers, Meadows, Marshall and Worrall, 'and by the Author, at Old Tom's Coffee-House in Birchin Lane'. The book was lengthy, and the price was six shillings, bound. This publication came twelve years after Drury's return to England. At this time he seems to have been a porter at East India House in Leadenhall Street, willing to

[1] John Cremer, *Ramblin' Jack*, vouches for these, p. 105.

[2] In 1756 Ebenezer Gilchrist, a Scottish doctor, published *The Use of Sea Voyages in Medicine*, and it went into a second edition in 1757. The humid and salty sea air was good for you, and so was the 'volutary and tossing motion of the ship', which provided excellent muscular exercise 'in order to preserve the equilibrium'. Even sea-sickness was exercise, and cleansed the passages of bad humours. All the same, in 1715 William Symson wrote that at Bombay, 'of twenty four Passengers we carry'd over, twenty were bury'd at this Place' (*New Voyage to the East-Indies*, p. 16).

demonstrate his accuracy in throwing the javelin.[3] He was also to be found at Old Tom's coffee-house round the corner, as the tail-piece to the book indicates.

I am every Day to be spoken with at *Old Tom*'s Coffee-house in *Birchin-Lane*; where I shall be ready to gratify any Gentleman with a further Account of any Thing herein contain'd; to stand the strictest Examination, or to confirm those Things which to some may seem doubtful.

*Madagascar* is surrounded by testimony to its authenticity and reliability, and its anxiety, as will be seen, had proved thoroughly counter-productive. The preface begins by remarking that 'at the first Appearance of this Treatise, I make no Doubt of its being taken for such another Romance as *Robinson Cruso*'. The author of this preface calls himself 'the Transcriber'. The original, he says, was written by Drury, 'which consisting of eight Quires in *Folio*, each of near an hundred Pages, it was necessary to contract it, and put it in a more agreeable Method'. Robert Drury 'constantly attended the Transcriber' during the redrafting. The transcriber, an enthusiastic enlightenment amateur theologian, had been fascinated by Drury's observations on religion in Madagascar, and confessed that on this subject he had put 'some Reflections in the Author's mouth'. Apart from that he had not been led to 'alter any Facts, or add any Fiction of his own'.

There is also a preliminary note by Captain William Mackett, dated 7 May 1728, certifying that Robert Drury, 'now living in *London*, was redeem'd from thence [Madagascar], and brought into *England*, his native Country, by Myself'. He believes 'that the Account he gives of his Strange and Surprising *Adventures* is Genuine and Authentick'.

Robert Drury was born in 1687 in London, son of a very respectable city innkeeper (a churchwarden of St Olave Jewry). From the age of eleven, he tells us, he wanted to go to sea, and when his parents could not dissuade him, they allowed him to go on a voyage to India in the Degrave, putting him in the care of the captain, William Young, and providing him with 'a Cargo to the Value of an hundred Pounds'. There was a cousin at Bengal, John Steel, to be visited. 'I went as a Passenger, well recommended to Capt. *William Younge*. My Passage, and Freight of the Cargo were agreed for' – and he embarked; he was thirteen years old. The Degrave left in February 1701. It took her three months and twenty days to reach 'Fort *St. George* in the *East Indies*' (Madras). Robert was not idle, for, at the end of the book, writing about his return visit to Madagascar, he says that 'when I was a Boy I had learn'd the Art of Navigation in our Voyage to *India*'.[4] At Fort St George there was a disaster. Among the fellow-passengers were

[3] Biographical details, when not taken from the *Journal*, are from Secord, '*Robert Drury's Journal*'.
[4] Drury, *Robert Drury's Journal*, 444.

'Monsieur *Lapie*, Jeweller, and his Son', who were going to settle at Madras. The boat taking them ashore capsized, and they were drowned, their stock-in-trade going down with them, 'to some thousand Pounds Value'.

In Bengal Drury met his cousin, who was a pilot, but Captain Young, acting for Robert's father, thought him unsuitable to take charge of the boy, and organized the sale of the cargo himself. Both the cousin and the captain were soon victims of the high European mortality. William Young's son Nicholas, the Degrave's second mate, took the ship over. (The fourth mate was John Benbow, son of the admiral.) It was eighteen months before they left Bengal. 'The only Good which I got at *Bengall*, and which prov'd of any Advantage to me afterwards', wrote Drury, 'was, that I here learnt to swim, which has two or three times since sav'd my Life and Liberty'.[5] Drury said they had 'about 120 Hands on board, besides two Women and myself and a few other Passengers'. The ship grounded going down the Hugli River near Calcutta, and sprang a leak. The leak worsened in the Indian Ocean, and they were forced to put in to Mauritius. But thereafter the ship's situation became desperate, and they were forced to make for Madagascar.

> The third Day in the Morning, they sent me and the Captain's Boy up the Mast-head to look out for Land, since they cou'd spare no Body else: In such Extremity of Life and Death, my being a Passenger was not consider'd.
>
> Drury, *Robert Drury's Journal*, 10.

It was Drury who spied the Madagascar coast. The ship was driven on shore, and broke up. One or two were drowned, but most got safely ashore.

> The Captain got on shoar with his Father's Heart in his Hand, which, according to his Request when dying, was put in a Bottle, to be brought to *England*, and bury'd at *Dover*.
>
> Drury, *Robert Drury's Journal*, 13.

The local population plundered the ship's substantial cargo and everyone's possessions. There was a surprise visit from a shipwrecked Englishman called Sam, and they were marched to meet the local king, Crindo, and found there two Scottish sea-captains, Drummond and Stewart (for whose supposed murder on the high seas the Scots hanged Captain Green of the Worcester). The enlarged British party staged a coup, kidnapped the king and his family, and set off for Fort Dauphin and the hoped-for protection of King Samuel. Most of them never made it. Their judgement weakened by hunger and intense thirst, they made foolish bargains with the pursuing army, and were massacred. Some got

[5] *Ibid.*, 7.

away; Drury and one or two other young ones were singled out and taken captive.

What happened in the following years is a very long story and not our immediate concern. His treatment varied greatly with the master he served. At the high point he could write, 'My Post here was a grand one, for I was made Captain of my Master's Guard'. And again, 'My Wife came also and lick'd my Feet, expressing her Concern for my Trouble, and Joy for my Deliverance. ... I had now about thirty head of Cattle, and liv'd very easy and happy.'[6]

Drury was eventually rescued by the slave-trader Captain William Mackett. His story is that during his years on the island he had met another shipwrecked English sailor, William Thornbury, who had got back to London and by sheer chance had been put in touch with Drury's father, who enlisted Mackett's help in locating and ransoming his son. Robert Drury got back to England in September 1717. He found that his father had died – his mother too, much earlier. So he went back to the island where he had spent fifteen years as a slave, this time as a slave-trader with a colleague of Mackett's. On their way they stopped in Natal. 'We bought in a Fortnight's Time, 74 Boys and Girls: These are better Slaves for working, than those of *Madagascar*, being stronger, also blacker.'[7] In Madagascar he donned native dress, visited the kindest of his Masters, Rer Moume, and licked his knees, and also bought large numbers of slaves. *Madagascar, or Robert Drury's Journal* ends with an eight-page vocabulary of the Madagascar language.

Over the years a number of people suspected the veracity and authenticity of *Robert Drury's Journal*, and once or twice it was suggested that it might have been the work of Defoe.[8] It was left to Professor John Robert Moore, who enormously inflated the supposed canon of Defoe's writing, to make out a case that the whole journal was a romance written by Defoe, based on many sources, but taking its departure from a news item of 1705, recording what has been called 'the most incredible part of the whole *Degrave* story'.[9] A ship arrived from India with the news of the wreck of the Degrave on the Madagascar coast and the massacre of her entire crew except 'a little Boy'. The diarist Narcissus Luttrell noted that the boy had arrived with the ship. (This boy is never mentioned by Drury, and his escape is very puzzling.) Moore's theory was that Defoe had built on the story of this boy to create his fictions. Moore's monograph of 1943, *Defoe's Sources for Robert Drury's Journal*, had very great influence, and soon major libraries – such as the London Library – were crossing Drury out of their author-catalogues and inserting 'See Defoe'. According to P. G. Adams,

6 *Ibid.*, 379 and 422. 7 *Ibid.*, 445.

8 Furbank and Owens, *The Canonisation of Daniel Defoe*, 109.

9 Secord, '*Robert Drury's Journal*', 22.

the *Encyclopedia Britannica* removed its references to Drury as an actual traveller. Adams himself called the *Journal* 'a fireside fabrication'.[10] Bonamy Dobrée, in the *Oxford History of English Literature*, volume VII, said that the *Journal* was 'almost certainly' Defoe's, but noted that this was 'contrary to the opinion of A. W. Secord'. Secord had been working away at the historical record and had shown in 1945 that a great deal of what was in the *Journal* was not romance at all but was factually true. He later wrote, 'Professor Moore was not impressed by my arguments' – a restrained understatement.[11] He went on with quite extraordinarily pertinacious and out-of-the-way researches, and was able to provide documentary confirmation for almost every event and person in the Drury story, though he could not throw much light on Thornbury. He was prepared to accept Defoe – quite unnecessarily, I think – as 'the Transcriber', but certainly not as the inventor Moore had made him out to be. Unfortunately, Secord did not live to publish these later researches, and they came out posthumously in 1961. The rather unpleasant story of Moore's indefensible methods in appropriating this and other works for Defoe is told by P. N. Furbank and W. R. Owens in their book, *The Canonisation of Daniel Defoe* (1988). In the standard biography of Defoe by Paula Backscheider, published in 1989, there is no mention whatsoever of *Madagascar, or Robert Drury's Journal* – even in the list of works 'by or attributed to Defoe'.

## George Whitefield

In August 1739 George Whitefield, at this time still a disciple of Wesley and under increasing opposition from authorities in England over his immensely popular preaching, was making a second journey across the Atlantic, mainly to continue the mission work begun by Wesley in Georgia. Although he was only twenty-four years old, he began to write the story of his life. 'Commenced writing an account of God's dealings with me from my infant days, which I have wanted to do these three years'.[12] He published this in 1740, and stated on the title-page that he had written it 'on board the *Elizabeth*, Captain Stephenson, bound from London to Philadelphia', and that the proceeds were for the benefit of his orphan-house in Georgia. His account describes how, as the son of a Gloucester innkeeper, he had been a drop-out from school but had been persuaded to return, and was admitted as a servitor at Pembroke College, Oxford (his earlier training as a bar-boy standing him in good stead in this ambiguous position.) He came under the influence of 'the despised

[10] Adams, *Travelers and Travel Liars*, 237.
[11] Secord, '*Robert Drury's Journal*', 6.
[12] Whitefield, *George Whitefield's Journals*, 232.

Methodists', met the Wesleys and began visiting the poor, the sick and prisoners, despite the Master of Pembroke threatening to expel him 'if I ever visited the poor again'. Having taken his degree and been ordained as deacon, he continued his work among the poor and in the gaols, and he discovered his forte as a preacher, drawing very large congregations and preaching nine times a week. This was 1737. The young man of twenty-two had been the boy who was 'very fond of reading plays' and fonder still of acting them – often (to his later shame) playing the women's parts.[13]

Wesley and Ingham had written from Georgia suggesting or half-suggesting that Whitefield should follow them, and he eventually made up his mind to go. Georgia was the brain-child of James Oglethorpe; it had been founded in 1732 out of public and private funds in order to give poor settlers a start with new land. Unfortunately, the land chosen south of the Savannah river was considered by the Spaniards as part of Florida, and they sent in armed scouting parties in 1736. The fact that Georgia was the frontier with Spain in an international friction that was soon to become war explains why Whitefield went to Georgia in the last days of 1737 in the Whitaker, which was being used as a transport for soldiers and their families.

Once aboard, Whitefield began to keep a journal. It was not a private diary; it was written for the information and edification of his friends and associates, one of whom took the liberty of publishing it. It was 'an account of what God has done for my soul since I left England', and we need to keep its audience in mind throughout. It is studded with exclamations and imprecations. 'Praise the Lord, O my soul!' 'May God give me a thankful heart!' 'What mercies have I received this week!' 'May God prosper the work of his hands!' 'Oh Drunkenness, what mischief thou hast done!' 'God give them a hearing ear, and an obedient heart!' Though written without vanity or pride, it is a triumphal record of a servant of the Lord, and it is not very easy to peer through the constant enthusiasm and discern what his fellow-passengers really thought of him.

But he must have been a dominating presence in that ship. He began at once to hold public prayers on deck, visit those who were sick, and catechize some of the younger soldiers. 'I was surprised they would submit to it.' Later he wrote that some of them 'answered most aptly, for which I distributed amongst them all something I knew would be agreeable. Oh! that I may catch them by a holy guile!'[14] On 24 January he noted that he had 'met with a little opposition', but his public prayers and preachings went from strength to strength. On Saturday, 4 February, for example, he notes that he took prayers in the great cabin in the morning, preached

13 These and other biographical details are from *a Short Account of God's Dealings*, 1740, ed. Iain Murray (London, 1960).

14 Whitefield, *George Whitefield's Journals*, 101 and 116.

twice to the soldiers 'as usual', and in the evening expounded the second lesson to 'the gentlemen' in the great cabin. The eternity of hell torments was the subject of his sermon to the soldiers on Wednesday, 8 February. He also performed marriage ceremonies, and he and an associate James Habersham (later president of Georgia) held reading classes for illiterate soldiers. At the end of March he was beginning to note 'more proofs of a thorough conversion being wrought in some in the ship', and he thought there was 'visible alteration' to be perceived through the whole ship; in the great cabin 'we talk of little else but God and Christ'.[15]

Whitefield constantly remarks on the help and encouragement that he received from both the captain of the ship and the military commander. And no wonder, for there was nothing whatsoever subversive in his practical Christianity. He was always on the side of obedience and submission. 'I took occasion, in my morning sermon, to exhort the soldiers to obey them that had the rule over them.' He particularly urged the women (there were sixteen of them) 'to be obedient to their own husbands, which they had lately been wanting in'.[16] There were some children on board and there are some unappealing entries in the journal about 'the benefit of breaking children's wills betimes'. A four-year-old-boy would not kneel and say his prayers, so Whitefield 'forced him down', and gave him 'several blows' until he had said the Lord's Prayer 'as well as could be expected'. Not unnaturally, at the time for evening prayers before Habersham, the child cried 'till he had said his too'. Whitefield took this as a sign of the success of his treatment, and wrote that the work of conversion would be much easier if the parents of children 'would but have resolution to break their wills thoroughly when young'.[17]

'I am never better than when I am on the full stretch for God', Whitefield wrote. It is very evident that on his return voyage to England in September from Charleston there was much less for him to do and that he had too much time for reflection. 'My sphere of action', he wrote, 'is now contracted into a very narrow compass'. For two days he was 'oppressed much in spirit'. It was a long and difficult voyage in very bad weather. Food ran short and Whitefield was unwell. He found his faith 'less lively', but 'blessed be God, though He slay me, yet will I put my trust in Him'.[18] His interpretation of the weather and their difficulties as heaven-sent was not always easy. During a bad storm on the voyage out he wrote that he had *endeavoured* to 'magnify God, for thus making His power to be known'. So on this awful journey home he writes that 'still God is pleased that the wind . . . should be contrary', and 'He has thought proper again to send us a contrary wind'. But after eight weeks he began to wonder whether the reason for their painful progress was that 'Satan

[15] *Ibid.*, 148. [16] *Ibid.*, 110 and 121. [17] *Ibid.*, 146. [18] *Ibid.*, 166 and 174.

hindered us. For I believe that it is he who is permitted to do this. ... O Satan, thou mayest toss me up and down ... but Jesus Christ is praying for me.'[19]

> My outward man sensibly decayeth, but the spiritual man, I trust, is renewed day by day. I have besought the Lord many times to send us a fair wind; but now I see He does not think fit to answer me. I am wholly resigned, knowing that His grace will be sufficient for me, and that His time is best.
>
> Whitefield, *George Whitefield's Journal*, 176.

The very next day they saw the coast of Ireland. On another prolonged transatlantic voyage he again felt the inaction a great strain. 'I never am so much tempted, as when confined on ship-board.' He wrote of 'many inward strugglings' and 'inexpressible agonies of soul'. But in 1741, at the end of a voyage back to England, he wrote as follows:

> This voyage has been a profitable voyage for my soul, because of my having had many opportunities for reading, meditation, and prayer. I cannot but adore the Providence of God in favouring me with such blessed retirements I have frequently enjoyed on the great waters.
>
> Whitefield, *George Whitefield's Journal*, 506.

Whitefield crossed the Atlantic thirteen times on his evangelical work, which extended far beyond Georgia into all the American colonies, and he died in Massachusetts in 1770, at the age of fifty-five. He had separated from Wesley on doctrinal grounds quite early on. Much of his life was spent on evangelical tours with punishing preaching schedules. His sermons were highly emotional and physically taxing. When advised to rest he said, 'I had rather wear out than rust out'. Surveying the reports of his sermons, Leslie Stephen thought that on the evidence of these 'tattered shreds of sensational rhetoric', the secret of Whitefield's success 'must have lain as much in the hearers as the orator'.[20]

## Robert Poole

Robert Poole, born in 1708, was a follower of Whitefield. He had studied medicine in London and in France, and was a physician at the Smallpox Hospital in London. He published a number of tracts under the name of Theophilus Philanthropos, as well as an account of a journey to France and Holland. It was for his own health, it would seem, that he paid his fare for a sea-journey in the Anna-Maria to Gibraltar and the West Indies in 1748. But he did not live to publish (or even, it would appear, to edit) his narrative, which came out in 1753 as *The Beneficent Bee: Or, Traveller's*

[19] *Ibid.*, 171 and 173.
[20] *History of English Thought in the Eighteenth Century* (London, 1876), XII, 103.

*Companion*. It is a journal which sets out with considerable self-confidence, and ends in pain and doubt.

Some of the entries are extremely pedestrian.

> We have been this Forenoon much incommoded, by great Plenty of Flies infesting the Cabin; which, though not very large, are very troublesome, and penetrating through the Stocking, much trouble one's Legs with their Stings.
>
> Poole, *Beneficent Bee*, 44.

His intention was not so much to record as to moralize and make spiritual use of what was happening. He constantly deplores the swearing that surrounded him. He made a fellow-passenger of his old pseudonym, Theophilus, and Theophilus is full of improving thoughts.

> We have been much becalm'd all this Afternoon; which, as it has put a stop to our Progress, it excites us to the Exercise of the Virtue of Patience. . . . Our Situation may now be compared to a barren Soul, in a sort of lifeless, useless State. . . . Oh! said *Theophilus*, that it might be his good Pleasure to come speedily, and shew himself gracious and merciful to us, granting us outward Wind and inward Grace . . .
>
> Poole, *Beneficent Bee*, 163–4.

To pass the time, Poole compiled for his reader's benefit forty-four rules of 'Polite Breeding'. The seventeenth is as follows:

> Polite Breeding forbids a Person's breaking Wind before Company, either upwards, by loud Belchings, if by any Means it can be prevented; but especially downwards, which must most carefully be avoided, however Necessity may require.
>
> Poole, *Beneficent Bee*, 85.

They had a very rough Atlantic crossing, and as the storms continued and fresh provisions gave out, there is much less moralizing from Poole and his alter-ego – 'being a good deal satiated with this tumbling, unsettled Situation'.

Poole recovered his judgemental poise in the West Indies, and recorded his disapproval of the ignorance, vice and profanity of the negroes, and their absence from divine service. But very soon there is a new note in his censoriousness. Noticing the well-dressed black 'kept Mistresses', he wrote that it was very wrong for men 'to chuse those for their companions in the Dark, which they are ashamed to be seen with in the Light'.[21] This remark may be partly against miscegenation, but it is also against racism and hypocrisy. He noted that although 'some Negroes are of a ready Wit and tractable Disposition' and could be introduced to Christianity, so far as their masters were concerned, 'the Labour of the Bodies of these poor Slaves will always be preferred to the Good of their Souls'.

[21] Poole, *Beneficent Bee*, 221.

The journal now begins to be haunted by the sight and sound of whipping. The slaves 'have no Instructor but the Whip and the Scourge, which, poor Wretches! is often exercised upon them in a very severe Manner'. 'Hardly a Day passes but the Noise thereof is sounding in one's Ears.' He describes the professional floggers, the jumpers, and their whips, in detail. When he was visiting a house the mistress prepared the tea and found the milk was spoilt. She leapt to the conclusion that her slaves were trying to poison her. Five or six were examined and denied the accusation. The jumper was sent for, with his 'long Whip', every stroke of which 'tares off the Surface of the Skin'. As one of the 'poor Wretches' was tied up, Poole intervened with the suggestion that they should test the milk. He managed to get a tame rabbit to consume some and it seemed to enjoy it. 'Thus I sav'd the Innocent from a severe Punishment.'

Poole travelled extensively through the islands, but though he dined with governors and leading officials, he was unwell, lonely and unhappy. He recorded as 'the most joyful Moment' since leaving London the receipt of letters from his friends there, 'but more especially from her, whom God has made the Companion of my Life'.[22] His increasing sympathy for the plight of the slaves is notable. In Antigua he found that a sale of Ibo slaves was heralded with flags flying and drums beating.

> I could not help being concerned to see my Fellow-Creatures thus attended, as Captives carried in Triumph, and conducted as Brutes to the Market for Sale; which, tho' not to be slaughtered like them, yet to render them perhaps far more wretched, by a Life of perpetual, cruel Slavery; and in which, by the great Inhumanity of some Masters, they are treated not as Fellow-Creatures, but worse than Beasts that perish.
>
> Poole, *Beneficent Bee*, 313.

The insistence, twice in this disordered sentence, that these African slaves were his fellow-creatures marks a great change in Poole from the pharisaical tone of the journal's beginning. However, he developed a fever in travelling between the islands, and, left to himself by the crew, he was at one point too ill to disembark. Eventually he got ashore and found some kind of a lodging 'in a place where Humanity is almost a Stranger, and where all proper Care is wanting'.[23] In the last entry he was feeling better and thanked God for his improvement, but the journal ends abruptly, giving no indication of how he got back to England. According to the *Dictionary of National Biography*, he died in Islington in 1752.

[22] *Ibid.*, 297. [23] *Ibid.*, 387.

## Henry Fielding

Henry Fielding, aged forty-seven, boarded a ship for Lisbon in June 1754, accompanied by his second wife and her companion, his eldest daughter and two servants. He was a very sick man, his body distended with dropsy, and in his own opinion, and in the opinion of others, he had not long to live. In fact he died in Portugal two months after the end of his voyage. When his ship, the Queen of Portugal, was in the Downs after leaving the Thames, Fielding found himself very much on his own; the women had retired feeling sea-sick and the other passengers were a fourteen-year-old boy and a Portuguese priest who spoke no English. It was at this time, he wrote, that he had 'the first serious thought . . . of enrolling myself among the voyage-writers'. The result, 'the production of the most disagreeable hours which ever haunted the author',[24] was *The Journal of a Voyage to Lisbon*, published posthumously in 1755.[25]

Strikingly, the great novelist turns against fiction. In the preface he argues that the best kind of travel-writing requires talent of the highest order, and it is not surprising that it is rarely found. What *is* surprising is that this genre alone 'should be overlooked by all men of great genius and erudition, and delivered up to the Goths and Vandals as their lawful property'.

> For my part, I must confess, I should have honoured and loved Homer more, had he written a true history of his own times in humble prose, than those noble poems that have so justly collected the praise of all ages; for though I read these with more admiration and astonishment, I still read Herodotus, Thucydides and Xenophon, with more amusement and more satisfaction.
>
> Fielding, *The Journal of a Voyage to Lisbon*, 173–5 (Preface).

Some would have it that Homer is in fact a voyage-writer, but the Odyssey 'and all of that kind' are to voyage-writing 'what romance is to true history, the former being the confounder and corrupter of the latter'.

In his conversion from instructive fiction to philosophic history, it is as though a very small taste of the sea has led Fielding to anticipate the spirit of Conrad, who spent the last thirty years of his life re-examining what had happened to him at sea in his younger manhood, and turning that earlier experience into myth. His whole outlook darkened by the misery of his ill-health and the expectation of death, by the additional confinement of the ship and his dislike of the company it forced upon him, Fielding began to see around him a new basic in humankind. Claude Rawson wrote of the

[24] Fielding, *The Journal of a Voyage to Lisbon*, 293 (2 August).

[25] Very curiously, two distinct versions were put out by the same publisher almost simultaneously. The shorter version, probably meant to supersede the other, may have been revised by Fielding's brother John. I quote from the fuller version, as given in vol. X of Fielding's complete works (1784).

*Journal* demonstrating the 'sense of pained betrayal' and 'the altogether less confident note' in Fielding's later writings.[26] I should put it rather more positively; the deep pessimism of the *Journal* (allowing for the qualification I shall later make) conveys to me the sense of discovery (however unwanted) more than the sense of loss.

All the incidents and all the people are turned into myth. Travel itself (in a remarkable passage) becomes a symbol of fallen humanity.[27] He had thought of including in his work a history of travel, until he heard of the discovery of 'a young antiquarian' that 'the first man was a traveller'; 'he and his family were scarce settled in Paradise before they disliked their own home, and became passengers to another place'.[28] This discovery greatly shortened his labours.

Perhaps the best-known passage of the *Journal* (it is discussed by Rawson) is the account of boarding the ship in the Thames, of how the helpless Fielding, being carried into a wherry and hoisted aboard, 'ran the gauntlope' through rows of sailors and watermen, 'few of whom failed of paying their compliments to me, by all manner of insults and jests on my misery'. This, wrote Fielding, 'was a lively picture of that cruelty and inhumanity, in the nature of men, which I have often contemplated with concern'. Such licentiousness 'never shews itself in men who are polished and refined', who have learned to 'purge away that malevolence of disposition, of which, at our birth, we partake in common with the savage creation'.[29] The verb 'purge away' seems to do combat with 'never shews itself'. The question is whether the basic malevolence is got rid of by civilized people or only covered up by them.

Running the gauntlope[30] through jeering watermen is a frightening image of leaving England, but it is more than that. It is an image of taking leave of mankind, as the author enters the boat to ferry him across the Styx. Charon is the captain of the Queen of Portugal (Richard Veal, though Fielding never names him). He is grotesque indeed; seventy years old, deaf, a cumbersome sword trailing by his side as testimony of former naval dignity, amorous enough to offer marriage to the Fieldings' maidservant, perpetually promising the fair wind that never arrives, and an arrogant despot in 'his little wooden world'. However, the journey is not a descent into the underworld. It is a kind of fortuitous joke that they can never leave England. The persistent contrary south-west wind keeps them groping their way along the south coast, putting in to haven after haven. After thirty-seven days and ninety-four pages of the journal the ship is still in English waters; then, eleven days and fifteen pages later – they are in

26 Rawson, *Henry Fielding and the Augustan Ideal under Stress*, 55.

27 Compare pp. 117–18. Perhaps George Forster had read Fielding as well as Seneca.

28 Fielding, *The Journal of a Voyage to Lisbon*, 201 (27 June).

29 *Ibid.*, 197 (26 June).

30 Properly so; 'gauntlet' is a later corruption.

Lisbon. So, this refocusing of the eyes upon human nature is a ship-board perspective of the old scene, as the dying man makes his last journey. The Isle of Wight landlady, the ill-humoured Mrs Francis (see Plate 9), is, like the captain, a grotesque inhabitant of Fielding's new world, but she belongs absolutely to old England, a lady of the land.

A main strategy is to contrast those who live by the sea with people of the land. For example, the boatmen of Deal, who regard passengers in distress as heaven-sent boons to increase their profits, make him wonder whether 'men, who live on the sea-shore, are of an amphibious kind, and do not entirely partake of human nature'. He wonders why it is that 'sailors in general should, of all others, think themselves entirely discharged from the common bands of humanity, and should seem to glory in the language and behaviour of savages!' And even naval officers – perhaps especially naval officers – consider themselves 'entirely free from all those rules of decency and civility, which direct and restrain the conduct of the members of a society on shore'.[31] This last takes us right into Conrad territory, with Marlow telling his listeners on the yacht in the Thames that if it were not for the policeman at the end of the street and the whispering of public opinion they would be capable of doing what Kurtz has done.

The society of the sea strikes the indignant landsman Fielding as a contravention of the society he is accustomed to, whose understood structure of law he as a magistrate had been responsible for enforcing. But the perverted maritime society is in fact a true mirror of normal society. It is therefore a mock conclusion that Fielding reaches, that 'all human flesh is not the same flesh, but that there is one kind of flesh of landmen, and another of seamen'.[32] Civil society appears to be usurped by the artificial society of the ship, reigned over by its petty tyrant, whose will is law. But it is not only in ships but in stage coaches in which the traveller is the victim of arbitrary despotism, having 'no more power over his own will, than an Asiatic slave, or an English wife'. *Verb. sap.* Insofar as we live in society, we are all travellers. A fleet at Spithead, Fielding notes, is a beautiful sight –

> And what, it may be said, are these men of war, which seem so delightful an object to our eyes? Are they not alike the support of tyranny, and oppression of innocence, carrying with them desolation and ruin wherever their masters please to send them?
>
> Fielding, *The Journal of a Voyage to Lisbon*, 255 (23 July).

In the passage about the 'gauntlope', and the malevolence of human nature which it revealed, Fielding wrote emphatically, 'This may be said, and this is all that can be said'. What that 'all' may be can be variously expressed. At one level, the journal is a baleful litany of discomfort, the

[31] Fielding *The Journal of a Voyage to Lisbon*, 220, 213 and 222 (4 July, 30 June and 5 July).
[32] *Ibid.*, 266 (26 July).

irritated outcry of a helpless and frustrated person. At another level, it is a sombre life-as-journey narrative informed with deep pessimism about human nature and civil society. But, at a third level, it is very amusing. The exasperated victim, physically unable to escape from the importunities and vulgarity of Mrs Francis and the captain, can still see his tormenters as grotesquely funny. Perhaps there is something of the malevolence of human nature in the way he laughs at them, but more certainly the humour saves the narrative from what might very well be despair. It is a saving grace.

## Elizabeth Justice

Fielding is one of the great literary artists of the eighteenth century; what is particularly interesting about the narrative of Elizabeth Justice is its complete artlessness. She gives her reason for enrolling herself among the voyage-writers in the introduction of her *Voyage to Russia*, published in York in 1739. She apologizes 'for my Presumption in attempting to engage in a WORK, which requires a more elegant and superior Hand to compleat, than any Female Abilities can pretend to'.

> The Occasion of my going into *Russia* was owing to my Husband, who was to have pay'd me an Annuity of Twenty Five Pounds a Year: Which he omitting to pay for Five Years, and a Quarter; I then ... was oblig'd ... to go to Law; and I did obtain a Verdict in my Favour.
>
> Justice, *A Voyage to Russia*, ii.

Her husband, however, threatened to proceed in Chancery against her if she did not pay the legal costs of the action. She gave in, and had to use up the annuity and get into debt to pay the costs. 'I resolv'd to go abroad to acquire a Support 'till my Creditors were satisfied.' A friend of hers, on her way back to Russia, knew of a Mr and Mrs Evans in St Petersburg who needed a governess for their three daughters. This was 1734. She stayed in Russia for three years, and then had to return because she learned that her husband was still not paying the annuity, and her own children needed her presence. Her husband's default has caused her, she writes, 'to go through great Hardships, which put me upon publishing this Performance'. She thanks her 215 subscribers, who include a 'Dr Johnson' and a 'Mrs Nutty Tankard'.

Mrs Justice sailed to St Petersburg in 'the Ship, call'd *The* PETERSBURGH *Frigat*; the Commander, Captain John Nansum'. The only other passengers were Mrs Trott and her daughter. I take Mrs Trott to be the friend who told her about the Evanses; her husband was a jeweller in St Petersburg (presumably a merchant). Her account of the two-month voyage via the Baltic qualifies her for a character in a Fielding novel.

Becalmed off Orford, they go ashore and drink tea with the clergyman and his lady. And she remembers very well, though as she says it is five years ago, that that night they had for dinner 'cold Leg of Lamb, Lobsters, and a Dish of Pease'. She was very much impressed with her accommodation aboard. The cabin, she writes –

> was exceeding neat, and very genteely furnished with a rich Crimson Damask; and very handsome China, Glass, and Sconces, with gilt Frames: the Mouldings of the Wainscot were gilt with Gold; and the Tea Things were in the same Order, as if we had been at land.
>
> Justice, *A Voyage to Russia*, 3.

All Sundays were observed 'in as solemn a Manner as the Place would permit'. The sailors 'were shav'd, and very clean', and 'the People of the Watch employed themselves in reading good Books'. By contrast, the soldiers exercising at Elsinore were 'little dirty Fellows'. She gives some local colour with the cries of the captain and the mate to the helmsman, 'Steady, my Lad, Steady!', and (in a storm), 'nothing but *Hard a Lee!*, and *Hard a Weather!*, an uncomfortable Command!'

On arrival at Kronstadt she was delighted to receive the hospitality of Admiral Gordon, 'a *Scotch* Gentleman'. 'He has a Daughter, who marry'd Sir *Henry Sterling*. They are bless'd with all the Perfections to be wish'd for; particularly Affability, which in Persons of their Rank is a great Beauty.' Her account of life in the large English community at St Petersburg is amusingly full of negatives and disclaimers. Some say the water works at the Imperial Palace exceed those of Versailles, but as she has not been to Versailles she can only say they are 'so fine, as they are beyond my Capacity to give a Description of'. The palace itself was 'very magnificent, but her Majesty being there, I did not see the Inside of it'. She describes travelling wagons: 'this is what I have been told; for I never went a Journey while I was there'. 'As to their Christenings, I never was at one: But, by what I have been told. . . .' 'I was not at one of their Weddings, but I saw Two or Three that were going to be married.' 'The Cathedral Church, I was told, was very magnificently adorned; but I was never in it.'[33]

It is sad. A sad life and a sad realization of her lack of talent – which she attributed to her gender. 'I think it is not possible for a Woman to paint the various Seasons of the Year in their proper Colours.'[34] Her return voyage she deals with quite briefly, though it too was long – over seven weeks. She was glad to find there were three ladies as fellow-passengers, but she soon found them a liability, 'they were so much frightened'. I have no later information on Elizabeth Justice.

[33] Justice, *A Voyage to Russia*, 10, 20, 27–8 and 37. [34] *Ibid.*, 41.

## Janet Schaw

There was no financial pressure on Janet Schaw, much better connected than Elizabeth Justice, to publish the narrative of her voyage to the West Indies and South Carolina in 1774–5. She had a considerable literary talent, but she posted off her journal in instalments to her relations in Scotland, and it was not published until 1921, when it appeared, edited by Evangeline and Charles Andrews, under the not very happy title of *Journal of a Lady of Quality*.

She was travelling with one brother, who was to become a customs official at St Kitts, to visit another brother, who was an official in North Carolina. She was in charge of the three Rutherfurd children who had been sent back to Scotland from the Carolinas seven years previously to be educated in Scotland. (The eldest, eighteen-year-old Fanny, notably proved the success of the scheme by reading Lord Kames's *Elements of Criticism* during a storm.) The ship was the Jamaica Packet (so called) sailing from the Firth of Forth round the north of Scotland.

Janet had understood that she and her party were the only passengers. It was a great shock to her when she came on deck for the first time after sailing to find 'the deck covered with people of all ages, from three weeks old to three score, men, women, children and suckling infants'. 'Never did my eyes behold so wretched, so disgusting a sight. They looked like a cargo of Dean Swift's Yahoos newly caught.' The captain explained that they were a company of emigrants, whom the ship's owner had asked him to take on board and keep them under hatches until they were safely at sea.

> I am resolved no more to encounter these wretched human beings. . . . Indeed you never beheld any thing like them. . . . The smell which came from the hole, where they had been confined, was sufficient to raise a plague aboard. I am besides not a little afraid, they may bestow upon me some of their live-stock, for I make no doubt they have brought thousands along with them. Faugh! let me not think of it; it affects my stomach more than this smooth sailing Vessel, or this shocking rough Sea, in which we are tumbling about so, that I can hardly hold the pen.
>
> Schaw, *Journal of a Lady of Quality*, 30.

However, when they have the Orkneys in sight (the captain has some mysterious score to settle at Fair Isle), Janet sees the emigrants crowding to the side of the ship, gazing at the islands. She writes that she had been too upset to enquire who these people were, 'but now find they are a company of hapless exiles, from the Islands we have just passed, forced by the hand of oppression from their native land'.

These people had been ejected by the new proprietor of their island. Janet Schaw's compassion was as great as her earlier disgust. 'Where are now the cargo of Yahoos?' She resolved to do 'all in my power to alleviate their misfortunes', which have sprung from 'the guilt and folly of others'.

She approached them, befriended a young mother, listened to their stories.[35] All communication ended, however, with an appalling Atlantic storm which lasted for days and ended with the ship broaching to, heeling over on her beam ends, and losing her masts. For twelve days Janet Schaw was unable to write her journal – the last entry, as the storm gathered strength, ending simply, 'Thy will be done'. She then wrote one of the most brilliant descriptions I know of a storm at sea. It is far too long to quote. The description of the awful conditions are punctuated with vivid touches, such as the little boy crying because he thought God would not be able to fish him out of the ocean if he drowned, Fanny Rutherfurd's harpsichord sliding across the deck, and 'the last of our poultry, a poor duck, squeezed as flat as a pancake'.

This lady of quality, for whom the voyage was a major learning experience, thought of others as much as herself. She noticed the sailors' hands raw with pulling on the ropes, and their clothes permanently wet – with nowhere to dry them because the owner had given so much space below decks to the emigrants and 'hard loading'. As for the emigrants, they were battened down under hatches during the whole period of the storm, except for one young married woman who had a miscarriage. Her husband, 'absolutely distracted, forced up the hatch, and carried her in his arms on deck, which saved her life'. She learned that for nine days the emigrant party were unable to lie down because of the water which had come into the hold, and had to live on raw potatoes and mouldy biscuit. (The food provided for them was in any event quite insufficient.) She learned this as they emerged when the storm ceased and jury-masts were being rigged. She also learned that with travelling from the Clyde to the Forth in search of a ship they had used up much of their financial resources and had been forced to bind themselves as indentured servants to the owner of the Jamaica Packet in order to pay for their passages – or, as Janet Schaw puts it, 'bound themselves slaves for a certain number of years'. Moreover, the wooden chests in which their worldly belongings were stowed were under water for fifteen days; the chests came apart and their contents were ruined or lost.[36]

Janet Schaw enjoyed the West Indies, but America was in turmoil with the gathering revolt of the colonies. She was deeply shocked by the activism of the 'rebels'. Her correspondent was urging her to return before things got worse. Her brother Alexander was returning with despatches for the British government, and in November 1775 she went back with him – taking back also the Rutherfurd children she had brought out!

[35] Schaw, *Journal of a Lady of Quality*, 33–7. [36] *Ibid.*, 42–55.

## Mary Wollstonecraft, and others

Oversea travel-narratives by women often have too little to say about the sea-journey to justify their inclusion here. Jemima Kindersley, for example, an army widow, published *Letters from the Island of Teneriffe* (etc) in 1777; all she has to say about travelling from Tenerife to Brazil is that it was a 'long, dangerous, and uncomfortable voyage'. Most of her book is in fact about India, through which she travelled extensively. Maria Riddell was fortunate in having the assistance of Robert Burns in getting her little book of travels and natural history published, *Voyages to the Madeira, and Leeward Caribbean Isles: with Sketches of the Natural History of these Islands* (Edinburgh, 1792). She went out to the West Indies in 1788 as a sixteen-year-old with her father, William Woodley, who had inherited an estate in Antigua and had been governor of the Leeward Islands. She married a widower estate-owner in St Kitts in 1790, and they returned to an estate they purchased in Scotland in 1792.[37] She writes about flying fish and a luminous sea ('sailing through an ocean of living fire'), about being chased by 'an Algerine' (a pirate), and hitting a coral reef. Most of her little book reproduces her notes on natural history, in which the plants are 'placed alphabetically according to the Linnaean names'. (Another tribute to Scottish education for girls.)

Mary Ann Parker's *Voyage Round the World in the Gorgon Man of War* was published in 1795, 'for the advantage of a numerous family'. Her husband, captain of the Gorgon, had died of yellow fever. John Parker had been commissioned to take the Gorgon to New South Wales with a new corps of soldiers for the convict colony, as well as Gidley King, who was returning to become the new governor of the infamous Norfolk Island. He asked his wife to come with him, and she had just a fortnight to decide and make all her arrangements. It was a fairly unadventurous voyage to Cape Town but she could never get used to the rolling and pitching of the ship, and rough weather was almost unendurable. She describes the social engagements at Cape Town in considerable detail. When she reached New South Wales, she noted the awful condition of the convicts being brought out in the transports; 'the poor miserable objects that were landed died in great numbers'. Her indignant husband visited the hospital and told her of 'mere skeletons of men', the dying lying by the dead. It made him shudder, she said, to reflect that 'this kind of human misery' would continue 'while the present method of transporting these miserable wretches is pursued'.[38] She is one of the few people to say good things about the aborigines.

37 Biographical details from Gladstone, *Maria Riddell*.

38 Parker, *A Voyage Round the World in the Gorgon Man of War*, 72.

They travelled back via Cape Horn, running into very cold weather and icebergs – with heating for the cabins being provided by 'hot shot'. At the Cape of Good Hope again, they took on board Captain Edwards, making his way home after the wreck of the Pandora (see p. 136). She notes that he had with him 'the convicts ... who had escaped from Port Jackson', though she does not name the famous escapee Mary Bryant, Boswell's 'Girl from Botany Bay'. [39] She does not mention that Captain Edwards also had with him some closely guarded members of the crew of the Bounty.

The most romantic story of a woman passenger is that of Elizabeth Wynne. Her parents, with their daughters and a large entourage, had been moving around Europe trying to keep out of Napoleon's way. But in Florence, in June 1796, they were forced to flee before the advancing French army, and at Leghorn were taken on board the frigate Inconstant, commanded by Captain Thomas Fremantle. The eighteen-year-old Elizabeth, or Betsey, was delighted with the comfort of the ship and deeply impressed by the captain. She wrote in her diary: 'How kind and amiable Captain Fremantle is. He pleases me more than any man I have yet seen. Not handsome, but there is something pleasing in his countenance and his fiery black eyes are quite captivating.'[40] Apparently attraction was mutual. They met at intervals during the next weeks as Fremantle pursued his duties in the Mediterranean and the Wynnes were guests in other ships while they awaited repatriation. Off Elba, Fremantle discreetly made his feelings known, and off Toulon he gave Betsey a ring. 'We parted with a broken heart.' Her parents would have preferred her to marry Captain Foley of the Britannia, who was wealthier. But she and Thomas were married in Naples with Sir William and Lady Hamilton in attendance. Betsey, an excellent sailor, then accompanied her husband as he played his part in the naval war.

*Sunday, April 30th* [1797]. A foul wind all day it had all the appearance of blowing hard in the night. Fremantle went on board with Admiral Nelson and I slept alone in the cabin all night, the first night I have slept alone since I have been married, did not like it.

Wynne, *The Wynne Diaries*, II, 176.

She was present at the blockade of Cadiz, and the disastrous failure of the attack on Tenerife, in which Nelson lost his arm, and her husband was badly wounded, also in the arm.

Mary Wollstonecraft's *Letters Written during a Short Residence in Sweden, Norway and Denmark* (1796) is hardly a voyage-narrative; passages relating to the sea occupy only a few pages in the first and the eleventh letters. But in terms of quality the little she has to say is as good as anything else in this

[39] Hughes, *The Fatal Shore*, 208. [40] Wynne, *The Wynne Diaries*, II, 98.

chapter. She made her journey and wrote her account of it between two attempts at suicide following the wreck of her relationship with the unfaithful Gilbert Imlay. In the introduction to his excellent Penguin Classics edition, Richard Holmes explains the extraordinary mission Mary Wollstonecraft was on. She was travelling on Imlay's behalf to Sweden and Norway to see what could be recovered of a ship and its cargo of silver which Imlay had smuggled out of France and which had vanished in the Baltic. Mary Wollstonecraft never mentions the nature of her mission in the *Letters*, nor the ostensible recipient of the letters (Imlay), which were written with publication in view. This absence of context gives her opening sentence a dark cryptic power:

> Eleven days of weariness on board a vessel not intended for the accommodation of passengers have so exhausted my spirits, to say nothing of the other causes, with which you are already sufficiently acquainted, that it is with some difficulty I adhere to my determination of giving you my observations, as I travel through new scenes, whilst warmed with the impression they have made on me.
>
> Wollstonecraft, *Letters*, 1.

The captain has been unable to put in to Arendal or Gothenburg to let his passenger off, and they have brought-to off the Swedish coast. The impatient Mary coaxes the sailors to row her ashore, where she transfers to a boat belonging to the chief pilot of the district, who looks after her and sets her on her way. We realize on the second page that she has a companion, a timid one, Marguerite, but we have several pages to go, and have seen her climb the rocks to view the departing ship with the lieutenant's telescope, before we realize that she also has an infant with her, 'my babe', the little Fanny Imlay.

All is energy, independence, self-sufficiency; comment is abrupt and caustic. 'The men stand up for the dignity of man, by oppressing the women.'[41] It is of course, as she admits disapprovingly in the Advertisement, a work of sensibility. Letter Eleven gives a quite remarkable claustrophobic account of a journey by boat along a section of the Norwegian coast. 'The view of this wild coast, as we sailed along it, afforded me a continual subject for meditation.' She meditated on 'the future improvement of the world', and the time when the world would be 'so completely peopled, as to render it necessary to inhabit every spot; yes; these bleak shores'. And then she 'pictured the state of man when the earth could no longer support him'. She 'became really distressed. ... The images fastened on me, and the world appeared a vast prison. I was soon to be in a smaller one – for no other name can I give to Risør.' Malthus yields to Piranesi. She describes the 'two hundred houses crowded together' as a bastille, shutting out 'all that opens the understanding, or

41 Wollstonecraft, *Letters*, 27.

enlarges the heart'. She felt confined and stifled between the 'tremendous bulwarks' of the cliffs and the 'boundless waste of water', and shuddered at the thought of having to remain there, 'in the solitude of ignorance', among mean-spirited inhabitants, who 'rest shut up . . . smoking, drinking brandy, and driving bargains'. It was a little better when she went out in a boat, climbed the rocks and listened to the echoing of a French horn – making her think she was on 'Shakespeare's magic island'. But she returned 'to be shut up in a warm room, only to view the vast shadows of the rocks extending on the slumbering waves'. She found her return to Helgeroa 'a sort of emancipation'.[42]

[42] *Ibid.*, 132–41.

# 10

# Autobiographies

As I am the Eldest of his four Children, my Father had a particular Regard to my Education, which he committed to the Care of Dr. *Wilding*, Head Master of the Free-school at *Sherborne*, founded by King *Edward* the Sixth; where, after I had passed through the usual Classes in *Latin* and *Greek*, he bound me Apprentice to Mr. *James Down*, Surgeon, at *Marn-hill*, in the aforesaid County.

This is from the opening page of *A Narrative of the very Extraordinary Adventures and Sufferings of Mr. William Wills, Late Surgeon on Board the Durrington Indiaman* (1751). One might be encouraged to think that the life-stories of real voyagers in the eighteenth century will be as good as those of the fictional ones. Unfortunately that is not the case. Most of the seamen who tried their hands at autobiography could manage a good beginning, but what happens after that is often disappointing – as it certainly is with William Wills, who has a tedious story to tell, full of recrimination and self-justification, about his relationship with a woman passenger at Madagascar and his quarrel with his captain.

It is ironic that Defoe, ruthlessly pillaging genuine accounts of life at sea to create his wholly inauthentic *Robinson Crusoe* and *Captain Singleton*, should have created a model of autobiography which taught nothing to English seamen aspiring to tell the story of their lives. The story of the voyage was the literary achievement of the real voyager, outclassing Defoe's effort in that genre, *A New Voyage Round the World* (1725). But in autobiography, fiction is supreme. The authentic autobiography is in general a late development; a number of the life-stories I shall be talking about look back at the eighteenth century from old age in the nineteenth. Dampier, of course, like a great many of his predecessors, has a strong autobiographical input, and indeed the success of the story of the voyage can depend on the way personal presence is handled.[1] But the sailor's life-story as such is an undeveloped genre, and those that exist, early or

[1] P. G. Adams has discussed the importance of the first-person travel narrative in the development of real and fictional autobiography in his chapter, 'The narrator' in *Travel Literature and the Evolution of the Novel*.

late, are usually clumsy compilations. So far as publication goes, it is an interesting question whether there was a lack of supply or a lack of demand. Probably both; certainly publishers were not fighting for copy. The narratives of John Cremer, Samuel Kelly and Jacob Nagle all remained unpublished until the twentieth century.

Nathaniel Uring's life-story begins well, too.

> My Parents were Shop-Keepers at *Walsingham* in the County of Norfolk, the Place of my Birth. My Father us'd the Sea until he was about Twenty Five Years of Age, and soon after married in that Town, where he was likewise born. I remaining at Home until I was about Fourteen Years old, and often hearing him make Relations of his Travels into the several Parts of the World with great Delight, it gave me a strong Desire to see those Countries; and tho' several Proposals had been made for my being bound Apprentice at *London* to some Trade, it was at last concluded to send me to Sea, that suiting most with my Inclinations; and I was accordingly sent to *London*, and put under the Care of a Relation, who had part of several Vessels, and traded abroad.
>
> Uring, *A History of the Voyages and Travels*, 1.

Uring's history as it develops is no better than any of the others. It is, however, important in that it is early, that it was published, and that it set itself up against the fictitious life-story – presumably with Defoe in mind. *A History of the Voyages and Travels of Capt. Nathaniel Uring* was published in 1726, with a second edition in 1727. The Advertisement to the Reader speaks of the 'Falsities and Inventions' in 'the many Sea-Voyages and Travels lately published by Persons unknown, which are all made Stories, on purpose to impose on the World, and to get Money'. (The life and adventures of Robinson Crusoe, 'Written by Himself', had appeared in 1719, and those of Captain Singleton in 1720). Uring was forty-four when he wrote his *History*. It was his second publishing venture; the year before, he had published an account of his troubled few months as Deputy Governor of St Lucia in the Windward Islands, which ended with the island being yielded to the French. The *History* is a great wad of reminiscences about his early years at sea, told in remorseless detail with almost no sense of the relative importance or interest of the various incidents. There is plenty of valuable material, such as the material on slaving already discussed in Chapter 8, but it has to be prised out of the block.

Veracity and authenticity are constant problems in the autobiographies of sailors. Veracity is after all not expected; one has to read in a constant state of sympathetic suspicion. Truth is squashed out of shape by all the expected pressures; chiefly the desire to impress, the need to think well of oneself, and the failure of memory. One expects distortion, and hopes one's judgement of what is true and what is false is not wholly fallible. Francis Bergh inspires great confidence in his honesty, but I am extremely uneasy about his account of spending 270 days cast away on a desert island with his dog Nero. The meticulous editing of Jacob Nagle's reminiscences by John Dann provides an extremely useful and cautionary demonstration of the mistakes, confusions and omissions which can be made in an author's recollections of a long life at sea.

Authenticity is a different matter. Although in my judgement there are no hoaxes among the autobiographies discussed in this chapter, there are difficult questions about ghosting and editorial intervention in each. It would be hard to think that the three before-the-mast seamen who published their own reminiscences, Francis Bergh, John Roach and William Spavens, did not seek and get some kind of assistance, even though what we have must basically be what they themselves wrote. Roach's third edition, however, published much later than its predecessors, was rewritten for him by his compassionate well-wishers, whose suppressions and additions are easily detectable. (See above, p. 151.) Bergh's narrative was first serialized in *Household Words* in 1851. 'We present it to our readers in the old man's own words. We may sometimes omit a few passages, and may sometimes alter his orthography, but we shall in no other respect interpose between him and the homely truth of his narrative.'[2] The missing passages can be restored from the book-publication (Gosport, 1852), but this edition contains some cautious revisions following the outrage of a banker who had supposed himself libelled in the serialized version.

John Nicol's *Life and Adventures* was published in 1822, with a prefatory note explaining to the public why 'an unlettered individual, at the advanced age of sixty-seven years, should sit down to give them a narrative of his life'. However, there is a postscript at the end of the book by 'the Editor', J. H. (John Howell), who says that having met the feeble and destitute old sailor, 'I thought of taking down a Narrative of his Life, from his own mouth. This I have done, as nearly as I could, in his own words.' The autobiography of John Cremer, *Ramblin' Jack*, was first published in 1936 from a manuscript preserved by his family but lacking quite a number of pages torn out at some point presumably because of their frankness. Samuel Kelly's autobiography, also published in the twentieth century from a privately held manuscript, has been cut down from its 300,000 words to 100,000. Not having seen the original, I cannot say how the editing has affected the spirit of the narrative.

George Walker's *Voyages and Cruises* (1760) offers a fascinating problem in establishing authorship, though its authenticity is not in doubt. Walker was a renowned privateer captain during the War of Jenkins' Ear (1740–8), and the book is full of information about his curious profession, by means of which the crews, the captains, and above all the business men who owned and fitted out the freelance but officially authorized fighting-

[2] Bergh, *The Story of a Sailor's Life*, 211.

ships made money out of war. Walker was ruined by the ending of hostilities and the financial malpractices of his employers, and spent four years in the King's Bench Prison as a bankrupt. The book was written as he struggled to re-establish himself as a trading captain.

In the introduction (unaccountably omitted from the 1928 reprint), the writer, calling himself 'the compiler of the following transactions', says that he has 'had the honour, for such I shall ever deem it, of having been with him [Captain Walker] on most of the cruises he made'. During his imprisonment he had often asked Walker's leave to publish, 'but I have more than once been checked in my purpose, with these words, *Have patience my friend, the public does not yet make my cause its concern*'. But Walker relented at last, and 'after having delivered the copy to him for his perusal, I must own I received it back from his hands much dissatisfied at the severity of his corrections, he having run his pen thro' very near one third of it'. The various incidents in the book 'were at all times beheld and noted down by me', but when he was absent he had carefully gathered the particulars from those who were present.

This is the style of the compiler's narrative:

> We then drawing nearer, saw they were all ships of force: and tho' on our side every thing was prepared for engaging; yet I believe, not a man in the ship thought of coming to one, the Sheerness being quite astern. Mr. Walker then, perhaps perceiving some suspence among his officers, as waiting his determination, delivered himself to us, nearly in these words: 'Gentlemen, I hope ... [etc.]'
>
> Walker, *The Voyages and Cruises*, I, 125.

The compiler is a very shadowy figure, and we never learn what position he held in the ship. When there is an account of a mutiny which involves the officers, it is a great puzzle to know which side the narrator is on until we read: 'This was the only cruise in which I did not attend Mr. Walker, having been detained at Dartmouth thro' illness'.[3]

'My intent is to give the character of my friend.'[4] The character he provides for his friend is impossibly good. The whole book is a hagiography, written for the greater glory of Walker. At the very beginning we learn that he 'always prevailed to the intire satisfaction of his employers, and of the officers and people under him', and we hear of 'that calmness of temper, and presence of mind, so prevalent in him on all occasions'. Amidst this tumult of compliments, it is astonishing to read that 'I have several reasons to pass over in silence many passages of politeness and generosity between Mr. Walker and his prisoners', the last of which being that 'I know Mr. Walker is prepared to quarrel with me, whenever I say a word, that seems to throw any compliment on himself'.[5]

[3] Walker, *The Voyages and Cruises*, I, 239. [4] *Ibid.*, II, 88–9. [5] *Ibid.*, I, 135–6.

If we were to suggest that the author of *Voyages and Cruises* was George Walker himself, and that this secret sharer, the compiler, was entirely his own invention, this last remark would show a nice sense of humour, and the remark about the compiler's absence from one of the cruises would be an interesting credibility-device. But the sense of humour and the narrator's cunning belong, I feel sure, not to Walker nor to one who had accompanied him, but to a Grub-Street collaborator whom he employed to work on his own journals and reminiscences, reckoning no doubt not only that a professional could tell the tale better but also that it would be more seemly for someone else to present the desired puffed-up image of himself. So the collaborator set himself up as a fly on the bulkhead; but, cleverly, not on every bulkhead.

> Mr. Walker went on board the Boscawen; and had a private conference with the captain; but was never heard to throw any censure publicly on his behaviour: what was the result of the conference no one knew; but we were soon sensible, that it produced no great effect.
>
> Walker, *Voyages and Cruises*, I, 54–5.

In his introduction, the narrator wrote that he had 'ventured sometimes to deviate from the common tract of the subject' and feared that some 'severe readers' might feel he was 'running out of the way too near the borders of romance'. He is probably referring to two occasions when, in the true fashion of the novel of the time, he has set apart the story of someone encountered. There is a separate heading for 'The Story of Madam — —', a French lady picked up when her ship from Martinique was sunk. It begins superbly, with every trapping of the skilled fiction writer. The lady's husband was killed in the Marlburian wars after less than a year of marriage. She, miscarrying, had no child to remember him by – but a mysterious woman turned up with an infant who was the image of her husband and she claimed that the lady's husband was the father. . . . The story is ever so well told, but suddenly one realizes that it has the plotlessness of reality and is going nowhere. Even better is 'the Spanish Gentleman's story', an extremely romantic tale of a fortune misappropriated by a wicked guardian, whose daughter falls in love with the victim. Both these insets read like fiction, but I think that they are basically from Walker's huge store of reminiscences, dressed up by his collaborator to give those reminiscences some of the appeal of fiction. It is odd that we have travel-fiction trying to pose as the real thing and the real thing trying to look like fiction.

Walker's is a boastful and vainglorious life-story; so is that of Jeffrey Raigersfeld, Rear Admiral of the Red, and a hereditary baron of the Holy Roman Empire. His autobiography was privately printed around 1830, and reprinted in 1929. He constantly praises his own actions and comments on his presence of mind etc. Such prolonged self-esteem is not common. Others write of themselves as unsuccessful and unhappy. Of his first going to sea (in 1778, aged fourteen), Samuel Kelly wrote 'I may date the beginning of the troubles of life from this period'.[6] Though he became a captain, he seems to have been a gloomy, lonely and sanctimonious individual incapable of inspiring loyalty in his crew. The value of the long narrative of his life that he wrote in his early thirties is in the sharpness of his recollection of his boyhood misery, as the perpetual underdog, seasick on lookout in the violently swaying fore-topmast head, plagued by rats, carrying wood through the broken reeds of marshes with his bare feet badly cut, hauling on ropes throughout a North Atlantic voyage with a whitlow that grew more and more painful. We are in his debt for a description of the ship being hit by lightning.

> As I came more to my senses I saw the men about me in various postures, but one after another began to speak as a man just awakened from sleep. There was a great emanation of a sulphury scent in our apartment and a sound of bells ringing in my ears all the night after.
>
> Kelly, *Samuel Kelly*, 116–17.

John Cremer too ('Ramblin' Jack'), writing his memoirs at the age of sixty-eight, tells his story as a life of unhappiness, though he is not morose like Kelly. 'Had I not been so thoughtless and negligent all my life I might have made a fortin and lived happy in my old Age; but I have always been a wandering, unhappy Chap.'[7] He tells his story up to the age of twenty-five; fostered out to an aunt as an infant he grew up (by his own account) as a rough, unruly, almost uncontrollable child and was picked out by a naval-lieutenant uncle to be sent to sea to relieve his mother's difficulties; 'we four sons being all at home, he took a liking to me, being the most Mischeafyous and prety active'. After a terrifying initiation into the 'Wooden World' (his own phrase), he settled into a career of scrapes and misfortunes which would have made an excellent picaresque tale if it were not so clumsily handled. The fantastic home-made spelling is easily forgiven; but he had no gift whatsoever for telling his tale. There is a kind of interest in the very crudity of the narrative, and in the realization that this must have been the sort of material which faced the editor of many narratives which appeared in a much more readable form.

Francis Bergh had as little education as Cremer, and suffered much more serious misfortunes – and unlike Cremer he never made his way up the ladder of command, but the whole spirit of his reminiscences, as well as the style, is utterly different. His unresentful tone and philosophic submissiveness in the face of extraordinary disasters and injustice are remarkable. The fact that he survived is apparently enough for him to introduce

6 Kelly, *Samuel Kelly*, 19. 7 Cremer, *Ramblin' Jack: The Journal of John Cremer*, 39.

his story as an account of 'the wonderful mercies the Lord has shown me'. He seems wholly unaware of the implications of the phrase he regularly uses when things go wrong: 'Men appoints, and the Almighty disappoints'.

Life before the mast in the eighteenth century produced by far the most interesting autobiographical material, and that goes for those who like Kelly and Cremer went on to command. The lives of the seamen were dominated by the violence of officers and captains as well as the violence of the elements and of war. Punishment, always excessive and often quite undeserved, is an unremitting theme in their recollections. Admiral Raigersfeld is very unusual in believing that it did him good when, as a midshipman, 'four of us were tied up one after the other to the breech of one of the guns, and flogged upon our bare bottoms with a cat-o'-nine-tails'. At first he was indignant at such treatment, but came to recognize that in so doing 'Captain Collingwood did his duty by me, as well as his country'.[8] Both Bergh and the American Jacob Nagle, pressed into the Navy, tellingly record their shock at the severity of naval discipline. 'I cannot describe the cruelty of this manawar', wrote Nagle, 'but I will endeavour to give a short sketch. ... Nothing was to be done without nocking down and thrashing in every duty that was to be done.' (And so on.)[9] Bergh was pressed into a frigate, the Brilliant.

> The very first night, at reefing topsail, I saw seven men flogged for not being smart enough; and me never seeing a man flogged before, I wished myself back again in my little brig. ... Our usage on board of the 'Brilliant' was very cruel ... there was starting and flogging all day long.
>
> Bergh, *The Story of a Sailor's Life*, 214.

William Spavens (see Plate 10) has a similar story to tell of the severity of Captain Cummings of the Blandford after he too had been impressed, but his story has the unusual ending that Cummings was court-martialled for cruelty (among other things) and dismissed from the service. It should also be added that Nagle wrote admiringly of the determination of Arthur Phillip, Commander of the First Fleet to Botany Bay in 1787, to stamp out 'starting' by the officers of the Sirius. He 'told them all if he new any officer to strike a man on board, he would brake him amediately'.[10]

The awful ritual of a flogging through the fleet was witnessed by both John Nicol ('a dreadful sight') and Samuel Kelly ('a most cruel punishment. ... I was informed one of the men expired on the same day').[11] Nicol also tells a vivid story (no doubt with Howell's assistance) of Kennedy, a marine who had been put on board an American prize, the Jason of

[8] Raigersfeld, *The Life of a Sea Officer*, 36. [9] Nagle, *The Nagle Journal*, 58.
[10] Nagle, *The Nagle Journal*, 85.
[11] Nicol, *The Life and Adventures*, 35; Kelly, *Samuel Kelly*, 27.

Boston. He was 'an intelligent lad, and well-behaved . . . and had not been long from home'. He was a favourite with the surgeon of his ship: 'they used to be constantly together reading and acquiring information'. Kennedy was put as sentinel over the spirit-room of the prize, but he allowed some of the men to get at the spirits. He was court-martialled and sentenced to be hanged. The surgeon drew up a petition for his pardon, but in vain.

He was taken to the place of execution, the rope round his neck, the match was lit, the clergyman at his post; we were all aloft and upon deck to see him run up to the yard-arm, amidst the smoke of the gun, the signal of death. When every one looked for the command to fire, the admiral was pleased to pardon him. He was sent on board the Surprise, more like a corpse than a living man; he could scarce walk, and seemed indifferent to every thing on board, as if he knew not whether he was dead or alive. He continued thus for a long time, scarce speaking to anyone; he was free, and did no duty, and was the same on board as a passenger.

Nicol, *The Life and Adventures*, 31.

Many of the writers discussed in this chapter spent their whole lives in the shadow of the press-gang.[12] As is to be expected, Raigersfeld supported the system of impressment. 'Although the duty of pressing is not the most agreeable, yet the necessity of the case authorised it. ... All men who choose a sea-faring life well know before they enter upon it that they are liable to this law of necessity. ... No better or readier way of manning the national fleet upon emergency has yet occurred.'[13] Raigersfeld's line of argument is typical of contemporary commentators and later historians: Britain came out on top of its century-long imperial contention with France because it had the ships and the crews to man them; there were insufficient volunteers, and conscription raised many problems; the press was an unfortunate necessity. The iniquity of the system may well have been exaggerated by what Linda Colley calls 'the black legends that have gathered around press gangs',[14] but it is as well to listen closely to the voices of those whose involuntary service was so necessary for the building of the empire.

Francis Bergh, impressed as we noted above, took the opportunity of deserting during the heat of an action at Tenerife in 1798 and got aboard an American schooner. Later, apprehensive that a Hamburg-bound ship he was in might call at London, where he would again be pressed, and 'having such a great dread of an English man-of-war, on account of the usage I had received', he got ashore at Guernsey and joined a privateer. Over several months this provided him not only with protection from the

[12] There are useful accounts of the system of impressment in N. A. M. Rodger's *The Wooden World*, chap. 5, and (more briefly) in J. C. Dann's edition of Nagle's journal, chap. 7.

[13] Raigersfeld, *The Life of a Sea Officer*, 39–40.

[14] Colley, *Britons*, 65.

press but also £350 in wages and prize-money. On the strength of this, he left the sea, got married, took 'a little house in Vine Yard, close to Pickle Herring Stairs', and set up a shop in which his wife served while he worked on the wharfs. Unfortunately, his wife's stepmother, 'a woman greatly given to drink', who sponged on them, struck his wife during a row, and he ordered her out of the house. She went to the lieutenant of the press-gang and informed them of Bergh's being a seafaring man.

About half-past ten o'clock that same evening, just when I was going to shut my shop up, the press-gang came, and took me. . . . I had a scuffle for it before I was taken, for I knocked the first two down that came into my house; but I was soon overpowered, and was taken by force, and taken down to the boat which they had brought to Pickle Herring Stairs; and from there I was taken on board the 'Enterprise', which lay at Tower Hill Stairs, where I was put both legs in irons and my hands tied behind me; and there I laid till the morning.

He was put on board other ships and taken round to Spithead.

And now having come a little to myself, you may depend my feelings and my mind was none of the best. The chief thing that grieved me was thinking about my wife; for I knew she was about seven months gone in the family way.

He managed to write a letter to a friend, his landlord, Mr Bland, instructing him to draw money from his banker and get two substitutes for him. But he got no answer before the ship he was now in, the Albion, sailed for the East Indies.

I left England with a heavy heart, not having heard from my friends. I often thought that none of my letters had gone; and being very careless of myself, I gave way to all sorts of badness, gambling, drunkenness, cursing and swearing, which brought me continually into trouble.

It was four and a half years before he got back to London and learned that on the day after he was taken, his wife had died in childbirth, after premature labour from the shock of his arrest.[15]

In the first two editions of John Roach's narrative, published in 1783/4 after getting back, crippled, from thirteen years captivity in Central America, he makes absolutely no mention of the fact that he had been pressed into the Navy and had deserted. Fourteen years later, when he was sixty-two (and quite safe), friends brought out a third edition where this information was given. 'The service of His Majesty was far from being agreeable to Roach; and, with the feelings natural to a pressed man, he anxiously meditated his escape [etc].' Living in fear of being retaken (as must have been the case with Roach) comes out very clearly in Nicol's narrative, which has many details of his devices and stratagems at various

[15] Bergh, *The Story of a Sailor's Life*, 215–16 and 227.

times to avoid being pressed – not always successful. In 1801 he left the sea, like Bergh, and married, following his trade as a cooper in Queensferry. His prospects were good, 'and I was as happy as ever I had been in my life'. But 'the war broke out again, and the press-gang came in quest of me. I could no longer remain in Edinburgh and avoid them. My wife was like a distracted women, and gave me no rest until I sold off my stock in trade and the greater part of my furniture, and retired to the country. Even until I got that accomplished I dared not to sleep in my own house, as I had more than one call from the gang.'[16]

William Spavens, a pressed man himself, had to serve as many others did as a member of a press-gang. He has a strange story of capturing a ship's crew in a raid on Liverpool and being set on and stoned by an angry crowd of citizens. He too deserted, and had some narrow escapes from being retaken. Once he found himself in a carriage with a naval lieutenant, and once, looking in a bookshop in London, he found the first lieutenant of his old ship standing by him. 'He never before having seen me in long clothes, I supposed he did not know me. ... I met him again another day in East Smithfield with a press-gang in his rear.'[17]

For the seaman's life ashore Jacob Nagle is an excellent informant. His colourful but enormously long and congested narrative suggests a seaman of unusual courage, intelligence, capability and dignity – and not much false modesty. He writes of his shore-doings with natural pride. On his first visit to England he had gone up to London 'as the sailor says, "to see what o'clock it was"'. His young Canadian friend had his money and Nagle's own watch stolen by a prostitute in a 'nany house' and Nagle explains just how he got the goods back. On a much later visit to London another friend was similarly robbed, and Nagle gives a very long account, full of absorbing detail about public houses, brothels and prostitutes, of how once again he got the money back. The young prostitute, Liddy, was terrified and 'nearly fainting' with Nagle pretending he had a constable with him, but all gratitude when she found that Nagle had no intention of turning her in. She 'said I was the best friend she ever fell in with and said I had saived hur from the gallos or transportation'. A little later he spent the night with Liddy, and on leaving missed his money belt with 35 guineas sown up in it. 'Well, thinks I, Liddy had done me with all my nowingness.' But the belt was among the bedclothes. 'She asked me if I had mistrusted her. I said I could not tell till I return'd to see. She cried. I pittied her. I gave hur two guineas. She refused, and I made hur take it.'[18]

The last of Nagle's prostitute stories tells (rather sentimentally) of his being accosted in a pub by a girl who could not be more than thirteen. He

[16] Nicol, *The Life and Adventures*, 200. [17] Spavens, *The Seaman's Narrative*, 69.
[18] Nagle, *The Nagle Journal*, 71–2, 154–7 and 160.

went home with her and found her widowed mother, who said she was forced 'to do what could not be helped' and live off her daughter's earnings. Nagle bought them a good dinner and went to bed with the girl. 'When she pulled her gown off, which was clean and deasent, . . . her shift was nothing but rags.' In the morning Nagle gave the girl half a guinea and the old woman a guinea, 'and bid them both good morning. I always thought I never done a better job in my life for the good of my own soul.'[19]

There is a story of a very different order about a seaman's sex-life in John Nicol's moving account of the voyage of the female convict ship, the Lady Juliana, to Botany Bay with the Second Fleet, and of his romantic liaison with one of the convicts, Sarah Whitlam.

> When we were fairly out at sea, every man on board took a wife from among the convicts, they nothing loath. The girl with whom I lived, for I was as bad in this point as the others, was named Sarah Whitelam. She was a native of Lincoln, a girl of a modest reserved turn, as kind and true a creature as ever lived. I courted her for a week and upwards, and would have married her upon the spot, had there been a clergyman on board. She had been banished for a mantle she had borrowed from an acquaintance. Her friend prosecuted her for stealing it, and she was transported for seven years. I had fixed my fancy upon her from the moment I knocked the rivet out of her irons upon my anvil, and as firmly resolved to bring her back to England, when her time was out, my lawful wife, as ever I did intend any thing in my life. She bore me a son in our voyage out. What is become of her, whether she is dead or alive, I know not. That I do not is no fault of mine, as my narrative will show.
>
> Nicol, *The Life and Adventures*, 119–20.

And indeed much of his life for years was devoted to getting into ships that might take him in search of Sarah, who, someone later told him, correctly or not, had left the colony and gone to Bombay.

As we are talking about the sex-life of sailors, this may be the time to mention a writer at the other end of the social scale, Augustus Hervey (1724–79), who became the third Earl of Bristol. His journal was printed from manuscript in 1953. It is an autobiographical fragment, covering the years 1746 to 1759, with two periods of war sandwiching a period of peace. Hervey is not much concerned with the life of the ship. Almost the only time he mentions a member of his crew is when he complains of a painfully swollen hand got through striking his steward. What mostly concerns him is the conduct of the fleet, and his sexual conquests. As regards the latter, there is an endless sequence of adventures in Lisbon and every Mediterranean port open to him with opera-singers who admitted him, wives who were unfaithful with him, countesses he seduced, duchesses who waylaid him, and girls he procured. He often has his mistress on board with him.

[19] *Ibid.*, 185–6 ('gown' apparently mis-written as 'gown'd').

His appetite seems phenomenal. As regards the conduct of the fleet, he is eloquent in his contempt for the Ministry and the Admiralty (especially Anson), and for Lord Hawke, but eloquent too in his defence of Admiral Byng, in his accounts both of the failure to relieve Minorca and the succeeding court-martial. His indignation on Byng's behalf, and his loyalty to him, do him more credit than anything else in the book.

I have chosen one autobiographical narrative to look at in some detail. It is that of John Roach of Whitehaven in Cumberland (now part of Cumbria). The narrative is almost unknown, it has an interesting publishing history, and it is an unusual story told in a language of its own.

In late 1783 or early 1784, Francis Briscoe, a Whitehaven printer, published the narrative as a book of sixty-four pages. There appear to be only three surviving copies; one in Trinity College, Cambridge, one in Carlisle Public Library, and one in the United States. The title-page runs as follows;

The Surprizing Adventures of John Roach, Mariner, of Whitehaven. Containing, A true and genuine Account of his barbarous and cruel Treatment, during a long Captivity amongst the savage *Indians*, and Imprisonment by the *Spaniards*, in South America. Together with his miraculous Preservation and Deliverance by divine Providence; and happy Return to the Place of his Nativity, after having been thirteen Years amongst his inhuman Enemies. Whitehaven: Printed by F. Briscoe: And sold by the Author: Price Six pence.

Roach was only thirty-five, but his sufferings had left him partly paralysed, and for a time his only income came from the sale of his book. Early in 1784 Briscoe brought out a second edition. Roach had added considerably to the rather meagre story of his life, but he had also made some interesting cuts. The book was enlarged from about 13,000 to 20,000 words. The wrapper to this edition contains a statement that the author has spent pains upon the improvement of his narrative, and the correction of some particulars 'in which his Memory was before deficient'. It goes on: 'The first small Impression ... did not enable him to exceed the Bounds of his native County', but the size of this new edition makes him hopeful of extending the sale 'to distant Parts of the Kingdom'. Then comes a solemn 'N. B.' 'The said J. Roach, warned by Insults already offered him', affirms that this publication, being 'his only present Means of Support, he will not fail to claim the protection of the British Laws' against any 'who may in future print or sell the same, except by his Appointment'. In spite of this warning the book was pirated, being published in Liverpool in 1785, and in both Dumfries and Glasgow in 1788.

In Whitehaven Public Library there is a copy of a much later authorized revision, dated 1810, printed by Edmund Bowness at Workington.[20] The circumstances of this edition, which are related in it, are as follows. Before John Roach left Whitehaven for the last time (about 1768) he had become engaged to Jane McCullen. She was still unmarried on his return, and now became his wife. For two years the pair travelled around selling the book, and receiving 'frequent donations from the charitable and humane'. They then set up a business, teasing oakum for Whitehaven shipbuilders and repairers, eventually employing four or five women. Roach took time out to travel round the borders exhibiting a monstrous fish caught off St Bees Head; it was four feet long, with two legs and feet, and had 'the testicles and penis of a man'.

Jane Roach died in 1808. The oakum business failed, and John Roach, now sixty, was once more destitute. Two brothers, William and Henry Gladders, teachers at different schools in nearby Workington, took an interest in him, and they helped him prepare an entirely new edition of those 'surprising adventures' as a means yet again of securing a livelihood. The preface says that the work was published to alleviate 'the distresses of the unfortunate man whose sufferings are related in it. . . . There remains to him, in fact, but the last consolation of the wretched, the power of making known his calamities, and of claiming for himself the compassion to which they so justly entitle him.' There are the names of twenty-nine subscribers who helped to finance the volume – mostly to the modest extent of one guinea: bankers, sailmakers, printers, a shipbuilder, an ironmonger, a tailor, a paper-maker, a gardener and so on. All the same, it is a very badly printed book on poor quality paper.

The editors, who, though they remain anonymous, must be the Gladders brothers, wrote that 'very considerable additions have been made' and 'several objectionable parts have been altered, or totally suppressed'. 'The whole has been written afresh' for the purpose of clarity; nevertheless, 'every fact in it has been taken, with much attention, from a verbal account of Roach himself, whose strength of memory is as surprising as his perspicuity and self-consistency are convincing of the truth of his relation'. We have already seen (in the chapter on the slave-trade, p. 151) something of the effect of the liberal-minded brothers on the tone of the narrative. The sale of the book may have kept the old mariner going for a time, but it did not save him from the Workington workhouse, where he died in May, 1819, aged seventy-one. There was a brief obituary in the Whitehaven Gazette.

In the three editions of Roach's life-story we have a narrative that both expands and contracts.

Roach was born in Whitehaven in 1748, the son of a sailor who was

20 I owe my knowledge of this to Mr Harry Fancy, Curator of the Whitehaven Museum, who also gave me a copy of the notice of Roach's death.

drowned when he was eleven. Nevertheless he followed his father's calling, and was wrecked when he was only fourteen. He was employed in the normal Whitehaven trade of shipping coal to Dublin, and (just once) he enlivened his existence by engaging himself for St Petersburg. Then, on a voyage from Workington to Cork, he was taken by the press-gang, and put on a sixty-four gun warship. This is the first major change in the narrative. The fact that he had been in the Navy at all was suppressed in the two early editions (see above, p. 195). In the 'Gladders edition', he deserted at Plymouth; he had only been allowed ashore by paying a deposit as a surety for his return. He got himself to Bristol and went aboard the first ship he could find. In the first edition, he wrote simply that from Cork he took his passage for Bristol. In the second edition, 'I took an adventurous passage to Bristol'.

Roach reached Bristol in July 1769. The ship he joined was the Jane, a slaver commanded by Captain Clarke. The account of the voyage and of the villainy of Clarke was hugely amplified and moralized by the Gladders brothers from the original noncommittal record, as we saw (p. 151). Roach left the Jane in Jamaica and served in various ships trading in the Caribbean – to Honduras, for example, for logwood and mahogany. The three narratives contradict each other on the names of the ships and the captains, but it is clear enough that some of the captains were pretty disreputable. The last was the worst, a rogue who loaded cattle in Darien and sailed off without paying for them. Roach went ashore to cut wood with a party of the slaves or former slaves who seem to have been common as crew-members on these trading ships. It looks as though they were on the coast of Costa Rica, west of Panama. They were suddenly attacked by Indians. The slaves were quicker than Roach in getting to the boat and making off.

Roach's captors were nomads wandering with some regularity from one chosen site to another. When they found he was incapable of using a bow and arrow they made him a beast of burden. He has a good deal to say about his sufferings from dysentery, lice, sore feet, abuse from the women and so on. It will be seen that Roach had a great love for adjectives, and these vary a good deal from edition to edition. 'This migratory crew' becomes 'this miscreant crew' in the second edition. 'Savage visages' disappears in the second, but 'frightful eyes' and 'frightful savages' remain. All these flourishes are curbed in the third edition, which keeps to such phrasing as 'wild and ungoverned barbarians'. More valuable than the terms of abuse is the mass of detail about his captors and their customs, considerably enlarged in the second edition. He calls the tribe the Woolaways – they are now usually referred to as the Uluas. He describes the procedures for flattening the heads of the babies between boards, the rituals for deciding on hunting grounds, methods of tattooing (he was tattooed himself), their pottery, ways of making bows – and above all the continual fear of the dreaded Mosquitomen raiding for slaves for the Jamaican market.

It does not appear that Roach was the victim of positive cruelty, but he wanted to escape. After ten months he got his chance when the hunters had been celebrating their success with plantain liquor. He made off, 'being greatly favoured by the enlightening rays of silver Luna'. (This phrase seems to have struck him as a little overdone, and in the second edition it became 'being greatly favoured by the enlightening rays of the full-orbed moon'.) After several days on the run, he was surprised to come across a saddled horse – a galloway, he calls it. He mounted it but it took charge of him, and carried him straight to an Indian encampment, and he was once more a prisoner, this time of a different tribe. He had had the bad luck to come across their one and only horse, which belonged to the chief. Roach calls his new captors the Buckeraws; I take these to be the Burucaca, about whom ethnologists seem to know little.[21]

In the second edition but not the first, Roach says that tattooed and painted as he was, with long black hair and his skin dark with ingrained dirt, his captors treated him well, supposing him an Indian of another tribe. But in a heavy rain-storm, the paint and dirt were so far washed off that they realized that what they had got was a white man, and thereafter he became once more an abused beast of burden. I am sceptical about this added story. It looks made-up. But the Gladders brothers included it although such racism on the part of the Indians worried them, and they added the reflection that 'the ravagers of America can best account for the detestation with which the whites are beheld by its inhabitants'. It is quite clear however, from Roach's own account, that he was not seriously maltreated. Once again, he has very interesting accounts of customs, and gives a full description of a great festival with what seem to be initiation rites.

Thinking of escape again, he did his best to make friends with the galloway nag, and, 'about the tenth month of my captivity, while the rest of the company were securely laid upon the verdant turf', he made off once more. (The ground is often verdant, though Roach tries a variant in the second edition, when the chief calls them up from their 'tufty beds'.) This second escape was also a failure; Roach was taken by yet another tribe. He calls these the Assenwasses, and I have not been able to identify them. They cultivated land and traded with the Spaniards. Roach escaped from them also, and for the first time in three years got clear of the forest. He was astonished and delighted to find a path, and that path led to

21 See Doris Stone, 'Synthesis of Lower Central American Indians', in *Handbook of Middle American Indians*, ed. R. Wauchope, vol. 4 (Austin, Tex., 1966), p. 210.

a house, in which there was a man in European clothes. But the man's face was undoubtedly that of a 'Woolaway' Indian. He spoke to Roach first in Spanish and then in English. He had been captured by the Mosquitomen when he was a boy, and sold as a slave in Jamaica to an English merchant who had settled on the Mosquito shore (Nicaragua), and who treated him well for many years. Eventually he went back to his old tribe, but he could not accustom himself to the old ways, and was now employed by the Spaniards, keeping a check on travellers.

This person looked after Roach and eventually sent him off to Matahualpa (or Matagalpa, in the heart of Nicaragua), obviously not appreciating the hostility of the Spaniards to the English. Roach was soon arrested as a spy, manacled and gaoled. This was the beginning of ten wretched years languishing in a succession of Spanish gaols, often depending for food on the charity of passers-by, and nearly always in chains. He was as much the victim of bureaucratic incompetence as anything else. Twelve months in one prison, six months in a second, six months in a third, twelve months in a fourth, twelve months in a fifth – it was four years before he had a proper hearing in front of a Spanish magistrate, in Comayagua, in central Honduras; he was listened to sympathetically but it did not do him any good in the end.

There is an extraordinary story of a ghost in the prison at Leon, in Nicaragua. Roach says he is aware he will not be believed, but 'my relation is a strict reality'. The prison was notorious for spirits and apparitions. They were all harmless except one, a 'turbulent visitant' who 'would frequently rattle the adamantine chains'. The malice of this apparition was directed against a single unfortunate person, a Spaniard who in terror at this persecution unfortunately took refuge in Roach's cell. The ghost followed him in, 'in the likeness of a man, drest in the white robes of a friar, with long hair hanging over his shoulders'. He assaulted the Spaniard so violently that he died of his wounds. Next night, Roach was horrified to see the ghost again, in the prison yard.

> He contracted his portly figure into the appearance of a diminutive star, permeated the chink thro' which my wondering sight was directed, alighted upon my chamber floor, resumed his manly shape, advanced towards me, and grasped my neck with the coldest hand I ever felt.
>
> Roach, *Surprizing Adventures* (1783/4), 53–61.

Roach was terrified, but 'to mine ineffable joy, my dread visitant peacably retracted his arm, and immediately quitted mine apartment, in the same manner in which he had entered it'. This performance was repeated on two more nights, after which Roach understandably appealed to the governor. The governor sent a 'venerable friar' who spent the night in his cell. 'His turbulent brother' appeared yet again. Roach's guest 'spoke a few words to him, in Latin: after which he instantaneously vanished, and I never saw him more'.

This entire story is omitted from the second edition. There is no mention of any ghost (and none in the third edition either). I imagine that Roach met a lot of scepticism about this part of the narrative, and he thought that thereby the credibility of the rest was put at risk. To save the whole, he sacrificed the part. In a way this is unfortunate; it seems to me that Roach cut out a very genuine part of his prison experience. It is not conceivable that Roach was fully in control of his mind during all those hideous years of painful and often solitary confinement. It is quite possible that a Spaniard really was beaten up in his cell and found dead in the morning. The whole context of that violent incident as Roach relates it is surely the effect of hallucination and not mendacity.

Of the later stages of his imprisonment, Roach wrote: 'I remained about three years in the subterraneous den, without ever beholding a glimps of solar light, except when I was conducted into the august presence of mine imperious judge'. He was, he says, 'flattered with the soothing hope that the same merciful Being who had graciously delivered me from the nemorivagous miscreants, would also work for me a deliverance from the tyrannical Spaniards'.[22] The word 'nemorivagous' does appear in the Oxford English Dictionary; it is applied to people who wander in woods. But the OED editors have no example of its actual use. It was found only in two early dictionaries. The word was deleted in Roach's second edition; 'nemorivagous miscreants' became 'the miscreant Indians'. One begins to wonder if there was an advisor who suggested changes for that second edition; who advised against 'silver Luna' and the ghost story as well as 'nemorivagous'. One also begins to wonder if the only English reading Roach could find in his American prisons was a dictionary.

Roach was sent to Guatemala, where they said they would have to seek instructions from Spain about him. This took them three years, and then the word was that he was to be sent to Spain to be imprisoned for life. On board the ship taking him to Europe Roach suffered a stroke and was put ashore at Havana. When he had sufficiently recovered, the Spaniards found him useful as an interpreter with English prisoners-of-war (taken by the Spaniards during the War of American Independence). Roach managed to mix in with a party of prisoners being exchanged for Spanish prisoners, and so got to Jamaica, a free man after thirteen years. But he was partly crippled and absolutely penniless. Fortunately he found a benefactor in Captain Thomas Cragg, in command of the Apollo from Workington. Cragg organized a free passage for him to London. He arrived in Whitehaven on 15 April 1783.

[22] Roach, *The Surprizing Adventures* (1783/4), 72–3.

# 11

# The infortunates

*The Infortunate* is the title of 'the voyage and adventures' of William Moraley, who went as an indentured servant to Philadelphia in 1729, and 'The infortunates' seems a suitable title for a chapter on the stories of those who went on voyages because they were down and out and had little option, or because they were sentenced to transportation and had no option. I add to these a sampling of the stories of sailors brought to extremes by disaster at sea.

## Indentured servants

William Moraley was a ne'er-do-well who published his own story, and I contrast his narrative with that of the very responsible John Harrower who kept a journal from the time of leaving his home in the Shetlands to search for work until his death in Virginia. His journal was not published until 1963.

There is a very full account of the practice of indentured service in the American colonies in Bernard Bailyn's *Voyagers to the West* (1986). Bailyn is particularly concerned with the three-year period 1773–6, and his statistics give a remarkable insight into who these servants were, where they came from, and why they went. Of the 9,364 registered emigrants from Britain to the colonies in that period, 4,472 were indentured servants or 'redemptioners'. Under the indenture system, a person made a contract with a ship's captain or an entrepreneur for a free passage to America in return for binding him or herself to work for a period of years (usually four) without provision for wages. On arrival in America the captain would sell his catch to employers for what he could get for them. If a 'redemptioner' could pay the passage-money within a limited period he or she was then free.

Moraley's book, published in Newcastle-upon-Tyne in 1743 after his return to England,[1] is a jaunty and cheeky piece of writing, emphasizing

[1] It is a very rare book; the only copy known to me in Britain is an imperfect one in the Newcastle public library. The work has recently been edited (1992) by S. E. Klepp and B. G. Smith from a copy in the Clements Library, Michigan.

more than the facts warrant both his gentility and his destitution. Born in London in 1698, he was first apprenticed to the law and then put to learn watchmaking. His father lost his money in the South-Sea Bubble and took his family north to Newcastle. He died in 1724. Having quarrelled with his mother, William went south again and was soon reduced to poverty.

> Not caring what became of me, it enter'd into my Head to leave *England*, and sell myself for a Term of Years into the *American* Plantations. Accordingly I repair'd to the *Royal Exchange*, to inform myself by the printed Advertisment fix'd against the Walls, of the Ships bound to *America*.
>
> Moraley, *The Infortunate* (1743), 8.

What he does not say, his recent American editors tell us, is that he had been imprisoned for debt and had just been released under the Insolvent Debtor's Act.[2] He was accosted by a tout who bought him beer and told him of a ship at Limehouse Dock about to sail to Philadelphia. He went before the Lord Mayor to swear he was neither married nor an apprentice and he signed his indenture in a stationer's shop on London Bridge. Soon he was aboard the Boneta, owned by Charles Hankin and commanded by James Reed. He wrote to 'Mr Stafford' to tell him what he was doing and got the reply that he must be mad as this person was about to get hold of money due to him by prosecuting his mother. At this point someone intervened, whether Mr Stafford or another, for the Boneta was intercepted as she made her way down the Thames and 'the Boatman ask'd if there was one *Moraley* on board', since there was an order from the Lord Mayor to bring him back. The mate swore there was no such person. Moraley claims he was fast asleep at the time and he cursed his fate that he knew nothing of this attempt to get him back. He made no fuss at Gravesend, however, when a Customs officer asked each one of them if they were going voluntarily.

They sailed for America on 7 September 1729 and arrived at Philadelphia the day after Christmas Day.

> I was sold for eleven Pounds, to one Mr *Isaac Pearson*, a Man of Humanity, by Trade a Smith, Clock-Maker and Goldsmith, living at *Burlington* in *New Jersey:* He was a Quaker, but a Wet one.
>
> Moraley, *The Infortunate* (1743), 13.

He spent three years with Pearson, and although he once attempted escape and was apprehended, he was forgiven two of the five years he was under contract to serve. He then wandered about, taking jobs here and there, getting into debt and avoiding his creditors, until he 'began to be heartily tir'd with these Ramblings' and decided to return to England. He struck a bargain with Captain Peel of the Sea Flower and got his passage

[2] Moraley, *The Infortunate* (1992), 10.

in return for acting as cook. There were several passengers, including an Irishman 'who had three Wives, one at *Dublin*, one at *Philadelphia*, and one at *London*'. They occupied themselves with relating their adventures; 'at other times we washed our Linen', though, he adds, he had little enough of that.

At Dublin he got aboard the Leviathan, a Workington collier, whose captain surprised him by reading prayers to the crew morning and evening. 'It was the only Ship I was ever in, where there was no Swearing or prophane Talking.'[3] It was just after Christmas, 1734, that he found himself in England again, and destitute again. 'I look'd not unlike the Picture of *Robinson Crusoe*.' He begged his way across England, in bitter weather, from Workington in Cumberland to Newcastle and then it appears that he so far made it up with his mother that he lived with her for three years until her death. 'Since that Time I have experienc'd the greatest Misfortune, occasion'd by the Mistake of her Executors, which is briefly as follows . . .'[4] But we leave him there.

The story of John Harrower is very sad. He did not write it as a story; it emerges from the entries he made, not always on the day, in his journal. He left his wife and children at home in the Shetlands in December 1773 and went to look for work, carrying with him £3 worth of Shetland knitted stockings and 8½d in cash. He thought of Holland, and when that did not prove simple he rejected the idea of North Carolina because of 'the thoughts of being so far from my family'. He kept himself going by selling his stockings, but his minute details of his lodgings and food show a very precarious existence. He sailed from Sunderland, hoping to get to Holland, but the ship diverted to Portsmouth. He made his way to London on foot, and *en route* wrote this verse in his journal.

My absent friends God bless, and those,
    my wife and Children dear;
I pray for pardon for my foes,
    And for them sheds a tear.
At Epsom here this day I ly,
    Repenting my past sins;
Praying to Jesus for his mercy,
    And success to my friends.

Harrower, *Journal*, 13–14.

It was quickly apparent that prospects for employment in London were very bad. He was looking for something in a merchant-house, a post as clerk or book-keeper (which seems to have been his profession), and was now willing to answer advertisements for such jobs in America, but every

[3] Moraley, *The Infortunate* (743), 56. [4] *Ibid.*, 63.

situation he applied for was already filled. 'Many good people are begging', he noted. He advertised himself, but it produced nothing.

Now at London in a garret room I am,
here friendless and forsaken;
But from the Lord my help will come,
Who trusts in him are not forsaken.

*

I'll unto God my prayer make,
to him my case make known;
And hope he will for Jesus sake,
Provide for me and soon.

Harrower, *Journal*, 16.

On Wednesday, 26 January 1774, he made the following entry.

This day, I being reduced to the last shilling I hade was oblidged to engage to go to Virginia for four years as a schoolmaster for Bedd, Board, washing and five pound during the whole time.

Harrower, *Journal*, 17.

He went aboard the Planter, and was surprised and pleased to find a fellow-Shetlander, and indeed there were enough fellow-Scots to form what he called the 'Scots Mace' (sc. mess). Captain Bowers was also a Scotsman, though it was a long time since he had been home, having been very busily employed in this lucrative Virginia trade. Harrower remarked that 'it was surprising to see the No. of good tradesmen of all kinds, that come on board every day'. Bailyn is able to tell us that the trades represented on the Planter included wig-makers, carpenters, clock-makers, bricklayers, cabinet-makers, hatters, weavers, breeches-makers, pipe-makers, farmers and grooms.[5] As the voyage began, with bad weather and adverse winds forcing laborious progress along the south coast, there were mutinous mutterings about the food, in which the Scots mess did not join. Harrower was soon called on by the captain to 'stand by the Mate' if there was any disturbance while he was ashore. A great deal of bartering went on among the passengers and crew. Harrower bought a penknife for six biscuits he had saved, and sold an old duffle-coat to the boatswain for four shillings.

As they get out to sea, he gives a graphic description of the scene below decks. (It is half-way to one of his rhymed lyrics.)

At 8 p.m. was oblidged to batten down both fore and main hatches, and a little after I really think there was the odest shene betwixt decks that ever I heard or seed.

There was some sleeping, some spewing, some pishing, some shiting, some farting, some flyting, some daming, some Blasting their leggs and thighs, some

[5] Bailyn, *Voyagers to the West*, 277.

their Liver, lungs, lights and eyes, And to make the shene the odder, some curs'd Father, Mother, Sister, and Brother.

Harrower, *Journal*, 24–5.

There was fever on board which spread widely, attacking his fellow-Shetlander, with whom he sat up all night, and himself, though he got off very lightly. Things were so bad that he was employed to write up the logs of both the stricken mate and the captain, and then to keep the log at the direction of the watchkeeper. As they neared the American coast he was also busy making out 'a Clean list' of all the 'servants' on board.

They entered the Rappahannock river and made their way to Fredericksburg.

This day severalls came on board to purchase servts. Indentures and among them there was two Soul drivers. They are men who make it their bussines to go on board all ships who have in either Servants or Convicts and buy sometimes the whole and sometimes a parcell of them as they can agree, and then they drive them through the Country like a parcell of Sheep untill they can sell them to advantage, but all went away without buying any.

Harrower, *Journal*, 39.

The captain rewarded Harrower by putting in a special word with 'Mr Anderson the Merchant', who undertook to do his best for him. So he waited until 'a great number of Gentlemen and Ladies' drove into town for the annual fair day and races. Mr Anderson begged him (it is Harrower's word) 'to settle as a schoolmaster' with his friend Colonel Daingerfield.

So John Harrower became tutor to Daingerfield's three sons.

In Virginia, now I am, at Belvidera settled,
but may they ever mercy find, who hade the cause
that I am from my sweet wife seperated
And Oblidged to leave my Infant Children, Fatherless.

As a schoolmaster, I am here;
and must for four years, remain so;
May I indeavour the Lord to fear,
and always his commands do.

For in Gods strength I do rely,
that he at his appointed time,
Will bring me back to my family,
if I his precepts do but mind.

Do thou enable me to labour,
and my fortune do thou mend
that what I get by thy favour

I to my family may send.

Harrower, *Journal*, 42–3.

There are three more stanzas. Harrower was very well treated by his employer, and was able to take other pupils. He began to entertain the idea of not going back home, and of saving enough to pay for his wife and children to join him. He copied out a letter he wrote to his wife.

I yet hope (please God) if I am spared, some time to make you a Virginian Lady among the woods of America which is by far more pleasent than the roaring of the raging seas round abot Zetland.

Harrower, *Journal*, 76.

She agreed to come, though they were both very worried about the effect of the approaching hostilities between the two countries. He saved £70. But the last entry in his diary is for July 1776, and he died in 1777, aged forty-four, without having seen his wife and family again.

## Convicts

One of the conveniences of empire was that overseas territories provided dustbins into which troublemakers could be tipped. This was not just an eighteenth-century idea; prominent in the Elizabethan colonizing propaganda was the argument that colonies could solve social problems in finding employment for the wastrels and layabouts of an overcrowded homeland. The logic of the system of transporting criminals to the colonies was obvious. The simple case was put with bland assurance by the author of *The Voyage of Governor Phillip to Botany Bay* (1789).

The colonies received by it, at an easy rate, an assistance very necessary; and the mother country was relieved from the burthen of subjects, who at home were not only useless but pernicious.

Phillip, *The Voyage of Governor Phillip*, 7.

It is estimated that from 1715 to 1775 between thirty thousand and fifty thousand convicts were transported to the American colonies.[6] But an independent America did not want the rejects of British society, and for some years there was a very worrying hiatus in the transportation system – worrying to the authorities, that is, who simply could not find space in rotting hulks for those felons whose crimes were not serious enough to hang them. An act for building prisons was passed, but the scheme was not much liked, and eventually the proposal of Joseph Banks and others that the south-east corner of Australia, which Cook had touched on in his first

[6] Ekirch, *Bound for America*, 23; Bailyn, *Voyagers to the West*, 295.

voyage, should be colonized and used for the disposal of convicts, was settled on. The 'First Fleet' sailed in 1787.

Quite early in the century 'the noted Street-Robber' James Dalton was sentenced to transportation to America. His narrative, *The Life and Actions of James Dalton . . . As taken from his Mouth in his Cell at Newgate* (1734) seems to be little known and so far as I know has never been reprinted. I have no doubt it is full of lies, from Dalton, and full of embellishment from his redactor, but it is brilliantly told. I have wondered if it is a hoax, but with Robert Drury in mind, we should be cautious in saying that good reporting is fiction because it is good. The address to the reader, dated Newgate, 1 May 1730, says that many people have wanted his story but he has given it to no one except Robert Walker (the publisher). There is indeed a 1728 publication, *A Genuine Narrative of all the Street Robberies Committed . . . by James Dalton*, which looks wholly fictitious.

'My Parents were Persons in very indifferent Circumstances, and suffered under very great Misfortunes (whether equal to their Deserts I am not a Judge) that are not proper for me to mention.' The last misfortune of his father was his execution, and that is mentioned. Dalton was born in 1700 – there are not many other dates in the narrative. The story of his early robberies is told with a marvellous insouciance. It was for the comparatively small affair of the theft of 39 shillings worth of linen that he was sentenced to transportation. There were thirty-six men and twenty women aboard the Honour, and when they ran into a gale which carried the main topmast away, the chief mate said 'if any of us were Sailors we should come upon Deck and lend a Hand, and that he would take our Irons off'. Twelve offered to help. 'The First Mate took a great Fancy to me, and made me Steward of the Prisoners.'[7] Their liberty had a not unexpected effect. They found that one of the prisoners had smuggled in considerable supplies of alcohol, including 'two Caggs of Geneva', which they ransacked. 'The Captain . . . threatn'd to whip us all round to find out the right Man, whereupon sixteen of us agreed to secure the whole Ship's Crew . . . before the *Whipping Gale blew harder*, which was accomplished.'

Having seized the ship, they headed for Cape Finisterre. They made a law 'among us sixteen commanding Men' that if anyone was drunk on watch, or 'caught in the Hold with the Women Prisoners', he should receive twelve lashes. They allowed the women 'the Benefit of the Air' and promised that they should go ashore with them. They did not keep their word. After fourteen days they were off Finisterre.

> We hoisted out our Long-Boat; and having supply'd ourselves with the most material Moveables that the Captain and Mate had, with their Watches and Money, the whole amounting to about 100*l*., we laid the Ship to. . . . Then we went

[7] Dalton, *The Life and Actions of James Dalton*, 25.

and drank with the Captain and Mate, and set them at Liberty, but lock'd down the nineteen Men that would not consent to the taking of the Ship, as also all the Women, and then went into the Boat to go ashore.

Dalton, *The Life and Actions of James Dalton*, 26.

They were arrested by the Spanish authorities who were prepared not to put them back on board the Honour if they joined the Spanish army. They wriggled out of *that* obligation, and eventually Dalton was thieving back in London. He was, however, betrayed by 'a Woman, whom I had left my Wife to live with', and sentenced to death for having returned from transportation. The sentence was reduced to fourteen years transportation, and this time he was taken to Virginia and sold to an Irishman. But he escaped, got to the Potomac, and 'enter'd myself on board a Ship bound for Bristol, and had 10*l.* paid me for my Service in the Voyage'.[8] He thieved in Bristol until he was arrested again, transported again, escaped again, was caught again – and so on, until he was living as a free man in America.

After this, I hired myself to a Pilot for 20*l. per annum*, with whom I remained for five Years: I got acquainted, being always trading in the River, with one Col. *Brown*'s Daughter, whose Fortune was 1500 Acres of Land and 200*l.* in Money. We lived together as Man and Wife for a long while, till the Money and Acres were all spent: In some short time after this I married a Carpenter's Daughter in *Mobgick-Bay*, with whom I lived for some time, and by her had one Son, if living, named *James Dalton*, but left her before Death parted us.

Dalton, *The Life and Actions of James Dalton*, 32.

Dalton took ship back to England, but in the Downs 'I was press'd and put on board the *Hampshire* Man of War, commanded by the Lord *Muskerry*, and went to the late Siege of *Gibraltar*' – this must have been 1727. When he came home, he was paid his wages, 'which supported my Extravagance for some time', but he fell to robbery again, and was now under sentence of death for a robbery he claimed he did not commit.

Dalton's narrative belongs to a genre of defiant rogue-literature, and there is no breath of repentance or contrition in it. At the opposite extreme is *The Sufferings of William Green, being a Sorrowful Account of his Seven Years Transportation ... Written by W. Green, the Unhappy Sufferer* (undated; perhaps 1775). It is full of unctuous contrition and sententious exhortations. These bleating repentance-narratives just copy one another. Phrases and themes in Green can also be found in *The Poor Unhappy Transported Felon's Sorrowful Account of his Fourteen Years Transportation at Virginia in America. By James Revel, the Unhappy Sufferer*. This also is undated. Green writes of the convict ship: 'There were twenty-six of us unhappy

8 *Ibid.*, 30.

felons, and a most wicked crew as ever went over, most of us did smoak, but all did swear'. Revel, in doggerel, says much the same thing:

> We were in number much about threescore,
> A wicked lousy crew as e'er went o'er,
> Oaths and tobacco with us plenty were,
> Most did smoak, but all did curse and swear.

The accounts of the market to buy the convicts are also very similar. Green writes: 'They search us there as the dealers in horses do their animals in this country, by looking at our teeth, viewing our limbs, to see if they are sound and fit for their labour'. Revel writes:

> Some view'd our limbs turning us around,
> Examining like horses if we were sound.

However, each has his own story of misery to tell, though for both of them, the later years were not too bad. Green was allowed to join a whaler and spent his last two years at sea. 'I liked it very well', but it would be 'too tedious for me to relate what is done at sea'. He got back to England in 1772, ten years after his sentencing. He was still only twenty-four – and we never learn exactly why he was condemned. He had been apprenticed to a weaver but had run away and joined a gang in Sherwood Forest. His parents died soon after his return, in 1773.

> Being thus left, and a wide world before me, I thought it most prudent to marry, which I accordingly did, and lived happy, having at this time a small family, and wrote this little book as a warning to all young and old people, to avoid the hardships I through my folly have suffered.
>
> Green, *Sufferings*, 14.

Most of the accounts of the voyages of the early convicts out to Botany Bay and Port Jackson are not from the convicts themselves. John Nicol, the cooper acting as steward on board the Lady Juliana in 1789–90, is a notable witness in his story of his relationship with Sarah Whitlam (see p. 197). His account of the Scottish girl who died before they sailed seems to have been heavily sentimentalized by his redactor, John Howell, but it is notable all the same.

> When we sailed, there were on board 245 female convicts. There were not a great many very bad characters; the greater number were for petty crimes, and a great proportion for only being disorderly, that is, street-walkers; the colony at the time being in great want of women.
>
> One, a Scottish girl, broke her heart, and died in the river; she was buried at Dartford. Four were pardoned on account of his Majesty's recovery. The poor young Scottish girl I have never yet got out of my mind; she was young and beautiful, even in the convict dress, but pale as death, and her eyes red with weeping. She never spoke to any of the other women, or came on deck. She was

constantly seen sitting in the same corner from morning to night; even the time of meals roused her not. My heart bled for her, – she was a countrywoman in misfortune. I offered her consolation, but her hopes and heart had sunk. When I spoke she heeded me not; if I spoke of Scotland she would wring her hands and sob, until I thought her heart would burst. I endeavoured to get her sad story from her lips, but she was silent as the grave to which she hastened. I lent her my Bible to comfort her, but she read it not; she laid it on her lap after kissing it, and only bedewed it with her tears. At length she sunk into the grave of no disease but a broken heart.

Nicol, *The Life and Adventures*, 111–12.

I prefer this account, maudlin as it is, to the brisk impersonality of Watkin Tench, an officer of marines on board the transport Charlotte in the First Fleet (1787–8). Before they left England, the prisoners were 'in high spirits', and 'an ardent wish for the hour of departure seemed generally to prevail'. He wanted to bear 'public testimony to the sobriety and decency' of the convicts, their behaviour being in general 'humble, submissive, and regular'. However, after thirty-six weeks in passage he confessed that 'we were over-joyed' at the prospect of an end to 'a service so peculiarly disgusting and troublesome'.[9]

The surgeon of the First Fleet, John White, was also in the Charlotte, and he gives a much more personal and sympathetic account in his *Journal of a Voyage to New South Wales* (1790). He noted by name the death of Isaac Coleman, who, 'worn out by lowness of spirits and debility, brought on by long and close confinement, resigned his breath without a pang'. That was near the beginning of the voyage. Very near the end, White recorded the death of Edward Thomson, 'worn out with a melancholy and long confinement. Had he lived, I think he would have proved a deserving member of society.'[10] There are many other examples of his awareness of the convicts as people, for example, William Brown, the 'poor fellow' who fell overboard. More general is his famous account of the anxiety of the men and the women in the ship to come to close quarters. In the tropics the heat was so great that the women were constantly fainting.

And yet, notwithstanding the enervating effects of the atmospheric heat, and the inconvenience they suffered from it; so predominant was the warmth of their constitutions, or the depravity of their hearts, that the hatches over the place where they were confined could not be suffered to lay off, during the night, without a promiscuous intercourse immediately taking place between them and the seamen and marines.

White, *Journal of a Voyage to New South Wales*, 30–1.

9 Tench, *A Narrative of the Expedition to Botany Bay*, 1, 2 and 43.
10 White, *Journal of a Voyage to New South Wales*, 12 and 112.

Anxious to solve both the moral and the physical problem, White got Captain Phillip to fix a grated hatch-cover with a wind-scoop to let air in and keep men out. But the women still found their way to the men, said White, and three men got through the hole made for the 'wind-sail'. White's general concern for the health of his charges is well shown in his indignation about the conditions which had been allowed to develop in the Alexander, where illness was becoming a serious problem. The 'noxious effluvia' of the accumulated water in the bilges was turning the officers' buttons black. 'When the hatches were lifted off, the stench was so powerful, that it was scarcely possible to stand over them.'[11]

The scanty information from the convicts themselves about conditions on the voyage has been collected by Robert Hughes in his outstanding and deeply distressing book, *The Fatal Shore*, particularly in his chapter 'The voyage', though some of this relates to the nineteenth century. He includes Thomas Milburn's account, in a letter to his father which was printed in 1790, of convicts keeping secret the death of those to whom they were chained in order to get their allowance of food. A much more formal publication, for which Hughes gives the background and context, was *A Narrative of the Sufferings of T. F. Palmer, and W. Skirving, During a Voyage to New South Wales, 1794, on the Surprise Transport* (1797). Palmer, 'late of Queen's College, Cambridge', was a Unitarian minister sentenced to seven years transportation on a charge of being involved in the circulation of a pamphlet opposing the war against France. The purpose of the pamphlet, published by Cambridge friends, was to free Palmer and Skirving from the trumped-up charge that they had tried to incite a mutiny on board the transport. The 'conspirators' had actually *paid* the master, Patrick Campbell, for their passage, so that they had decent accommodation to start with, and their gentility saved them from the floggings and irons meted out to their supposed associates in the wholly fictional plot to murder the captain and take the ship to America. But they were locked up and deprived of all possessions, including paper, and proper food; and they were subjected to constant abuse. Campbell was a scoundrel. The outcome, however, was in their favour. Though there are no details of proceedings, Hughes is able to show that Palmer did quite well in the convict colony.[12]

## In extremis

In 1726, John Dean, who, we are told, had for some years been 'His Majesty's Consul for the Ports of Flanders, Residing at Ostend', published an account of the wreck of the Nottingham Galley off the New Hampshire

[11] *Ibid.*, 39. [12] Hughes, *The Fatal Shore*, 178.

coast fifteen years earlier. John Dean had been the captain of the ship. His motives for publication are not stated. I assume that even after fifteen years the scandal surrounding the shipwreck still clung to Dean, or that he feared its reappearance, and since at this time 'the Master alone survives of all that he particularly knew', he thought it would be a good idea to provide a final and authoritative narrative that would put his own conduct in the best imaginable light. I cannot think of any other reason for publication than apprehension about his future career. Certainly not a bad conscience.

There had been three narratives already about the wreck of the Nottingham, all published in 1711; the first by John Dean himself, the second by his brother Jasper, the third by the mate, the boatswain and a sailor (Christopher Langman, Nicholas Mellen and George White). This last was accompanied by a whole wad of affidavits sworn before a Justice of the Peace in Portsmouth, New Hampshire, in February 1711, after they were rescued, and before notaries in London in August. The two issues of scandal were, first, the reason for the wreck, on an island near the mouth of the Piscataqua river, not far from Portsmouth, New Hampshire; and secondly, responsibility for deciding to eat the carpenter, who had died.

As regards the first, Dean's account in 1726 runs like this.

> The Mate being slightly indisposed, the Master, upon Deck, going forward, saw, to his infinite surprize, the Breakers a-head very near them; and instantly calling out to the Steersman, to put the Helm hard a Starboard, was so ill obey'd in the sudden Astonishment, as to have the very reverse perform'd.
>
> Dean, *A Narrative of the Shipwreck*, 4.

This story of the helmsman's error is quite absent from Dean's much more direct earlier version.

> I saw the *Breakers* a Head, whereupon I call'd out to put the Helm hard a Starboard, but 'ere the Ship cou'd wear, we were struck upon the East End of the Rock called *Boon Island.*
>
> Dean, *A Narrative of the Sufferings*, 2.

But Langman and the others deny that the captain was on deck at all. 'He was then undressing himself to go to Bed.'

The Nottingham was owned by John's brother Jasper (seven-eighths) and a young man called Whitworth (one-eighth). It was the contention of Langman, Mellen and White that the owners were out to get the ship's insurance either by getting her captured by a French privateer, or by running her ashore. They gave detailed reports of conversations they claim to have overheard between Dean and Whitworth. That these charges were in circulation was the reason given for Dean's first publication. This first account was brief, clumsy and poorly printed. The second, put out by Jasper as a first-person narrative by John, is fuller and more circumspect. The three Dean versions are full of contradictions, with the last being extensively rewritten to provide the captain with nobility, resourcefulness and courage. He takes advantage of the 'Ignorance and Credulity' of the crew to tell them of the likelihood of their rescue, though he does not believe it himself, 'since he already too plainly observ'd their great Dejection, and frequent Relapses into an utter distrust of Divine Providence'.

> As it pleased God to indulge the Master in a greater Share of Health and Strength of Body, and likewise a proportionate Vigour of Mind; so he eventually endeavour'd to instill into the Hearts of the dispirited People a Reliance on that Almighty Being . . . (etc)
>
> Dean, *A Narrative of the Shipwreck*, 11.

As regards eating the carpenter, Dean's gradual distancing of himself from the repulsive act would be amusing if it were not so degrading. In the first version, the men 'began to request of him to eat of the Dead Body', and, 'after abundance of mature Thought and Consultation', he 'was oblig'd to submit'. In the second version, he elaborates on his grief and shock at being reduced 'to eat the Dead' and he debates with himself about the lawfulness on the one hand and 'absolute Necessity' on the other. But the account in both versions of his serving out slices of the dead body is disgusting. How changed all this is in the latest version! There the captain is absent for some time, and he finds the crew have held a confabulation.

> After some Pause, Mr. *Whitworth*, a young Gentleman, his Mother's darling Son, delicately educated, amidst so great an Affluence, as to despise common Food . . . began, in the Name of the Assembly, to court the Master's Concurrence in converting the Humane Carcase into the Matter of their Nourishment.
>
> Dean, *A Narrative of the Shipwreck*, 16.

It was only after much more prolonged hesitation that the captain agreed. However, Langman and his colleagues say curtly that it was the captain himself who proposed the flaying and eating of the carpenter's body, assuring them '*It was no Sin, since God was pleas'd to take him out of the World, and that we had not laid violent Hands upon him*'.[13] The boatswain refused to help him cut the body up, and all three authors of the pamphlet say they refused to touch the food at first, but gave in on the second day.

It is impossible to say what exactly happened on that little island off the New England coast in 1711, but the account by the mate, the boatswain and White carries much greater conviction of honesty than the constantly amended account of the captain. Often enough one feels that a smooth

[13] Langman, *A True Account of the Voyage*, 18.

and self-righteous account of trouble at sea is full of suppressions and perversions of the facts, but it is rare to have the evidence of doctoring provided by Dean's three versions.

There is only one account, so far as I know, of the much more terrible cannibalism aboard the sloop Peggy of New York in 1766, and this was from the captain, David Harrison, who affirmed his story 'by repeated Depositions, before the Right Hon. George Nelson, Esq., Lord-Mayor of the City of London, and Mr Robert Shank, Notary Public'.[14] The Peggy left Fayal in the Azores to return to New York with a cargo chiefly of wine and brandy. She ran into a violent storm in mid-Atlantic which lasted for several days and left her drifting helplessly. The crew broached the brandy and got drunk, but food ran out completely – they had eaten the cat and the leather off the pumps.

The weather did not improve. 'It blew "black December" as Shakespeare phrases it.' (A nice near-recollection of 'the rain and wind beat dark December' from *Cymbeline*.) On Christmas Day a ship came near but 'the inexorable captain pursued his course without regarding us'.[15] Harrison became very ill, and was unable to leave his bunk. The crew went on drinking, but Harrison 'imbibed the strongest aversion imaginable to wine'. He was told he was no longer in charge; the mate, Archibald Nicolson, insisted that a sacrifice must be made of one of themselves, and that lots should be drawn. Interestingly, the loser was Wiltshire, a 'negro slave or black man', who had formed part of Harrison's cargo, but whom he had been unable to sell in Fayal. They shot him and cut up the body. James Campbell could not wait, and ate the liver raw; three days later, 'he died raving mad'. The captain refused his share in utter revulsion.

> Add also to this, that the stench of their stewing and frying threw me into an absolute fever, and that this fever was aggravated by a strong scurvy and a violent swelling in my legs.
>
> Harrison, *The Melancholy Narrative*, 27.

As the crew fed upon the flesh of the first victim, the captain began to fear that he would be the next. 'In proportion as the negro grew less, so in proportion my apprehensions were encreased.' There were now seven of them left in the ship. At the end of January, they told Harrison they were going to draw lots again. The lot fell on David Flatt, 'a foremastman, the only man in the ship on whom I could place any dependence'. 'The fire already blazed in the steerage.' Flatt appeared resigned, and asked James Doud, who had shot the negro, to shoot him, begging first 'a small time to prepare himself for death'. He was given until the morning. But by midnight, Harrison wrote, he had gone deaf, and by 4 a.m. he was 'quite delirious'. At 8 a.m. a sail was sighted.

[14] Harrison, *The Melancholy Narrative*, title-page. [15] *Ibid.*, 14.

The Susanna, commanded by Thomas Evers, returning from Virginia to London, came up and sent a boat to take off the crew of the Peggy. They were horrified by their appearance, with their 'hollow eyes, shrivelled cheeks, long beards, and squallid complexions'. Harrison had to be lowered into the boat. Then they found that they had not got the mate, who was discovered blind drunk. Harrison is full of praise for the care taken of them by Evers, all the more generous as his ship too had suffered in the storms and was short of provisions. They reached Dartmouth at the beginning of March. Nicolson the mate, Doud and John Warner all died during the passage. Only Harrison, Lemuel Ashley, Samuel Wentworth and Flatt survived, though Flatt continued 'out of his senses'. Harrison went up to London and, in the interest of his owners, made his statement to the Public Notary. He arranged a passage back home, and presumably while he was waiting wrote his *Melancholy Narrative of the Distressful Voyage and Miraculous Deliverance of Captain David Harrison*. 'I am now returning to New York, in the ship Hope, captain Benjamin Davis.'[16] He does not say what happened to David Flatt.

16 *Ibid.*, 49.

# 12

# Conclusion

To render his relation agreeable to the man of sense, it is therefore necessary, that the voyager should possess several eminent and rare talents ...

It would appear, therefore, somewhat strange, if such writers as these should be found extremely common. ... But on the other hand, why there should scarce exist a single writer of this kind worthy our regard; and whilst there is no other branch of history (for this is history) which hath not exercised the greatest pens, why this alone should be overlooked by all men of great genius and erudition, and delivered up to the Goths and Vandals as their lawful property, is altogether as difficult to determine.

And yet, that this is the case, with some very few exceptions, is most manifest.

Henry Fielding, *Journal of a Voyage to Lisbon.*

It remains to ask: what is the value of the writings collected and described in this book? As we saw, when Fielding was writing his *Voyage to Lisbon* during his last illness, he said that 'romance' (in which term he included the work of Homer) was 'the confounder and corrupter' of 'true history'. Why then, he asked, should 'voyage-writing', which is a branch of history, not engage the talents of the best writers? The 'original poets' may have had some excuse. 'They found the limits of nature too strait for the immensity of their genius, which they had not room to exert, without extending fact by fiction.'[1] The human scene, Fielding went on, has now grown larger and more complex, and there can be no more excuses.

Fielding was thinking of travel-writing in a broad sense. In my more restricted area of the sea-voyage, one obvious reason for the dearth of great writing is that few people of real literary talent ever went to sea. Smollett, Melville, Marryat, Conrad, Dana, Stevenson, Golding – the list can be extended but it remains small. This 'technical' explanation does not really face the issue, however, for even these writers tended to turn their experiences into fiction. The appeal of fiction has not grown any less, as Fielding thought it should have done, even for those comparatively few first-class writers qualified to write voyage-narratives.

[1] Fielding, *The Journal of a Voyage to Lisbon*, Preface.

Why does the devil have all the best tunes? If we were to insist on answering Fielding's question, we should have to ask why it is that the greatest writing, recognized in a majesty of language which seems to crystallize human experience and enshrine it for generation after generation, should for the most part be embedded in fictional or invented human situations. 'To know my deed, 'twere best not know myself.' It is as though every time great artists want to say, 'This is how life *is*', they find themselves saying, 'This is how I *imagine* life to be'. A very few lyric writers hold tenaciously to the narrow path of personal experience. But the life of the imagination remains richer, ampler, more fertile, more tempting than the life of incident, whatever Fielding thought. As Cleopatra said,

> Nature wants stuff
> To vie strange forms with fancy.

If we were concerned with the sea as a force operating on the literary imagination, this would be a totally different book. But my concern has been with writers reporting on real events at sea which they had participated in, and, though we may protest against Fielding calling them Goths and Vandals, we have to accept that they were not great writers. However, in trying to bring back from the shadows a once very popular branch of literature, it was never my thought to uncover a forgotten literary masterpiece. None was sought, none was found.

So what claim does this kind of literature have on our attention? The first and most obvious claim, and in the end the most important claim, is that we are in the presence of flesh and blood. These men and women are not the figments of anyone's imagination; these ships were real and sailed the real seas. Contact may be tenuous and uncertain, but even lying does not invalidate that stamp of actuality. These writings originate in lives that were lived; they testify to a real not a symbolic presence. Captain Cheap facing his opponents outside his tent on Wager Island, and the twelve-year-old Thomas Caple dying of hunger in the Speedwell, had their existence; and they still have it in the pages of Bulkeley's narrative. This narrative has gone far beyond the office of a parish register or court document which preserves the memory of a human being from extinction and oblivion. Its unremarkable, matter-of-fact writing has brought Captain Cheap and Thomas Caple to life. They were there in the real drama on Wager Island which Bulkeley took part in and helped to shape, but we see them as actors in the written drama which he created, for his own purposes, out of the real events. It is because these narratives are dynamic re-creations by the actors of the real dramas they lived through that they have a right to exist alongside fiction which may be much better written, with much more insight into human psychology.

It is not that there is a competition between the two kinds of writing.

Each serves its own ends. One can go back to and reread imaginative literature in a way one is rarely invited to by the literature of report. At the same time, one can grow impatient with the free-wheeling arbitrariness with which fiction-writers move their characters into and out of their moral predicaments. Kierkegaard rudely said that aesthetics was 'a courteous and sentimental science which knows of more expedients than a pawnbroker.'[2] The moral predicaments which constantly present themselves in the stories collected in this book are real, however weakly described and analysed; and they do not admit of manufactured conclusions.

These voyage-writings originate in the real, and that is where their claim for attention originates; but much of the time they are evading the truth. The art of the voyage-narrative is an art of disguise. In his great poem 'The Castaway', arising from an incident recorded in Anson's *Voyage*, William Cowper wrote that 'the page / Of narrative sincere' was 'wet with Anson's tear'. 'Sincere' here means honest, uncorrupt, not dissembling. There are very few narratives with that kind of innocence; certainly not Anson's, as we saw. Voyage-narratives, which get their value from their proximity to real events, are all the time moving away from those real events into an account that will best serve the interests of the writer. But, if half their value is in their contact with the real, the other half is in their manner of evading the real. This is where they really come alive.

John Hawkesworth's plastic surgery on the narratives of Cook and his other victims is rather a special case in that he was not a participant, and was not (as many Grub-Street hacks were) employed by a participant to perform a cosmetic operation. But Hawkesworth's editing is only an extreme example of the 'improvement' that went on in one form or another in almost every narrative, in order to produce something acceptable to the author and the reader. 'What name is my journal of the voyage to come out in?' was the question which John Marra asked his bookseller. An ingenuous enquiry which illustrates something of the deviousness of the path which lay between observation and publication.

Actually, the midwifery of the booksellers and their hirelings was the least important (though often disastrously obvious) of the manipulations of the record which I have been demonstrating in *The Story of the Voyage*. At the other extreme from the tinkering of Hawkesworth, an outsider, is the sheer mendacity of George Shelvocke or John Dean, captains who had much to conceal. I do not want to rehearse what I have already written about the ways in which the assembled writers have sought to adjust the record and escape from the event, from Dampier at the end of the

[2] Kierkegaard, *Fear and Trembling*, 95.

seventeenth century to Bligh at the end of the eighteenth. But, as I say, it is in the adjustment that they come alive.

There is a curious antithesis. Great art, while indisputably the supreme expression of personality, is also as T. S. Eliot insisted the extinction of personality, an abdication of the creator in favour of the creation. In the literature of report, the personality of the writer comes alive in the process of writing. I hope it does not seem a sentimentality to say that a major pleasure in writing this book has been the presence of the authors, men and women waking from the dead and reassembling themselves in their writings. Not always likeable people, but astonishingly real, often because in their efforts to present a good picture of themselves they do not have the art to conceal themselves. They weld themselves into the reality they were part of in the very act of trying to escape from it in their writing.

All my writers re-create the events, they re-create their colleagues, their enemies, their victims, and themselves. They try to re-create all this on their own terms; and to some extent we accept what they have to say for its great interest in itself as a subjective record of encounters and vicissitudes – all the more valuable for its context of imperial expansion and the collision of cultures. But we are all the time conscious that our access to people and events is through a mist arising from the energy of partisan re-creation.

In reading voyage-narratives we are the audience in a kind of theatre – a theatre of writing. We are not watching original people and events, which are forever irrecoverable, nor, simply, a subjective version of events. We are watching events being written about, written for an audience: the Lords of the Admiralty, perhaps, and the reading public. And this version of events is then challenged – by someone else presenting *his* version of the same expedition, or by a superseded manuscript that confronts the writer with contradictory words of his own. It is a complex show, full of perspectives which move and shift and reshape themselves. The writing may be amateurish, but it is the writing which provides this fascinating show of imperfect, inadequate, dissolving images.

I suggested (pp. 176–9) that in his pain and discomfort Fielding turned his sea-voyage into a symbol of the unhappy life of fallen humanity, Adam being the first traveller. He also saw travel, whether in ship or stage-coach, as a kind of imprisonment.

> This subjection is absolute, and consists of a perfect resignation both of body and soul to the disposal of another; after which resignation, during a certain time, his subject retains no more power over his own will, than an Asiatic slave, or an English wife.
>
> Fielding, *The Journal of a Voyage to Lisbon*, 203.

Mary Wollstonecraft, in an impressive and all-too-short passage, wrote of the intense claustrophobia which a journey by sea along the Norwegian coast produced in her, and of her vision of a future when there would not be standing-room on the over-populated earth. 'The images fastened upon me, and the world appeared a vast prison.' You would expect these two highly literate passengers to engage themselves with the time-honoured symbolism of the sea. Two other well-educated writers had the equipment to pursue these analogies: both the Forsters, as we have seen. It was the young George Forster who went furthest, with his published epigraph from Seneca, in which Cook's explorations become symbols of the aimless frenzy of modern life. Although less literate writers frequently use the term 'the wooden world' for the ship, few of them made much of the symbolic applications of the life they were leading.

I quoted Dr Johnson's comment on a ship being a jail in my introduction. In that same tour Johnson and Boswell were being taken from Skye by Donald Maclean in Mr Simpson's vessel, 'with the prospect of seeing Mull, and Icolmkill and Inchkenneth, which lie near to it'. A change in the weather made Mr Simpson change the destination from Iona (Icolmkill) to Tobermory on the island of Mull. The weather changed again and worsened. Various new possibilities and destinations were proposed by Mr Simpson and his skipper. Then it got very rough and they decided to run for the island of Coll. Boswell gives a fine description of their passage in the violent storm, with himself, anxious to help, being given a rope to hold which he later discovered was of no use: 'his object was to keep me out of the way'.

> Piety afforded me comfort; yet I was disturbed by the objections that have been made against a particular providence, . . . objections which have often been made, and which Dr Hawkesworth has lately revived, in his Preface to the Voyages to the South Seas; but Dr. Ogden's excellent doctrine on the efficacy of intercession prevailed.

Well, they made it to Coll.

> Dr Johnson had all this time been quiet and unconcerned. He had lain down on one of the beds, and having got free from sickness, was satisfied. The truth is, he knew nothing of the danger we were in: but, fearless and unconcerned, might have said, in the words which he has chosen for the motto to his *Rambler*,
>
> *Quo me cunque rapit tempestas, deferor hospes.*
>
> Boswell, *Journal of a Tour to the Hebrides*, 349–50.

This tag is from the Epistles of Horace: Wherever the storm takes me, I put in and become a guest.

On this occasion, Johnson was very fortunate in his experience of being an involuntary passenger, taken where the wind forced the skipper to steer. For many people at sea, the ship really was a jail: all the convicts transported first to America and then to New South Wales, all the slaves in their shackles on the middle passage, and one must add all those like Francis Bergh snatched away from family and friends by the press-gang. But it is remarkable how few people in the wooden world had any control over what they were doing or where they were going. Officers and men might not be told where they were heading until they were well out to sea, and even then an often quite vaguely formulated mission would be subject to all the alterations and diversions which the weather and the captain might bring about. A great deal of time on voyages of every kind was spent on improvising and making the best of new circumstances. Privateers went 'cruising' on the offchance of meeting a vessel to plunder or fight; merchant-vessels sought markets for a cargo; ships of all kinds put into unintended harbours because of bad weather or lack of water; discoverers failed to find the land they sought but came across uncharted islands; colonists set out with only the faintest idea of whether the territory they were heading for was suitable for settlement. In this respect, with mission so vaguely defined, course changed and destination altered, the terms success or failure for a voyage could be adventitious – and here once again the importance of the *written* voyage comes in, for on paper purposefulness in fulfilling an objective could be a lot clearer than it ever was from within the ship.

Most of those within the ship had no say at all in where they were going. The designs of the owners, or the Lords of the Admiralty, were entirely subject, as regards their fulfilment, to the quality of the ships, the knowledge and temperament of the captain and the officers, and the vagaries of the weather. The captain's determination to get from A to B was dependent on wind and weather, and the health and cooperativeness of officers and men. Who or what else was involved in governing and directing those who travelled by sea? It was a remarkable act of the otherwise conventionally minded Hawkesworth to refuse to attribute fortunate outcomes of critical situations to the intervention of Providence. He was severely castigated for this apparent lack of faith in a protective divinity. He certainly makes George Whitefield and John Newton look foolish in their determination to attribute every change in wind and weather to the direct intervention of God. At the other end of the scale is the quite unintended darkness of Francis Bergh's words when he was trying to be philosophical about plans going awry: 'Men appoints, and the Almighty disappoints'.

Whether God was in it or not, and if He was whether He was favourably inclined or not, the destiny of those who travelled by sea was not in the control of the travellers. Or rather, they shaped their ends only after they had been rough-hewn by other people, other forces. Most of Dampier's life seems to have been a series of improvisations; almost literally jumping from one ship to another as they touched. The records of several of our writers are records of exile, loneliness, unhappy wandering – perhaps Roger Poole and John Harrower in particular. There is also Nicholas Owen on the west coast of Africa, 'scrapeing the world for money, the uneversal God of man kind, untill death overtakes us'. There is John Marra the dispossessed (another Irishman), picked up by Cook and alternately caressed and flogged by him. There is John Cremer, 'Ramblin' Jack': 'I have always been a wandering, unhappy Chap'.

The mythical dimensions of the wooden world are not far to seek in the writings I have brought together. Even if the writers themselves make little of them, it is their writing which lets us see them. Especially perhaps the autobiographies of sailors such as William Spavens and Francis Bergh. In writing with so little artistry and literary skill the story of lives of continuous resourceful and philosophic response to almost continuous adversity they tell more truth than they are aware of, and a different truth from that which they constantly, with all their fellows, lay claim to.

# Bibliography

The following is a list of the writings referred to in the text, both the primary voyage-narratives (prefaced with an asterisk), and the secondary works. Dates within round brackets are those of first publication. The names of publishers are given for modern secondary works only. For information, I give the titles of further editions, not specifically referred to in my text, after the word ALSO.


Abbott, J. L. *John Hawkesworth: Eighteenth-Century Man of Letters*. Madison, Wis.: University of Wisconsin Press, 1982.

Adams, Percy G. *Travelers and Travel Liars* (1962). Revised edition, New York: Dover, 1980.

Adams, Percy G. *Travel Literature and the Evolution of the Novel*. Lexington, Ky: University Press of Kentucky, 1983.

**An Affecting Narrative of the Unfortunate Voyage and Catastrophe of his Majesty's Ship Wager*. London, 1751.

*Anson, George. *A Voyage Round the World in the Years MDCCXL, I, II, III, IV. By George Anson, Esq. ... Compiled from Papers and other Materials of the Right Honourable George Lord Anson, and Published under his Direction. By Richard Walter, M.A.* London, 1748.

Anson, George. *A Voyage* ... Ed. Glyndwr Williams. London: Oxford University Press, 1974.

*Atkins, John. *A Voyage to Guinea, Brasil, and the West-Indies in His Majesty's Ships, the Swallow and the Weymouth*. London, 1735.

ALSO: Reprinted, London: Frank Cass, 1970.

Bach, John. *See* Bligh, *The Bligh Notebook*.

Bailyn, Bernard. *Voyagers to the West: A Passage in the Peopling of America on the Eve of the Revolution* (1986). New York: Vintage Books, 1988.

*Banks, Joseph. *The Endeavour Journal of Joseph Banks 1768–1771*. Ed. J. C. Beaglehole. 2 vols. Sydney: Public Library of New South Wales, in assoc. with Angus and Robertson, 1962.

*Barker, Robert. *The Unfortunate Shipwright, or Cruel Captain*. London, [1760?].

Barrow, Sir John. *The Mutiny and Piratical Seizure of H. M. S. Bounty* (1831). Introd. by Sir Cyprian Bridge. London: Oxford University Press, 1951.

Batten, Charles L. *Pleasurable Instruction: Form and Convention in Eighteenth-Century Travel Literature*. Berkeley: University of California Press, 1978.

Beaglehole, J. C. *The Exploration of the Pacific* (1934). Third edition, London: Black, 1966.

Beaglehole, J. C. *The Life of Captain James Cook*. London: Black, 1974.
*See also* Cook, James; Banks, Joseph.

*Bergh, Francis. *The Story of a Sailor's Life*. In *Household Words* III (1851), 211–16, 222–8, 256–61, 306–10, 353–4.
ALSO: *The Story of a Sailor's Life, or, Fifty Years at Sea*. As related by Francis Bergh. Third edition, Gosport, 1852.

*Betagh, William. *A Voyage Round the World. Being an Account of a Remarkable Enterprize begun in the Year 1719*. London, 1728.

*Bligh, William. *A Narrative of the Mutiny on Board His Majesty's Ship Bounty*. London, 1790.

*Bligh, William. *A Voyage to the South Sea ... in His Majesty's Ship the Bounty*. London, 1792.

*Bligh, William *The Log of the Bounty*. Ed. Owen Rutter. London: Golden Cockerel Press, 1937.

*Bligh, William, and others. *A Book of the Bounty*. Ed. George Mackaness (1938). Introd. by Gavin Kennedy. London: Dent, 1981.

*Bligh, William. *The Bligh Notebook ... 18 April to June 1789*. Transcription and facsimile, ed. John Bach. Sydney: Allen and Unwin in assoc. with the National Library of Australia, 1987.
ALSO: *The Log of H. M. S. Bounty 1787–1789*. Facsimile. Guildford: Genesis, 1975.

Bonner, W. H. *Captain William Dampier: Buccaneer and Author*. Stanford University, Calif.: Stanford University Press, and London: Oxford University Press, 1934.

Boswell, James. *Journal of a Tour to the Hebrides with Samuel Johnson, LL.D* (1786). Ed. R. W. Chapman, with Johnson's *Journey to the Western Islands of Scotland*. Oxford: Oxford University Press, 1979.
*See also* Hill, G. B.

*Bougainville, Louis de. *A Voyage Round the World ... in the Years 1766, 1767, 1768, and 1769*. Translated by J. R. Forster. London, 1772.

Braidwood, S. J. 'Initiatives and organisation of the Black poor 1786–1787'. *Slavery and Abolition*, 3 (1982), 211–27.

Brosses, Charles de. *Histoire des navigations aux terres australes*, 1756. *See* Callander, John.

*Bulkeley, John and Cummins, John. *A Voyage to the South-Seas, In the Years 1740–1. Containing, A Faithful Narrative of the Loss of His Majesty's Ship the Wager*. London, 1743.

*Bulkeley, John and Cummins, John. *A Voyage to the South Seas, In the Years 1740–1*. Second edition, with additions, London and Philadelphia, 1757.

Bulkeley, John and Cummins, John. *A Voyage* ... Ed. A. D. Howden-Smith. The Argonaut Series. London: Harrap, 1927.

Burney, Fanny (Mme d'Arblay). *The Early Journals and Letters*. Ed. Lars E. Troide. 2 vols. Oxford: Clarendon Press, 1988.

Burney, James. *A Chronological History of the Discoveries in the South Sea or Pacific Ocean*. 5 vols. London, 1803, 1806, 1813 and 1817.

*Byron, John. *The Narrative of the Honourable John Byron* .... London, 1768.

Byron, John. *Byron's Journal of his Circumnavigation, 1764–66*. Ed. Robert C. Gallagher. Cambridge: Cambridge University Press for the Hakluyt Society, 1964.

Callander, John. *Terra Australis Cognita: Or, Voyages to the Terra Australis, or Southern Hemisphere.* 3 vols. Edinburgh, 1766–8. [Free Translation of Charles de Brosses].

*Campbell, Alexander. *The Sequel to Bulkeley and Cummins's Voyage to the South-Seas.* London, 1747.

Campbell, John. *See* Harris, John.

*Carteret, Philip. *Carteret's Voyage Round the World 1766–1769.* Ed. Helen Wallis. 2 vols. Cambridge: Cambridge University Press for the Hakluyt Society, 1965.

Colley, Linda. *Britons: Forging the Nation 1707–1837.* New Haven and London: Yale University Press, 1992.

*Colnett, James. *A Voyage to the South Atlantic and Round Cape Horn into the Pacific Ocean.* London, 1798.

*Cook, James. *The Journals of Captain James Cook on his Voyages of Discovery.* Ed. J. C. Beaglehole. I. *The Voyage of the Endeavour 1768–1771.* Cambridge: Cambridge University Press for the Hakluyt Society, 1955.

*Cook, James. *The Journals* ... II. *The Voyage of the Resolution and Adventure 1772–1775.* Cambridge: Cambridge University Press for the Hayluyt Society, 1961.

*Cook, James. *A Voyage Towards the South Pole and Round the World. Performed in His Majesty's Ships the Resolution and Adventure. In the Years 1772, 1773, 1774, and 1775.* 2 vols. (1777). Second edition, London, 1777.

*See also* Hawkesworth, John.

Cox, E. G. *A Reference Guide to the Literature of Travel (in English).* 3 Vols. Seattle: University of Washington, 1935–49.

*Cremer, John. *Ramblin' Jack: The Journal of John Cremer.* Transcribed by R. Raynell Bellamy. London: Jonathan Cape, 1936.

Crone, G. R., and Skelton, R. A. 'English collections of voyages and travels, 1625–1846'. In *Richard Hakluyt and his Successors*, ed. Edward Lynam. London: Hakluyt Society, 1946, pp. 65–140.

*Dalton, James, *The Life and Actions of James Dalton, (The Noted Street-Robber) ... As Taken from his Own Mouth in his Cell in Newgate.* London, [1730].

*Dampier, William. *A New Voyage Round the World.* London, 1697.

ALSO: Ed. Sir Albert Gray (Argonaut Press, 1927). London: A. C. Black, 1937.

*Dampier, William. *Voyages and Descriptions. Vol. II. In Three Parts.* London, 1699. ['Vol II' means the second volume of Dampier's works.]

ALSO: *Voyages and Discoveries* [*sic*]. Ed. Clennell Wilkinson. London: Argonaut Press, 1931.

*Dampier, William. *A Voyage to New Holland, &c. In the Year 1699 ... Vol. III.* London, 1703.

*A Continuation of a Voyage to New Holland, &c..* London, 1709.

ALSO: Ed. J. A. Williamson. London: The Argonaut Press, 1939.

ALSO: Ed. James Spencer. Gloucester: Alan Sutton, 1981.

*See also* Masefield, John.

*Dean, John. *A Sad and Deplorable but True Account of the Dreadful Hardships, and Sufferings of Capt. John Dean, and his Company, on Board the Nottingham Galley.* London, 1711.

*Dean, Jasper. *A Narrative of the Sufferings, Preservation and Deliverance of Capt. John Dean and Company; in the Nottingham-Gally of London*. London, [1711].

*Dean, John. *A Narrative of the Shipwreck of the Nottingham Galley, &c. Published in 1711. Revis'd, and Re-printed with Additions in 1726*. London, 1726.

Defoe, Daniel. *A New Voyage Round the World. By a Course Never Sailed Before*. London, 1725.

Dening, Greg. *Mr. Bligh's Bad Language: Passion, Power and Theatre on the Bounty*. Cambridge: Cambridge University Press, 1992.

*Dixon, George. *A Voyage Round the World: But more Particularly to the North-West Coast of America*. London, 1789.

*Dixon, George. *Remarks on the Voyages of John Meares, Esq*. London, 1790.

*Dixon, George. *Further Remarks on the Voyages of John Meares, Esq*. London, 1791.

*Drury, Robert. *Madagascar: or, Robert Drury's Journal, During Fifteen Years Captivity on that Island*. London, 1729.

ALSO: *The Adventures of Robert Drury, During Fifteen Years Captivity on the Island of Madagascar*. London, 1743.

ALSO: *The Adventures* .... Reprinted, Hull, 1807.

Ekirch, A. Roger. *Bound for America: The Transportation of British Convicts to the Colonies, 1718–1775*. Oxford: Clarendon Press, 1987.

*Elliott, John, and Pickersgill, Richard. *Captain Cook's Second Voyage: The Journal of Elliott and Pickersgill*. Ed. Christine Holmes. London: Caliban Books, 1984.

Equiano, Olaudah. *See* Olaudah Equiano.

*Falconbridge, Anna Maria. *Narrative of Two Voyages to the River Sierra Leone, During the Years 1791–2–3* (1794). Second edition, London, 1802.

ALSO: Reprinted, London: Frank Cass, 1967.

*Falconer, William. *The Shipwreck. A Poem in Three Cantos*. In *The British Poets* (Chiswick Press), vol. 58, 1822.

*Fielding, Henry. *The Journal of a Voyage to Lisbon* (1755). In *The Works of Henry Fielding, Esq.*. London, 1784. Vol. 10, pp. 167–304.

Firth, C. H. ed. *Naval Songs and Ballads*. London: Navy Records Society, 1908.

Floyd, Troy S. *The Anglo-Spanish Struggle for Mosquitia*. Albuquerque: University of New Mexico Press, 1967.

*Forster, George. *A Voyage Round the World, in His Majesty's Sloop, Resolution*. 2 vols. London, 1777.

ALSO: Ed. Robert L. Kahn, in *Georg Forsters Werke*. Vol. 1. Berlin: Akademie Verlag, 1968.

*Forster, George. *A Letter to the Right Honourable the Earl of Sandwich*. London, 1778.

Forster, George. *Reply to Mr. Wales's Remarks*. London, 1778.

ALSO: *Streitschriften und Fragments zur Weltreise*. Ed. R. L. Kahn. *Sämtliche Werke*, vol. 4. Berlin, 1972.

*Forster, J. R. *Observations Made During a Voyage Round the World on Physical Geography, Natural History, and Ethic Philosophy*. London, 1778.

*Forster, J. R. *The Resolution Journal of of Johann Reinhold Forster, 1772–1775*. Ed. Michael E. Hoare. 4 vols. London: Hakluyt Society, 1982.

Forster, J. R. and G. *Characteres generum plantarum*. London, 1775.

Frantz, R. W. *The English Traveller and the Movement of Ideas, 1660–1732* (1934). Lincoln, Neb.: University of Nebraska Press, 1967.

Fremantle, Elizabeth. *See* Wynne.

*Fryer, John. *The Voyage of the Bounty's Launch as Related in William Bligh's Despatch to the Admiralty. And the Journal of John Fryer.* Ed. Owen Rutter. London: Golden Cockerel Press, 1934.

*Funnell, William. *A Voyage Round the World. Containing an Account of Captain Dampier's Expedition into the South-Seas in the Ship St. George. In the Years 1703 and 1704.* London, 1707.

Furbank, P. N. and Owens, W. R. *The Canonisation of Daniel Defoe.* New Haven and London: Yale University Press, 1988.

Fyfe, Christopher. *A History of Sierra Leone.* Oxford: Oxford University Press, 1962.

Gallagher, R. E. *See* Byron, John.

Gilchrist, Ebenezer. *The Use of Sea Voyages in Medicine* (1756). Second edition, with a Supplement, London, 1757.

Gladstone, Hugh S. *Maria Riddell, the Friend of Burns.* Dumfries: Private Circulation, 1915.

*Green, William. *The Sufferings of William Green, Being a Sorrowful Account of his Seven Years Transportation.* London, [1775?].

Hale, C. R. and Gordon, C. T. 'Costeno demography: historical and contemporary demography of Nicaragua's Atlantic coast'. In *Ethnic Groups and the Nation State: The Case of the Atlantic Coast of Nicaragua.* Ed. CIDCA/Development Study Unit. Stockholm: University of Stockholm, 1987.

Hamilton, George. *A Voyage Round the World in His Majesty's Frigate Pandora. Performed under the Direction of Captain Edwards.* Berwick, 1793.

Harris, John. *Navigantium atque Itinerantium Bibliotheca. Or, A Complete Collection of Voyages and Travels.* Now Carefully Revised, with Large Additions. London, 1744. [Revision by John Campbell. 1st ed. 2 vols. 1705; 1st 1 vol. folio edn 1715.]

*Harrison, David. *The Melancholy Narrative of the Distressful Voyage and Miraculous Deliverance of Captain David Harrison, of the Sloop, Peggy, of New York.* London, 1766.

*Harrower, John. *The Journal of John Harrower, an Indentured Servant in the Colony of Virginia, 1773–78.* Ed. Edward M. Riley. Williamsburg, Va.: Colonial Williamsburg Foundation, 1963.

*Hawkesworth, John. *An Account of the Voyages Undertaken . . . for Making Discoveries in the Southern Hemisphere . . . by Commodore Byron, Captain Wallis, Captain Carteret, and Captain Cook.* 3 vols. London, 1773.

*Hervey, Augustus (3rd Earl of Bristol). *Augustus Hervey's Journal . . . 1746–1759.* Ed. David Erskine (1953). London: William Kimber, 1954.

Hill, George Birkbeck. *Boswell's Life of Johnson.* Revised L. F. Powell. 6 vols. Oxford: Clarendon Press, 1935–50.

Hill, George Birkbeck. *Johnsonian Miscellanies.* 2 vols. Oxford: Clarendon Press, 1897.

Hoare, Michael E. *The Tactless Philosopher: Johann Reinhold Forster (1728–1798).* Melbourne: Hawthorn Press, 1976.

Hughes, Robert. *The Fatal Shore: A History of the Transportation of Convicts to Australia 1787–1868* (1987). London: Pan Books, 1988.

Hulme, Peter, and Whitehead, Neil L., eds. *Wild Majesty: Encounters with Caribs from Columbus to the Present Day. An Anthology*. Oxford: Clarendon Press, 1992.

Joppien, Rüdiger, and Smith, Bernard. *The Art of Captain Cook's Voyages*. Volume Two. *The Voyage of the Resolution and Adventure 1772–1775*. New Haven and London: Yale University Press in assoc. with the Australian Academy of the Humanities for the Paul Mellon Centre for Studies in British Art, 1985.

**A Journal of a Voyage Round the World, in His Majesty's Ship Endeavour*. London, 1771.

*Justice, Elizabeth. *A Voyage to Russia*, York. 1739.

*Kelly, Samuel. *Samuel Kelly: An Eighteenth Century Seaman*. Ed. Crosbie Garstin. London: Jonathan Cape, 1925.

Kennedy, Gavin. *Bligh*. London: Duckworth, 1978.

ALSO: *Captain Bligh: The Man and his Mutineers*. London: Duckworth, 1989.

Kierkegaard, Søren. *Fear and Trembling* and *The Sickness unto Death*. Trans. Walter Lowrie (1941). New York: Doubleday Anchor, 1954.

*Kindersley, Jemima. *Letters from the Island of Teneriffe, Brazil, the Cape of Good Hope, and the East Indies*. London, 1777.

*Langman, Christopher (and others). *A True Account of the Voyage of the Nottingham-Galley of London*. London, 1711.

Lowes, John Livingston. *The Road to Xanadu* (1927). New York: Vintage Books, 1959.

Mackaness, George. *The Life of Vice-Admiral William Bligh, R. N., F.R.S.*. 2 vols. Sydney: Angus and Roberston, 1931.

Mackay, David. *In the Wake of Cook: Exploration, Science and Empire, 1780–1801*. London: Croom Helm, 1985.

*Marra, John. *Journal of the Resolution's Voyage*. London, 1775.

Martin, Bernard. *John Newton: A Biography*. London: Heinemann, 1950.

*Masefield, John, ed. *Dampier's Voyages*. 2 vols. London: Grant Richards, 1906.

*Meares, John. *Voyages Made in the Years 1788 and 1789, from China to the North West Coast of America*. London, 1790.

Meares, John. *An Answer to Mr. George Dixon*. London, 1791.

*Moraley, William. *The Infortunate: Or, The Voyage and Adventures of William Moraley*. Newcastle, 1743.

Moraley, William. *The Infortunate* ... Ed. Susan E. Klepp and Billy G. Smith. Philadelphia: Pennsylvania State University Press, 1992.

*Morris, Isaac. *A Narrative of the Dangers and Distresses which Befel Isaac Morris and Seven More of the Crew, Belonging to the Wager Store-Ship*. London, [1750?].

*Morrison, James. *The Journal of James Morrison, Boatswain's Mate of the Bounty*. Ed. Owen Rutter. London: Golden Cockerel Press, 1935.

*Nagle, Jacob. *The Nagle Journal: A Diary of the Life of Jacob Nagle, from the Year 1775 to 1841*. Ed. John C. Dann. New York: Weidenfeld and Nicolson, 1988.

Narborough, Sir John [and others]. *An Account of Several Late Voyages and Discoveries to the South and North*. London, 1694.

Newson, Linda. *The Cost of Conquest: Indian Decline in Honduras under Spanish Rule*. Boulder and London: Westview Press, 1986.

*Newton, John. *An Authentic Narrative of Some Remarkable and Interesting Particulars in* *the life of* * * * * * * * *. Communicated in a Series of Letters to the Rev. Haweis.* London, 1764.

*Newton, John. *Thoughts upon the African Slave Trade.* London, 1788.

*Newton, John. *Letters to a Wife.* London, 1793.

*Newton, John. *The Journal of a Slave-Trader (John Newton) 1750–1754.* London: Epworth Press, 1962.

ALSO: *The Works of the Rev. John Newton* (1827). Edinburgh, 1841.

*Nicol, John. *The Life and Adventures of John Nicol, Mariner.* Edinburgh, 1822.

ALSO: Ed. Alexander Laing. London: Cassell, 1937.

*Olaudah Equiano. *The Interesting Narrative of the Life of Olaudah Equiano, or Gustavus Vasa, the African. Written by Himself.* 2 vols. London, [1789].

ALSO: Abridged and edited by Paul Edwards. London: Heinemann, 1967.

*Owen, Nicholas. *Journal of a Slave-Dealer.* Ed. Eveline Martin. London: Routledge, 1930.

Pack, S. W. C. *The Wager Mutiny.* London: Alvin Redman, 1964.

*Palmer, Rev. Thomas Fyshe. *A Narrative of the Sufferings of T. F. Palmer, and W. Skirving During a Voyage to New South Wales, 1794, on the Surprise Transport.* Cambridge, 1797.

*Parker, Mary Ann. *A Voyage Round the World in the Gorgon Man of War.* London, 1795.

Parks, G. B. 'Travel'. In *The New Cambridge Bibliography of English Literature.* Cambridge: Cambridge University Press, 1971. Vol. 2. 1389–1486.

Pearson, W. H. 'Hawkesworth's alterations', *Journal of Pacific History,* 7 (1972), 45–72.

Phillip, Arthur, *The Voyage of Governor Phillip to Botany Bay* (1789). Third edition. London, 1790.

Phipps, C. J. *A Voyage Towards the North Pole Undertaken by His Majesty's Command, 1773.* London, 1774.

Pickersgill, Richard. *See* Elliott, John.

*Poole, Robert. *The Beneficent Bee: Or, Traveller's Companion.* London, 1753.

*Portlock, Nathaniel.*A Voyage Round the World: But More Particularly to the North-West Coast of America.* London, 1789.

Pratt, Mary Louise. *Imperial Eyes: Travel Writing and Transculturation.* London and New York: Routledge, 1992.

Prebble, John. *The Darien Disaster* (1968). Edinburgh: Mainstream, 1978.

*Raigersfeld, Jeffrey, Baron de. *The Life of a Sea Officer.* (1830?) Ed. L. G. Carr Laughton. London: Cassell, 1929.

Rawson, C. J. *Henry Fielding and the Augustan Ideal under Stress.* London and Boston: Routledge and Kegan Paul, 1972.

Rediker, Marcus. *Between the Devil and the Deep Blue Sea: Merchant Seamen, Pirates, and the Anglo-American Maritime World, 1700–1750.* Cambridge: Cambridge University Press, 1987; reprinted 1993.

*Revel, James. *The Poor Unhappy Transported Felon's Sorrowful Account of his Fourteen Years Transportation at Virginia in America.* London, [1800?].

*Richardson, R. *The Dolphin's Journal Epitomized, in a Poetical Essay.* London, 1768.

*Riddell, Maria. *Voyages to the Madeira, and Leeward Caribbean Isles: with Sketches of the Natural History of These Islands.* Edinburgh, 1792.

*(Ringrose, Basil.) John Esquemeling, *Bucaniers of America*. The Second Volume ... Written by Mr Basil Ringrose, Gent. London, 1685.

ALSO: Ed. W. S. Stallybrass. London: Routledge, and New York: E. P. Dutton, [1923].

*Roach, John. *The Surprizing Adventures of John Roach, Mariner, of Whitehaven*. Whitehaven, [1783 or 1784].

*Roach, John. *The Surprizing Adventures* ... Second edition, Whitehaven, [1784].

*Roach, John. *A Narrative of the Surprising Adventures and Sufferings of John Roach, Mariner, of Whitehaven*. Workington, 1810.

*Robertson, George. *The Discovery of Tahiti: A Journal of of the Second Voyage of H. M. S. Dolphin Round the World, Under the Command of Captain Wallis, R. N. in the Years 1766, 1767 and 1768*. Ed. Hugh Carrington. London: Hakluyt Society, 1948.

Robinson, Tancred. *See* Narborough.

Rodger, N. A. M. *The Wooden World: An Anatomy of the Georgian Navy*. London: Collins, 1986.

*Rogers, Woodes. *A Cruising Voyage Round the World*. London, 1712.

ALSO: Ed. G. E. Manwaring. London: Cassell, 1928.

Saine, Thomas P. *Georg Forster*. New York: Twayne, 1972.

*Schaw, Janet. *Journal of a Lady of Quality*. Ed. Evangeline W. Andrews and Charles McL. Andrews (1921). Third edition, emended and enlarged, New Haven: Yale University Press, 1939.

**A Second Voyage Round the World in the Years MDCCLXXII, LXXIII, LXXIV, LXXV, by James Cook, Esq. ... Drawn up from Authentic Papers*. London, 1776.

Secord, A. W. *'Robert Drury's Journal' and Other Studies*. Ed. R. W. Rogers and G. Sherburn. Urbana: University of Illinois Press, 1961.

*Shelvocke, George. *A Voyage Round the World by the Way of the Great South Sea, Performed in the Years 1719, 20, 21, 22, in the Speedwell of London*. London, 1726.

Shelvocke, George. *A Voyage Round the World* ... Ed. W. G. Perrin. London: Cassell, 1928.

Shipman, Joseph C. *William Dampier: Seaman–Scientist*. Lawrence, Kan.: University of Kansas Libraries, 1962.

Skelton, R. A. *See* Crone, G. R.

Sloane, Hans. *A Voyage to the Islands Madera, Barbados, Nieves, S. Christophers and Jamaica*. 2 vols. London, 1707, 1725.

Smith, Bernard. *European Vision and the South Pacific 1760–1850: A Study in the History of Art and Ideas*. Oxford: Clarendon Press, 1960.

*See also* Joppien, R.

*Snelgrave, William. *A New Account of some Parts of Guinea, and the Slave-Trade*. London, 1734.

Sparrman, Anders. *A Voyage to the Cape of Good Hope, Towards the Antarctic, and Round the World*. Translated from the Swedish Original. 2 vols. London, 1785.

ALSO: Ed. V. S. Forbes, Cape Town: Van Riebeck Society, 1975.

*Spavens, William. *The Seaman's Narrative*. Louth, 1796.

Stafford, Barbara Maria. *Voyage into Substance: Art, Science, Nature, and the Illustrated Travel Account, 1760–1840*. Cambridge, Mass., and London: MIT Press, 1984.

*Stanfield, James Field. *The Guinea Voyage. A Poem. In three Books*. London, 1789.

*Stanfield, James Field. *The Guinea Voyage. A Poem, in Three Books. ... To Which are Added Observations on a Voyage to the Coast of Africa*. Edinburgh, 1807.

*Symson, William. *A New Voyage to the East Indies*. London, 1715.

*Tench, Watkin. *A Narrative of the Expedition to Botany Bay*. London, 1789.

*Thomas, Pascoe. *A True and Impartial Journal of a Voyage to the South-Seas and Round the Globe in His Majesty's Ship the Centurion, under the Command of Commodore George Anson*. London, 1745.

*Thompson, Edward. *Sailors Letters. Written to his Select Friends in England During his Voyages and Travels ... from the Year 1754 to 1759*. 2 vols. (1766). Second edition, Corrected, London, 1767.

*Uring, Nathaniel. *A History of the Voyages and Travels of Capt. Nathaniel Uring* (1726). Second edition, London, 1727.

ALSO: Ed. A. Dewar, London: Cassell, 1928.

Vancouver, George. *A Voyage of Discovery to the North Pacific Ocean and Round the World 1791–1795*. Ed. W. Kaye Lamb. 4 vols. London: Hakluyt Society, 1984.

Villiers, Alan, *Captain Cook: The Seamen's Seaman*. London, 1967.

*Wafer, Lionel. *A New Voyage and Description of the Isthmus of America*. (1699). Ed. L. E. Elliott Joyce. Oxford: Hakluyt Society, 1934.

*Wales, William. *Remarks on Mr. Forster's Account of Captain Cook's Last Voyage*. London, 1778.

*Walker, George. *The Voyages and Cruises of Commodore Walker, During the Late Spanish and French Wars*, 2 vols. London, 1760.

ALSO: Ed. H. S. Vaughan. London: Cassell, 1928.

Wallis, Helen. 'The Patagonian Giants'. In *Byron's Journal* (1964).

Walter, Richard. *See* Anson.

West, Richard. *Back to Africa. A History of Sierra Leone and Liberia*. London: Jonathan Cape, 1970.

*White, John. *Journal of a Voyage to New South Wales*. London, 1790.

*Whitefield, George. *George Whitefield's Journals*. Ed. Iain Murray. London: The Banner of Truth Trust, 1960.

Whitehead, Neil L. *See* Hulme, Peter.

Wilkinson, Clennel. *William Dampier*. London: John Lane, The Bodley Head, 1929.

*Wills, William. *Narrative of the Very Extraordinary Adventures and Sufferings of Mr William Wills, Late Surgeon on Board the Durrington Indiaman, Captain Robert Crabb, in his Late Voyage to the East Indies*. London, 1751.

Withey, Lynne. *Voyages of Discovery: Captain Cook and the Exploration of the Pacific* (1987). London: Hutchinson, 1988.

*Wollstonecraft, Mary. *Letters Written during a Short Residence in Sweden, Norway, and Denmark*. London, 1796.

ALSO: Ed. Richard Holme. Harmondsworth: Penguin, 1987.

*Wynne, Elizabeth (later Fremantle). *The Wynne Diaries*. Ed. Anne Fremantle. 3 vols. London: Oxford University Press, 1935, 1937 and 1940.

Young, John. *See Affecting Narrative*.

# Index

*NOTE: See 'Ships' for names of all ships.*

CAMBRIDGE STUDIES IN EIGHTEENTH-CENTURY ENGLISH LITERATURE AND THOUGHT

1 *The Transformation of* The Decline and Fall of the Roman Empire
by David Womersley

2 *Women's Place in Pope's World*
by Valerie Rumbold

3 *Sterne's Fiction and the Double Principle*
by Jonathan Lamb

4 *Warrior Women and Popular Balladry, 1650–1850*
by Dianne Dugaw

5 *The Body in Swift and Defoe*
by Carol Flynn

6 *The Rhetoric of Berkeley's Philosophy*
by Peter Walmsley

7 *Space and the Eighteenth-Century English Novel*
by Simon Varcy

8 *Reason, Grace, and Sentiment: A Study of the Language of Religion and Ethics in England, 1660–1780*
by Isabel Rivers

9 *Defoe's Politics: Parliament, Power, Kingship and* Robinson Crusoe
by Manuel Schonhorn

10 *Sentimental Comedy: Theory & Practice*
by Frank Ellis

11 *Arguments of Augustan Wit*
by John Sitter

12 *Robert South (1634–1716): An Introduction to his Life and Sermons*
by Gerard Reedy, SJ

13 *Richardson's* Clarissa *and the Eighteenth-Century Reader*
by Tom Keymer

14 *Eighteenth-Century Sensibility and the Novel: The Senses in Social Context*
by Ann Jessie Van Sant

15 *Family and the Law in Eighteenth-Century Fiction: The Public Conscience in the Private Sphere*
by John P. Zomchick

16 *Crime and Defoe: A New Kind of Writing*
by Lincoln B. Faller

17 *Literary Transmission and Authority: Dryden and Other Writers*
edited by Earl Miner and Jennifer Brady

18 *Plots and Counterplots: Sexual Politics and the Body Politic in English Literature, 1660–1730*
by Richard Braverman

19 *The Eighteenth-Century Hymn in England*
by Donald Davie

20 *Swift's Politics: A Study in Disaffection*
by Ian Higgins

21 *Writing and the Rise of Finance: Capital Satires of the Early Eighteenth Century*
by Colin Nicholson

22 *Locke, Literary Criticism, and Philosophy*
by William Walker

23 *Poetry and Jacobite Politics in Eighteenth-Century Britain and Ireland*
by Murray G. H. Pittock

24 *The Story of the Voyage: Sea-narratives in Eighteenth-Century England*
by Philip Edwards